THE FURNITURE FACTORY OUTLET GUIDE

THIRD EDITION

BY KIMBERLY CAUSEY

HOME DECOR PRESS

Published by: Home Decor Press
                 1000 Peachtree Industrial Blvd., Suite 6333
                 Suwanee, GA 30024

To order single copies of this book, or any other books published by Home Decor Press, please call (800) 829-1203, visit our website at **www.smartdecorating.com**, or use the order form given in the back of this book. All major credit cards accepted.

Quantity discounts are available. Please call the publisher at (678) 947-1750 for a discount schedule. Our titles are also available through Ingram Book Co.

If you have any questions or comments regarding this book, please write to the author in care of the publisher at the above address.

Publisher's Cataloging-in-Publication Data

Causey, Kimberly,

   The Furniture Factory Outlet Guide, Third Edition

   Includes index.
   1. Interior decoration--United States   2. Consumer education--United States   3. Shopping--United States

ISBN 1-888229-43-8

TABLE OF CONTENTS

Factory Outlets And Discounters (Cont.)

FACTORY OUTLETS AND DISCOUNTERS (CONT.)

FACTORY OUTLETS AND DISCOUNTERS (CONT.)

FACTORY OUTLETS AND DISCOUNTERS (CONT.)

FREQUENTLY ASKED QUESTIONS

What are "factory outlets" and "discounters"?

The term "factory outlet", in this book, refers to any factory-owned store that sells floor samples, overstock furniture, photography samples, customer returns, discontinued styles, and seconds. These outlets are set up by most major furniture manufacturers to sell off furniture that can't be sold to their regular wholesale customers, primarily furniture stores and interior designers.

Except for seconds, the vast majority of the furniture in stock at a typical factory outlet is in new first-quality condition. Factory outlet furniture is normally just as high-quality and in just as good condition as the furniture sold by your local furniture retailer. Seconds do have small flaws, but they are very clearly identified as such and usually make up a very small percentage of the furniture in stock at a typical factory outlet.

"Discounters", such as Boyles and Furnitureland South, are not factory-owned stores. They are retailers that buy furniture from the factories and resell it to the public.

Unlike your local furniture retailer, however, discounters have made a conscious decision to drastically lower their prices by reducing their overhead. They typically don't offer "free" design services in your home, as your local furniture retailer usually does, nor do they have large advertising budgets or big brightly-lit stores in the high-rent district of every major city. Discounters cut costs even further by having just one central location, usually just a few miles from the furniture factories in North Carolina, instead of having multiple stores all over the country.

By eliminating the huge budget a typical local furniture retailer spends on rent, advertising, utilities, and a staff of interior designers, a furniture discounter is able to pass those savings on to you. Typically, the very same piece of furniture made by the very same manufacturer will cost you about half as much if you order it through a discounter as it would if you ordered it through a local furniture retailer.

Simply put, local furniture retailers attempt to get more customers by offering more "free" services while keeping prices at or near full retail. Furniture discounters attempt to get more customers by cutting overhead costs and reducing prices to near-wholesale. Factory outlets exist to sell off furniture that can't be sold through the normal retail channels, at prices below the normal wholesale price.

How much money will I save if I buy my furniture from a factory outlet or discounter?

The typical savings at a factory-owned factory outlet run from 50%-80% off the normal retail price you would pay at your local furniture retailer for the very same furniture. New first-quality furniture normally runs 50%-75% less than the prices you would pay at a local furniture retailer. Discontinued styles, floor samples, photography samples, overstock furniture, and customer returns are usually new first-quality and account for the vast majority of the furniture at a typical outlet.

Seconds, or furniture with small flaws, normally costs 75%-80% less than the prices you would pay for the same style if you purchased it through a local furniture store. Most outlets have very few second-quality pieces, and many outlets have none at all.

The typical savings on new first-quality furniture ordered through a discounter run from 40%-60% off retail, with most brands discounted about 40%-50% off the prices charged by local furniture retailers.

My local furniture retailer is having a big sale. Does this mean that I'll get just as much of a bargain from the local retailer as I would from a true factory outlet or discounter?

No. It is an unfortunate fact that many local furniture retailers misrepresent the discounts on their furniture. It is a common practice for local furniture retailers to mark the regular price of a piece of furniture up right before a sale, and then mark it right back down, leading their customers to believe that they're getting a big discount when they really aren't. In the industry, this is called "marking it up to mark it down".

In fact, one major furniture retail chain was recently sued by the California State Attorney General and seven other states over exactly this practice. As reported in the Los Angeles Times, Levitz Furniture Co. paid $1.2 million dollars in 1996 to settle charges brought by the State of California that it "misled consumers with phony discounts". Arizona, Connecticut, Maryland, Missouri, Pennsylvania, Texas, and Washington also took part in the suit against Levitz. Levitz admitted no wrongdoing in its settlement of the lawsuit, although it should be noted that the company was also sued by the State of California on similar false-advertising charges back in 1973.

According to the CBS Morning News, in its reporting of the same lawsuit, Levitz "was accused of posting false regular prices on sale items to give consumers the impression they were getting a great deal when they were actually paying full price".

According to the allegations by the State of California, "Levitz duped customers by comparing 'sale' prices to 'regular' prices that never existed". As a part of the settlement, Levitz agreed not to advertise "regular" prices unless the item is available at that price at least 60% of the time and is sold at that price at least 20% of the time.

California Deputy Attorney General Albert Shelden told the Los Angeles Times, "We are hoping these standards will lead [furniture retailers] to not engage in as much phony advertising. It is a problem we see a lot and we are concerned about".

It is a problem that I, and many of the consumers I've spoken with all over the U. S., have seen frequently as well. My family owned a factory that sold to local furniture retailers all over the U. S. for over twenty years. We saw this problem contantly among local furniture retailers in every state. The problem of phony discounts is so prevalent in the home furnishings industry that it even has a special name: "borax pricing", named after similar shady practices in the mining industry.

Occasionally, I speak with consumers at my seminars who have seen this type of phony pricing first hand. Typically, these are consumers who check and record prices over several months before making a purchase. One man related this story at a seminar:

> *"I saw a chair I wanted at a local retailer and wrote the price down: $500.00. Then, a few weeks later, I noticed that the store was having a "40% off sale". I went to buy the chair expecting it to be marked 40% off of the original $500.00 price. When I got to the sale, I found that the chair's original retail price had been marked up, and the new SALE price was $515.00!"*

Research is the best defense. Although some local furniture retailers do advertise their sales honestly, many don't. Don't take any chances. Always compare the ACTUAL PRICE among many different retailers, including the factory outlets and discounters in North Carolina, before you buy. Completely ignore any claims of percentages off and focus on the actual dollar amount, including freight and sales tax, that you'll actually have to pay for the furniture. As long as you do this every time you shop, you can't be fooled into paying more than you should.

If I see a piece of furniture I like at a local furniture retailer, how can I get the accurate item number so I can compare the price with factory outlets and discounters?

This is, unfortunately, a growing problem. Some local furniture retailers will actually hide, remove, or alter the original manufacturer's item numbers and names to prevent customers from comparing prices with factory outlets and discounters. This is hardly what could be called a "fair trade practice".

Fortunately, there are several ways around this problem:

1. Ask to see the manufacturer's catalog. Most furniture stores do have the original manufacturer's catalog and will bring it out on request. One customer told me that she always gets the store salespeople to bring out the catalog by asking them what other items the manufacturer has that match the one she is considering buying. Usually, the manufacturer's catalog has all of the correct item numbers and names.

2. Ask for a product sheet. Many furniture manufacturers provide stores with color product sheets for their furniture. Often, these sheets have the accurate item number, or at least the accurate style name. If the product sheet doesn't have the item number shown, you can usually fax or mail the entire sheet to a discounter and get them to properly identify the product for you so they can give you a comparison price.

3. Take a photograph of the furniture. Many local furniture retailers won't object to photographs. Many people do take photographs of furniture to show their husbands, wives, children, etc., when shopping for furniture alone. Then, send the photograph to a discounter and let them help you identify the product.

Never allow a local furniture retailer's hiding or falsification of product information to cause you to pay too much for your furniture. No customer would tolerate this practice at a car dealership, computer store, or electronics store, so why should anyone put up with this from furniture stores? Consumers deserve accurate product information, and they have every right to compare prices among different sources before they buy.

What is the quickest and easiest way to find the best price available on a specific piece of furniture?

Contact me. I am now offering free price checking through my Web site, **www.smartdecorating.com**. Please use my Web site to provide as much information as possible on the furniture you wish to price. I'll be happy to check my sources for the best bargain, including factory outlets and clearance centers. Discounts range from 40% to 80% off retail.

On certain brands, I have been able to negotiate special discounts and/or rebates available to my readers only. These extra discounts are not available to the general public.

Please note that I am unable to conduct price checks over the phone or by mail. Please use my Web site for this service.

My local retailer told me the manufacturer of the furniture I'm interested in has set a "minimum retail price" that even the North Carolina discounters can't beat. Is this true?

A small number of furniture manufacturers use what is called "minimum retail pricing" or MRPs. In these few cases, all stores nationwide that carry the line have a certain set minimum price which they are not allowed to go under.

Even the deep discounters in North Carolina who normally discount brands by 40%-50% are not allowed to go below these manufacturer minimums, or they may lose the privilege of selling that brand.

There is a lot of debate going on in the industry right now over this practice. Some feel that this is a form of illegal price fixing. Attorneys general in several states are investigating this issue right now.

It is my hope that this practice will be declared illegal in the near future. It is certainly not consumer friendly. Open price competition is what keeps prices low on all kinds of products.

Until that happens, what can consumers do when they run into this situation? First, they can refuse to pay artificially fixed prices. For every manufacturer who fixes their prices at an point higher than the market would normally bear, there are a dozen competitors who make similar or identical styles to the same level of quality and allow the deep discounters in North Carolina to mark their prices as low as the market demands. Don't let brand loyalty or a famous name on the tag (which you will remove as soon as the furniture is in your home) cause you to pay more than a product is really worth.

Also, don't just assume that because a particular brand has an MRP, your local furniture retailer is necessarily charging the minimum possible price. In major cities with lots of open competition, many retailers do mark these brands down to the minimum possible price, which means that ++their prices on that particular brand will be as good
as you can get through a North Carolina deep discounter.

However, in many smaller markets where a given retailer may be the only source of that brand in town, I have found that many stores charge at or near full retail. In these cases, you can still save substantially by ordering even these restricted brands from a North Carolina deep discounter. Plus, most deep discounters ship MRP brands free of charge to help offset the manufacturer's prohibition against giving the customer a better price.

Please note that even brands with MRPs do not restrict the discounts they charge in their own factory owned factory outlets. For instance, Thomasville currently uses MRPs. Discounts on Thomasville furniture are restricted, even at the deep discounters. However, Thomasville does not apply those restrictions to their own company owned factory outlets. You can still buy Thomasville furniture at the factory outlet for the usual factory outlet discounts of 60%-75% off retail, frequently in new first-quality condition.

What brands and types of furniture are available at a discount?

Nearly every brand of furniture at your local furniture retailer is also available through factory outlets and discounters.

There are factory-owned factory outlets for most major furniture brands, including Baker, Century, Hickory White, Hooker, Lane, Wellington Hall, Henredon, Hickory Chair, Councill-Craftsmen, Clayton Marcus, Maitland Smith, La Barge, and many more. They are all listed in this book. If there is a factory-owned factory outlet for the brand of furniture you want, you'll normally get the best deal there.

About 99% of the other brands sold by local furniture retailers and interior designers are available through one or more of the discounters listed in this book. Most of the individual discounter descriptions in this book include a list of the brands they carry. If you don't find the brand you want listed with any discounters in this book, call several of the largest discounters, such as Thomas Home Furnishings or Boyles. Frequently, discounters can also order brands other than those listed here, and many discounters add new brands all the time.

If you can't find the brand you want through any of the discounters listed here, and this will happen with about 1% of the brands on the market, there are a couple of alternatives:

1. Let the discounters help you find an identical product from another brand.

    A few brands greatly restrict the availability of their products in order to keep prices high. For instance, Ethan Allen furniture is normally carried only by Ethan Allen's corporately-owned retail stores. No discounter carries that line, so Ethan Allen stores have no price competition and can charge full retail for their furniture.

    Fortunately, there are other brands that have identical or nearly identical furniture to Ethan Allen's that are available through discounters and factory outlets. You might particularly want to check out Pennsylvania House, which is Ethan Allen's biggest competitor nationwide, and Hitchcock Chair, which specializes in early American furniture. Both of these brands have factory-owned factory outlets and are widely available through discounters.

Stickley is another brand that can be difficult to find at a discount. They do not have a factory outlet anymore, and they do not allow deep discounters to sell their products. Several other brands manufacture furniture in the same style and quality as Stickley: Robert Bergelin Co., Arts & Crafts Industries, and Richardson Brothers, to name a few. Each of these lines produces furniture that is identical in looks and quality to many Stickley products, and they're all a lot cheaper. As with many designer products, sometimes you really do pay more for the name.

If you can't find the brand you want from a factory outlet or discounter, contact several discounters and let them identify other brands that have the same look and quality you want. Frequently, you can find a product from another manufacturer that is absolutely identical to the one you originally picked out.

2. Shop wholesale. There are some lines that aren't available through discounters or factory outlets that are available through wholesale showrooms. There are wholesale showrooms in most major cities that sell primarily to interior designers and interior decorators. Many members of the public get into these showrooms to shop, too. This is a very common practice in the industry.

For many years, my family's factory had showrooms at the world trade centers in Atlanta and Dallas, and we also showed at the International Home Furnishings Market in High Point, NC. During all the years I worked in those showrooms, I watched many consumers come in and shop for themselves. Some were friends and relatives of furniture store owners and others in the trade, but many had simply figured out how to get in on their own.

The Los Angeles Times recently interviewed Elaine M. Redfield, president of the American Society Of Interior Designers (ASID) for the Los Angeles area, about consumers getting into design centers and wholesale showrooms to buy directly from manufacturers. She had this to say: "It's a simple matter for someone to get a resale number and go shop at the showrooms, and many do."

The Los Angeles Times also interviewed Pat Stamps, the former head of the ASID for the Los Angeles area. She had this to say about retail customers getting into the wholesale showrooms to shop: "We all know it happens because our customers tell us they've shopped here. I've seen women who come in who use their husband's resale number, and he sells plants."

In my experience, about 3/4 of the manufacturers out there will sell directly to consumers at their wholesale showrooms. Of course, it is important to know how to get into the showrooms and how to properly conduct business once you get there. Wholesale shopping is not at all like shopping at a local retail store. It's also important to have the proper credentials, including a resale number.

For more detailed information on how to get into wholesale showrooms and design centers, and how to shop properly once you get there, please read chapter 19 of my book, _The Insider's Guide To Buying Home Furnishings_.

Do I have to travel to North Carolina to save a lot of money on furniture?

Not necessarily. It is true that you'll get the very best deals if you go in person. If you want to save 75% to 80% off retail on new first-quality furniture, you'll have to go in person to the factory outlets and clearance centers, the vast majority of which are located in North Carolina where most of the furniture factories are. There are a few factory outlets in other states, including New York, Missouri, Wisconsin, and Virginia.

Or, you can utilize my price checking service at my Web site, **www.smartdecorating.com**. I keep files of the bargains I've found at the various factory outlets and clearance centers. If I happen to have found a bargain on the piece you're looking for, I'll be happy to arrange your purchase and save you the trip to North Carolina.

If you do decide to travel to North Carolina to shop, be sure to contact the discounters and outlets you intend to visit in advance of your trip. Some offer travel discounts from time to time. A few discounters will rebate all or part of your travel expense up to a certain amount if you buy your furniture from them. Other discounters have arranged for package deals on airfare and hotel rooms that can save you quite a bit. Please read the individual listings in this book for more information.

If you aren't able to travel to North Carolina, you can still save around 50% off retail on most brands by ordering your furniture from those discounters who accept phone orders and having it shipped to you. This is how most people buy their furniture from North Carolina. This is a very safe and reliable way of buying your furniture, and it can save most people thousands of dollars on their purchases.

Again, readers may always use my price checking service at my Web site to quickly find the best deal from a deep discounter on a particular piece of furniture.

Are there group tours to North Carolina that can help me cut my travel costs?

Absolutely! Please check my Web site, **www.smartdecorating.com**, for information on upcoming group tours to North Carolina. By going on a group tour, you can save at least 50% off your hotel and transportation. Plus, I go along on each tour to teach all of our group members how to spot the best deals, and I negotiate special extra discounts and freebies just for my own tour members.. Please check the Web site for more information.

Are there ever any special sales at the outlets in North Carolina?

Yes! Many outlets have special sales right after the wholesale furniture markets in High Point, which happen every April and October. When the wholesale markets end, many manufacturers send all their floor samples to the factory outlets, and most outlets have special sales to move out all the extra furniture. Discounts frequently run 75% to 80% off retail during these times.

Some factory outlets have sales right before the High Point market. Typically, you'll save an extra 10%-20% off the already discounted outlet price of 50%-80% off retail.

Some factory outlets also have sales in January and July when business is slow. No matter what time of year you're shopping for furniture, there will be some very good sales coming up within the next month or two.

Please check our Web site, **www.smartdecorating.com**, for free information about upcoming sales at factory outlets and furniture factories.

If I order my furniture over the phone, do I have to pay sales tax on it?

If you order your furniture over the phone from outside of North Carolina, you will not have to pay any North Carolina sales tax.

Whether or not you will have to pay sales tax to your own home state depends on the laws where you live. At this writing, most states have laws requiring consumers to pay "use tax" on any items purchased from an out of state vendor if no sales tax was paid at the time of purchase. This applies to any kind of purchase, from books at Amazon.com to furniture from North Carolina. Use tax rates are normally exactly the same as sales tax rates.

States are becoming more aggressive recently in enforcing existing use tax laws. At this writing in February 2004, I am aware of two states which inspect trucks bringing furniture into the state and assess use tax and penalties against the purchaser if sales tax has not been paid: Florida and Texas. By the time you read this book and order your furniture, more states may be stepping up their enforcement.

California has recently mailed booklets to all state taxpayers explaining their use tax responsibilities. Maryland recently sued a major furniture discounter in an effort to force them to charge and remit Maryland sales tax on furniture sales to Maryland residents.

The best course of action for any consumer is to contact the sales tax office in your state. Most states now have information and forms online spelling out exactly what you need to do to comply with the law. As long as you file and pay any use tax owed on your order before your furniture is delivered, you should have no problems.

Can I use a professional interior designer and still get my furniture at a discount?

Certainly. I've found that some consumers believe that they must make a trade-off between price and service. They think that if they choose to buy their furniture from a factory outlet or discounter which doesn't provide an in-home design service, they can't have any in-home design help. This isn't at all the case.

There are many interior designers who work on an hourly basis. It is a simple matter to hire a designer at an hourly rate for her design advice only, and then go buy your furniture directly from the factory outlets and discounters. In this way, you still get the best possible price, and you can get the service you need.

Another advantage to hiring a designer this way is that you only pay for the help you actually need and no more. If you buy your furniture through a local retailer and use their "free" in-home design help, what you're actually doing is paying a large mark-up on everything you buy to compensate the designer for his or her time. Everyone pays the same mark-up whether they need to consult with the designer for an hour, a week, or a month. So, customers who only need a little help choosing their colors and arranging their furniture pay the same hefty commission as those customers who need far more assistance. This is hardly a fair system.

You can't go wrong hiring a designer by the hour. This way, you only pay for exactly the help you actually need and receive.

For detailed information on locating a reputable and qualified designer in your area, negotiating a fair hourly rate, putting together a contract, and making sure the job is done properly, please read chapter 14 of my book, _The Insider's Guide To Buying Home Furnishings_.

How can I make sure I'm buying high-quality furniture?

It is important to make sure you are choosing the correct type of wood, and the correct type of fabric in the case of upholstered furniture. Making sure your furniture is made from the highest-quality and most appropriate materials is the best way to make sure it will last for a long time.

This is too broad a subject to go into here. For detailed information on furniture construction, wood types, and fabric types, please read chapters 2 and 3 of my book, _The Insider's Guide To Buying Home Furnishings_.

If I do decide to visit a factory outlet in person, what should I be sure to bring with me?

1. Simple sketches of each room you intend to decorate, with the basic room dimensions shown. Snapshots of each room are very useful, as well.

2. Measurements of all doorways and hallways that your furniture will have to go through to reach the correct room. Before you buy that unreturnable entertainment center at the factory outlet in North Carolina, it's very important to make sure it will fit through the door when you get it home.

3. Swatches of any fabrics, carpeting, or paint that you'll need when choosing upholstered furniture.

4. Photographs torn from magazines or copied from books that show the basic styles you like (and those you hate). This can be a very useful way to narrow down the look you want (and the looks you want to avoid).

5. Tape measure to measure any furniture you are considering buying. Outlets generally don't have any to lend.

6. A camera to take snapshots of furniture before you buy. It can be very helpful to take snapshots of everything that appeals to you as you shop around the various outlets, and then spread out the pictures back at your hotel room to make your final decision before going back to make your actual purchases. You may also want to be able to fax a picture to a relative back home for a second opinion.

How long will it take to receive my furniture?

If you're shopping in person at the factory outlet or discounter, you can normally have your furniture shipped to you the same day. This is another big advantage to going to North Carolina in person. Not only do you get substantially better discounts, there's no wait for your furniture.

If you order your furniture over the phone from a discounter, you will normally have to wait 8-12 weeks for your furniture to be delivered. Just like local furniture retailers, furniture discounters custom-order your furniture directly from the manufacturer. Medium to high-end furniture is just too expensive for any store to keep in stock waiting for a buyer.

How will my furniture be shipped to me?

Most factory outlets and discounters use special furniture delivery services that will unpack your furniture and set it up in the correct place in your home, including carrying it up or down stairs if needed. It's important to be aware, though, that there are some things you need to do before your new furniture arrives.

1. Move your old furniture. It's important to have the spot where your new furniture is to go already cleared.

2. Remove pictures and other items from hallway walls. It's too easy for them to be bumped or broken as the delivery people carry your furniture down the hall. It's a good idea to remove any nails from the walls, too. Yes, this is a nuisance, but not nearly as much of a nuisance as having your brand-new upholstery repaired.

Furniture delivery people will generally not provide the following services: moving your old furniture, taking away packing materials, and putting electronic equipment into entertainment centers.

How much will the freight charges be to have my furniture shipped home?

The freight charges will depend on the weight of the furniture. The factory outlet or discounter will be able to give you a written quote at the time you place your order or buy your furniture in person.

Occasionally, I am asked if the cost of having furniture shipped to you from North Carolina will outweigh or cancel out the savings. No.

The normal savings on furniture purchased from factory outlets and discounters is 50% to 80% off retail. The usual freight charge to have your furniture shipped home normally runs about 5% of the retail cost of the furniture. So, you are still far ahead to order your furniture directly rather than through a local retailer.

Another thing to bear in mind is that whether you order your furniture through a local furniture store or directly from a North Carolina factory outlet or discounter, it all has to be shipped from North Carolina either way. That's where the vast majority of the furniture factories are. No matter how you order it, the furniture will have to be shipped from North Carolina, and the cost of that freight will be passed on to you.

Can I buy custom draperies, fabrics, wallcoverings, carpeting, rugs, blinds, accessories, and other furnishings at a discount, too?

Absolutely. All of these things can be purchased directly from manufacturers, discounters, factory outlets, and local wholesale workrooms. For more information, please read chapters 3 through 18 of my book, _The Insider's Guide To Buying Home Furnishings_.

What do I do if there's a problem with my order?

Statistically, you are far less likely to have a problem with a factory outlet or discounter than you are with your local furniture dealer. Just ask anyone who put down a deposit for furniture at Sears Homelife, Heilig-Meyers, Krause's, Castro Convertibles, or any of the hundreds of other furniture retailers who have gone bankrupt in the last few years. Still, every year a few problems do occur with furniture ordered from North Carolina.

The best defense is prevention. Avoiding problems before they happen and troubleshooting them after they happen is too broad a subject to go into here. For more information on this subject, please read chapter 20 of my book, _The Insider's Guide To Buying Home Furnishings_.

How can I obtain updated information on the outlets and discounters in this book?

Visit my Web site, **www.smartdecorating.com**, and subscribe to the SmartDecorating.com Newsletter. Each newsletter has any necessary updates on the sources in this book.

I always let my readers know which stores may have moved, closed, or received customer service complaints since the last book printing. I also let my readers know about new sources I've found, special sales coming up, bargains on hotel rooms, etc.

Why don't you list Web sites that sell furniture in this book?

This book lists "brick and mortar" stores only. The only Web sites listed in this book are those run by companies which also have a storefront open to the public.

Any company that sells furniture only on the Web, without a storefront open to the public, will not be listed here. Some of these Web sites are legitimate. Many are not.

I am currently researching a separate guide for Web sites that sell furniture. It will be available in electronic form only at my Web site, www.smartdecorating.com, later in 2004.

FOR MORE INFORMATION ON

GROUP SHOPPING TOURS TO NORTH CAROLINA

AND

SPECIAL SALES AT FACTORY OUTLETS

PLEASE CHECK OUR WEB SITE AT:

WWW.SMARTDECORATING.COM

FACTORY OUTLETS
AND
DISCOUNTERS

A & H Wayside Furniture

1086 Freeway Dr.
Reidsville, NC 27320

Phone:	**(336) 342-0717**	**Hours:**	**M-F 8:30-5:30, Sat 9:00-5:00**
Toll Free:	**(800) 334-0369**	**E-mail:**	**wayside@netmcr.com**
Fax:	**(336) 342-6524**	**Web site:**	**www.ahwayside.com**

A & H Wayside Furniture has been discounting furniture by phone since 1974. They are a very well established company with a good reputation for service.

If you visit this source in person, don't forget to check out their clearance center about a mile down the road!

Lines carried:

2nd Ave	Bevan Funnell, Ltd.	Conover Chair	Hekman
A. A. Laun	Black Hawk	Cox Furniture Mfg.	Hickory Hill
Action/Lane	Bradington Young	C. R. Laine	Highland House
Alexvale	Braxton Culler	Craftique	Hooker
American Drew	Brown-Jordan	Distinctive Designs	Howard Miller Clocks
Artistica Metal Design	Broyhill	Fairfax	Johnston Casuals
Ashley	Cebu	Fairfield Chair Co.	Keller
Athol Table	Charleston Forge	Fashion Bed Group	Key City
Barcalounger	Cherry Valley Furniture	Ficks-Reed	Kimball
Barn Door	Classic Leather	Flat Rock Furniture	Klaussner
Benchcraft	Clayton-Marcus	Flexsteel	Koch Originals
Berkline	Cochrane	Friendship Upholstery	Lane
Bermex	Comfort Designs	Hammary	Lea Industries

Phone orders accepted:	**Yes**
Discount:	**40%-50% off mfrs. suggested retail**
Payment methods:	**VISA, MC, Discover, AMEX, personal checks**
In-house financing available:	**No**
Deposits required:	**50% deposit when order is placed, balance due when furniture is ready to be shipped**
Catalog available:	**No**
Clearance center:	**Yes - See *A & H Wayside Clearance Center***
Delivery:	**Full service in-home delivery and set-up. Customer pays freight company directly for shipping costs.**

Directions: From I-40, near Greensboro, NC, take Hwy. 29 north at exit #127. After about 30 miles you will come to the Reidsville area. Take the first Reidsville exit, and go west on Business 29. After about 8 miles, you will come to a major intersection where Business 29 will bear left. Stay on Business 29. About 1/2 mile after the intersection, you will see A & H Wayside on the right side of the road next to an Oldsmobile dealership.

A & H Wayside Furniture (cont.)

Lines carried (cont.):

Leather Trend
Legacy Classic Furniture
Lexington
Lloyd Flanders
Millennium
New England Clock Co.
Nichols & Stone
Pennsylvania House
Peters-Revington
Powell
Pulaski
Regency House
Richardson Bros.
Riverside
Royal Patina
Saloom
Sam Moore
Schnadig
Serta Mattress
Sligh Clocks
Sligh Furniture
South Sea Rattan
Southwood
Spring Air Mattress
Statesville Chair
Statton
Taylor-King
Tropitone
Universal
Uwharrie Chair
Vanguard
Vaughan
Virginia Metalcrafters
Webb
Weiman
Wesley Allen
Wesley Hall
Whitaker
Winners Only
Winston
Woodmark Originals
Yesteryear Wicker

A & H Wayside Clearance Center

1550 Freeway Dr.
Reidsville, NC 27320

Phone:	(336) 342-4532	**Hours:**	M-F 8:30-5:30, Sat 9:00-5:00
Toll Free:	None	**E-mail:**	wayside@netmcr.com
Fax:	None	**Web site:**	None

A & H Wayside Clearance Center carries discontinued styles, floor samples, and customer returns from A & H Wayside's main showroom and telephone sales center just up the street. They have a nice selection of contemporary and traditional furniture, the vast majority of which is in new first-quality condition.

A & H Wayside also has a spotless record of customer service. I've never heard a single delivery related complaint about them.

This clearance center is definitely worth checking out if you are in the Greensboro, NC, area. Reidsville is only about a half hour drive northeast of Greensboro.

Lines carried:	See listings under *A & H Wayside Furniture*
Phone orders accepted:	No
Discount:	50%-70% off mfrs. suggested retail
Payment methods:	VISA, MC, Discover, AMEX, personal checks
In-house financing available:	No
Deposits required:	Not applicable
Catalog available:	No
Clearance center:	Not applicable
Delivery:	Full service in-home delivery and set-up. Customer pays freight company directly for shipping costs.

Directions: From I-40, near Greensboro, NC, take Hwy. 29 north at exit #127. After about 30 miles you will come to the Reidsville area. Take the first Reidsville exit, and go west on Business 29. After about 8 miles, you will come to a major intersection where Business 29 will bear left. Stay on Business 29. About 2 miles after the intersection, you will see the A & H Wayside Clearance Center on the right side of the road across the street from a Lowes grocery store, approximately 1 1/2 miles past A & H Wayside's main store.

A Land Of Furniture

The Atrium
430 S. Main St.
High Point, NC 27260

Phone:	(336) 882-3876	**Hours:**	M-Sat 9:00-6:00
Toll Free:	None	**E-mail:**	alandoffurniture@atriumfurniture.com
Fax:	(336) 882-3866	**Web site:**	www.atriumfurniture.com

A Land Of Furniture just opened in 2003 at the Atrium Furniture Mall in High Point, NC. They have a good reputation for honesty and service in their first year of business.

They stock medium quality casegoods and upholstery from some lesser known lines: Aspen, Hillcraft, Rodi, and Fraenkel. Styles represented include Shaker, Mission, contemporary, transitional, and traditional. The quality on these lines is comparable to Bassett or Broyhill.

This is a new store on the block, but I've found them to be honest and eager to please their customers. If you're in the market for medium-quality furnishings, do give them a call.

Lines carried:

Aspen
Fraenkel
Hillcraft
Rodi

Phone orders accepted:	Yes
Discount:	25%-40% off mfrs. suggested retail
Payment methods:	VISA, MC, Discover, AMEX, personal checks
In-house financing available:	Yes
Deposits required:	50% deposit when order is placed, balance due when furniture is ready to be shipped
Catalog available:	No
Clearance center:	No
Delivery:	Full service in-home delivery and set-up. Customer pays freight company directly for shipping costs.

Directions: A Land Of Furniture is located inside the Atrium complex in downtown High Point. Please see *The Atrium* for complete directions.

About Last Nite

Catawba Furniture Mall
377 Hwy. 70 SW
Hickory, NC 28602

Phone:	**(828) 324-2830**	**Hours:**	**M-Sat 9:00-6:00**
Toll Free:	**None**	**E-mail:**	**aln@twave.net**
Fax:	**(828) 324-2866**	**Web site:**	**www.catawbafurniture.com**

About Last Nite at the Catawba Furniture Mall has a great selection of high end linens, beds, cribs, and bed & bath accessories. You could do a great job decorating a nursery or an adult bedroom with the lines they carry.

The linens are priced as low as the manufacturers will permit. As with some furniture lines, most linens manufacturers set a minimum discount which they will not allow discounters to price their lines below. You'll find a better deal here than you will just about anywhere else.

About Last Nite has a great reputation for customer service, and a very helpful staff. If you're interested in fine linens or beautiful beds you really should check prices with this source.

Lines carried:

Aubergine Bedding	Fleur de Lis Linens	Old Biscayne Design	Style Craft
Basil's Linens	Frette	One Thousand Islands	Sweet Dreams Linens
Bella Notte Bedding	Good Home	Peacock Alley	Urban Evolutions
Bradshaw Kirchofer	J. Clayton Int'l Linens	Pine Cone Hill Bedding	Wildcat Territory
California Kids Bedding	K. Hall	Purist Linens	Bedding
Chandler Collection	Lady Primrose	Robert Domond	
Christy Linens	Legacy Linens	SDH Linens	
Eastern Accents	Matteo	Sferra Bros.	
Fino Lino Linens	Mystic Valley Traders	Stone Country Iron Works	

Phone orders accepted:	**Yes**
Discount:	**20% off mfrs. suggested retail price on furniture lines. Discount varies on linens.**
Payment methods:	**VISA, MC, Discover, AMEX, personal checks**
In-house financing available:	**Yes**
Deposits required:	**50% deposit when order is placed, balance due when furniture is ready to be shipped**
Catalog available:	**No**
Clearance center:	**No**
Delivery:	**Full service in-home delivery and set-up. Customer pays freight company directly for shipping costs.**

Directions: Please see *Catawba Furniture Mall* for complete directions.

About Last Nite

The Atrium
430 S. Main St.
High Point, NC 27260

Phone:	**(336) 885-9737**	**Hours:**	**M-Sat 9:00-6:00**
Toll Free:	**None**	**E-mail:**	**aln@twave.net**
Fax:	**(336) 885-1098**	**Web site:**	**www.atriumfurniture.com**

About Last Nite at the Atrium Furniture Mall has a great selection of high end linens, beds, cribs, and bed & bath accessories. You could do a great job decorating a nursery or an adult bedroom with the lines they carry.

The linens are priced as low as the manufacturers will permit. As with some furniture lines, most linens manufacturers set a minimum discount which they will not allow discounters to price their lines below. You'll find a better deal here than you will just about anywhere else.

About Last Nite has a great reputation for customer service, and a very helpful staff. If you're interested in fine linens or beautiful beds you really should check prices with this source.

Lines carried:

Aubergine Bedding	Fleur de Lis Linens	Old Biscayne Design	Style Craft
Basil's Linens	Frette	One Thousand Islands	Sweet Dreams Linens
Bella Notte Bedding	Good Home	Peacock Alley	Urban Evolutions
Bradshaw Kirchofer	J. Clayton Int'l Linens	Pine Cone Hill Bedding	Wildcat Territory
California Kids Bedding	K. Hall	Purist Linens	Bedding
Chandler Collection	Lady Primrose	Robert Domond	
Christy Linens	Legacy Linens	SDH Linens	
Eastern Accents	Matteo	Sferra Bros.	
Fino Lino Linens	Mystic Valley Traders	Stone Country Iron Works	

Phone orders accepted:	**Yes**
Discount:	**20% off mfrs. suggested retail price on furniture lines. Discount varies on linens.**
Payment methods:	**VISA, MC, Discover, AMEX, personal checks**
In-house financing available:	**Yes**
Deposits required:	**50% deposit when order is placed, balance due when furniture is ready to be shipped**
Catalog available:	**No**
Clearance center:	**No**
Delivery:	**Full service in-home delivery and set-up. Customer pays freight company directly for shipping costs.**

Directions: Please see *The Atrium* for complete directions.

Adams Furniture

301 North Main St
High Point, NC 27262

Phone:	(336) 889-0807	**Hours:**	**M-F 9:30-5:30, Sat 9:00-5:00**
Toll Free:	None	**E-mail:**	**adamsfurn@aol.com**
Fax:	(336) 889-0827	**Web site:**	**www.adamsfurniture.com**

Adams Furniture is a factory direct source for lovely high-end 18th century English reproduction furniture. All of their furniture is manufactured from mahogany, walnut, oak, cherry, and yew. Their entire line is made in England.

Their quality and style is top of the line. Although this is their main showroom to the furniture trade, the public is also permitted to shop here at a 30%-40% discount.

They also have a clearance center just down the street with deeper discounts on selected items: up to 70% off retail. Please note that the clearance center is open by appointment only. Please call the main store if you wish to visit the clearance center.

From time to time, Adams Furniture purchases antique pieces at auction in England and brings them to their High Point showroom as well. Of course, the prices vary on these pieces.

On a recent visit, I found a gorgeous mahogany breakfront bookcase with yew inlay (pictured on the following page). This is a new piece, available by special order. The retail price is $15,795.00, and the discounted price available to the public is $9,477.00. For a bookcase of this style and quality, that's a real bargain.

If you're in the market for high-end English reproduction furniture, you absolutely should visit this showroom!

Phone orders accepted:	**Yes**
Discount:	**30%-40% off mfrs. suggested retail**
Payment methods:	**VISA, MC, personal checks**
Deposits required:	**50% deposit when order is placed, balance due when furniture is ready to be shipped**
Catalog available:	**Yes, a limited catalog is on their Web site**
Clearance center:	**Yes**
Delivery:	**Full service in-home delivery and set-up. Customer pays freight company directly for shipping costs.**

Directions: **Adams Furniture is in downtown High Point, NC. From I-85, take exit #111 (Hwy. 311), and head northwest into High Point. After several miles, when you reach downtown High Point, Hwy. 311 will become Main St. Adams Furniture will be on the far left corner at the intersection of N. Main St. and English Rd.**

Adams Furniture (cont.)

Mahogany breakfront bookcase from Adams Furniture

Retail: $15,795.00   Discounted price: $9,477.00
Savings at Adams Furniture: $6,318.00 = 40% off retail

Alan Ferguson Associates

422 South Main St.
High Point, NC 27260

Phone:	**(336) 889-3866**	**Hours:**	**M-F 9:00-5:00, Sat 10:00-4:00**
Toll Free:	**None**	**E-mail:**	**john@alanferguson.com**
Fax:	**(336) 889-6271**	**Web site:**	**Under construction**

This is a wonderful source for high-end contemporary and traditional furnishings. The ground floor has a beautifully decorated traditional showroom. There are some lovely antiques, as well as new pieces from Thayer Coggin, Wellington Hall, Bevan-Funnell and many other lines. Most of the furniture here is 40-50% off retail.

Alan Ferguson Associates specializes in the unusual, even among their traditional lines. If you're looking for an 8 1/2 foot tall entertainment center for a high-ceilinged room, for instance, they've got one.

The entire second floor is devoted to contemporary furnishings. They have a particularly nice selection of contemporary dining room sets and occasional chairs.

If you're on the lookout for contemporary furniture and accessories, or something just a bit out of the ordinary in the traditional vein, you should definitely visit this source!

Lines carried:

Accessories International	Currey & Co.	Hart Associates	Piage & Pieta
Allusions	Dale Tiffany Inc.	Italmond	Planum
Ambience	DIA Metal Furniture	John Richard	Preview Upholstery
Arte De Mexico	Directional Upholstery	Johnston Casuals	Quoizel
AXI	Elements By Grapevine	Lane	Robert Abbey
Bevan-Funnell	Elite	Lee Upholstery	Speer Lamps
Cambridge Lamps	Ello Casegoods & Chairs	Leeazanne	Swaim
Carvers Guild	Emerson et Cie	Lorts	Thayer Coggin
Casa Bique	Fabrica Rugs	Maitland-Smith	Theodore Alexander
Casa Stradivari	Fine Art Lamps	Masland	Van Teal
Corsican	Furniture Guild Casegoods	Mila Glassware	Wasserklar
Country Affaire/Elden	George Kovacs Lamps	Phoenix Art Group	

Phone orders accepted:	**Yes**
Discount:	**40%-50% off mfrs. suggested retail**
Payment methods:	**VISA, MC, personal checks**
Deposits required:	**50% deposit when order is placed, balance due when furniture is ready to be shipped**
Catalog available:	**No**
Clearance center:	**No**
Delivery:	**Full service in-home delivery and set-up. Customer pays freight company directly for shipping costs.**

Directions: Alan Ferguson Associates is in downtown High Point, NC. From I-85, take exit #111 (Hwy. 311), and head northwest into High Point. After several miles, when you reach downtown High Point, Hwy. 311 will become S. Main St. Alan Ferguson Associates is on the left hand side of the road, right past the Atrium furniture mall.

Alan Ferguson Associates (cont.)

Alan Ferguson Associates

Alman's Home Furnishings

110 E. First St.
Newton, NC 28658

Phone:	**(828) 464-3204**	**Hours:**	**M-F 9:00-5:00, Sat. 9:00-3:00**
Toll Free:	**(888) 729-5082**	**E-mail:**	**joelharris@charter.net**
Fax:	**(828) 464-3208**	**Web site:**	**www.almanfurniture.com**

Family owned and operated since 1946, Alman's is a well-established discounter for many medium to high end lines including Hooker, Bassett, Natuzzi, and Lexington, among many others.

Their galleries occupy four large buildings in downtown Newton, NC, about ten miles southeast of Hickory, NC. Alman's is certainly worth a visit if you're in the Hickory area.

If you're ordering furniture by phone, definitely check Alman's prices. They have one of the best phone order policies I've ever seen: they accept credit cards for your final payment as well as your deposit, they have a written satisfaction guarantee, etc. Their reputation for customer service is excellent.

Lines carried:

Action /Lane	Chromcraft	Klaussner	Pulaski
American Drew	Clark Casual	Lane	Rex
Ashley	Cochrane	Lea	Ridgewood
Barcalounger	Craftique	Lexington	Riverside
Bassett	Flexsteel	Lloyd Flanders	Richardson Brothers
Benchcraft	Hammary	Lyon Shaw	Singer Furniture
Berkline	Henry Link	Morgan Stewart	Southern Furniture
Berkshire	Highland House	Morganton Chair	Universal
Broyhill	Hooker	National Mt. Airy	Vanguard
Clayton Marcus	J. Royale	Natuzzi	Vaughan
Classic Leather	Keller	Nichols and Stone	Wesley Allen
Charleston Forge	Kincaid	Palliser	

Phone orders accepted:	**Yes**
Discount:	**Approximately 50% off mfrs. suggested retail**
Payment methods:	**VISA, MC, AMEX, Discover, cash**
In-house financing available:	**Yes**
Deposits required:	**50% deposit when order is placed, balance due when furniture is ready to be shipped**
Catalog available:	**No**
Clearance center:	**No**
Delivery:	**Full service in-home delivery and set-up. Customer pays freight company directly for shipping costs.**

Directions: Alman's is located near Hickory, NC. From I-40, take the Hwy. 16 exit (exit #131). Go south five miles to downtown Newton. Turn left at the courthouse.

American Accents

The Atrium
430 S. Main St.
High Point, NC 27260

Phone:	**(336) 885-7412**	**Hours:**	**M-F 9:00-6:00, Sat 9:00-5:00**
Toll Free:	**None**	**E-mail:**	**AmericanAccents@atriumfurniture.com**
Fax:	**(336) 885-8879**	**Web site:**	**www.atriumfurniture.com**

American Accents is definitely a great source to check out. They specialize in high-quality shaker and country reproductions, so if you want the early American look, this is the place to go.

This source also carries a nice variety of high-quality but lesser known lines that have the same look as better known brands. For instance, they had a very nice solid oak arts & crafts dining room set on display from Arts & Crafts Industries that was indistinguishable from the identical dining room set I viewed at the Stickley factory sale. The only thing that wasn't identical was the price tag. Arts & Crafts Industries was considerably less expensive than Stickley for the very same quality and appearance.

Pictured on the following page, the Arts & Crafts Industries dining room set I viewed at American Accents was priced at $7,689.00 for the table, four side chairs, two arm chairs, the hutch, and a separate buffet. I was then able to haggle the salesman down to $7,000.00 even if I made the purchase that day. Compare that to Stickley's prices on the identical products! American Accents also carries some very nice arts & crafts style furniture from Brown Street and Skillcraft.

If you're looking for the "Bob Timberlake" look, you might want to check out pieces by Chatham County at American Accents instead of the pricier, but nearly identical, authorized Bob Timberlake line by Lexington. The quality was excellent, and I seriously doubt that anyone could tell the difference without looking inside the drawers for the Bob Timberlake tag.

I was very impressed with American Accents. If you're looking for the "latest in-thing" by Stickley, Bob Timberlake, or any other line, you would be doing yourself a big favor to call American Accents and see what they have to offer. If you'll be in High Point in person, don't forget to check out their clearance center!

Phone orders accepted:	**Yes**
Discount:	**40%-55% off mfrs. suggested retail**
Payment methods:	**Cash or personal checks. No credit cards.**
In-house financing available:	**No**
Deposits required:	**1\3 deposit when order is placed, balance due when furniture is ready to be shipped**
Catalog available:	**No**
Clearance center:	**Yes - See *American Accents Clearance Center***
Delivery:	**Full service in-home delivery and set-up. Customer pays freight company directly for shipping costs.**

Directions: American Accents is located inside the Atrium complex in downtown High Point. Please see *The Atrium* for complete directions.

American Accents (cont.)

Mission oak dining room set from Arts & Crafts Industries

Retail: $12,815.00   Discounted price: $7,000.00
Savings at American Accents: $5,815.00 = 45% off retail

Lines carried:

Arts and Crafts Ind.	Carper's	Leisters	Park Place
Artisan's Lamps	Cassady	LT Moses Willard	Philips Furniture Co.
Ashton Pictures	Cast Classics	Marshfield	Royal Craftsman
Bermex	Chatham	Masterfield	Spectra Wood Products
Big Sky Carvers	Classic Rattan	Murry Feiss	Taos Drum
Borkholder	Comfort Air	Null Ind.	Towne Square
Bradco Chair Co.	Edrich Mills Wood Shop	Oak Heritage	Vermont Tubbs
Brent Jacobs	Hubbardton Forge	Orderest Bedding	Villageois
Brown Street	Kingsley Bates	P & P Chair	

American Accents Clearance Center

1300 S. Main St.
High Point, NC 27260

Phone:	**(336) 885-1304**	**Hours:**	**M-F 9:00-6:00, Sat 9:00-5:30**
Toll Free:	**None**	**E-mail:**	**None**
Fax:	**(336) 884-4171**	**Web site:**	**None**

American Accents Clearance Center carries customer returns, discontinued items, and floor samples from the American Accents showroom in the Atrium complex in High Point. Most of their stock is early American and shaker, but there are also some other traditional styles mixed in.

The deals here are very good. Pictured on the following page is a terrific deal they had on a solid pine entertainment center. It was in perfect condition and only $549.00.

They will also sell by phone if you know what you want and they have it on the sale floor. If you're in High Point, definitely stop in here.

Lines carried:	**Please see listings under *American Accents***
Phone orders accepted:	**Yes**
Discount:	**50%-60% off mfrs. suggested retail**
Payment methods:	**Cash or personal checks. No credit cards.**
In-house financing available:	**No**
Deposits required:	**Payment in full required at time of purchase**
Catalog available:	**No**
Clearance center:	**Not applicable**
Delivery:	**Company's own trucks in some areas, otherwise a full-service delivery company. Customer pays freight company directly for shipping costs.**

Directions: **American Accents Clearance Center is in downtown High Point, NC. From I-85, take exit #111 (Hwy. 311), and head northwest into High Point. After several miles, when you reach downtown High Point, Hwy. 311 will become S. Main St. American Accents Clearance Center is on the left hand side of the road, at the intersection of S. Main St. and Kearns Ave. Turn left on Kearns Ave., and park behind the store.**

American Accents Clearance Center (cont.)

American Accents Clearance Center

Solid pine entertainment center from American Accents

Retail: $1,099.00   Discounted price: $549.00
Savings at American Accents: $550.00 = 50% off retail

American Reproductions

The Atrium
430 S. Main St.
High Point, NC 27260

Phone:	**(336) 889-8305**	**Hours:**	**M-F 9:00-6:00, Sat 9:00-5:00**
Toll Free:	**(800) 334-0369**	**E-mail:**	**american@northstate.net**
Fax:	**(336) 889-8302**	**Web site:**	**www.americanreproductions.com**

American Reproductions has a gorgeous showroom in the Atrium furniture complex in High Point. They have a very nice selection of high end traditional reproduction furniture. They are owned by A & H Wayside Furniture of Reidsville, NC, which has had an excellent reputation for service for many years.

On a recent visit, I found a great deal on a beautiful mahogany canopy bed and matching mahogany chest on chest from Lloyd Buxton (pictured on the following page). The bed retails for $6,305.00, and the chest retails for $7,665.00. The price at American Reproductions was only $3,105.00 for the bed and $3,775.00 for the chest. That's a savings of 51% off retail!

Most pieces are marked at about 40%-50% off retail, with a few lines as much as 70% off retail.

If you are looking for something unique in high-end traditional furniture, definitely visit this showroom. This source also accepts phone orders and ships nationwide.

Lines carried:

Action by Lane	Big Sky Carvers	Cox Furniture Mfg.	Finkel Outdoor
Alexvale	Black Hawk Furniture Inc.	Craftmaster	Flat Rock
American Reproductions	Bradington Young	Crawford Furniture Co.	Furniture Classics
Armando Rho	Braxton Culler	C. R. Laine Upholstery	Gat Creek
Ashley	British Traditions	Custom Shoppe	Hammary
Baker	Butler Specialty Co.	Designer Wicker	Hooker
Bassett	Charleston Forge	Designmaster Furniture	James River
Benchcraft	Christopher Coleson	Distinctive Imports	John Richard Collection
Benetti's Italia USA	Conestoga Wood Inc.	Eastern Accents	Kings Road
Benicia Foundry	Cooper Classics	Elliott's Designs Inc.	Lane Co.
Bentwood	Corsican Brass	Fairfield Chair Co.	Ligo Products Inc.

Phone orders accepted:	**Yes**
Discount:	**40%-70% off mfrs. suggested retail**
Payment methods:	**VISA, MC, Discover, AMEX, personal checks**
In-house financing available:	**No**
Deposits required:	**50% deposit when order is placed, balance due when furniture is ready to be shipped**
Catalog available:	**No**
Clearance center:	**No**
Delivery:	**Full service in-home delivery and set-up. Customer pays freight company directly for shipping costs.**

Directions: American Reproductions is located inside the Atrium complex in downtown High Point. Please see *The Atrium* for complete directions.

American Reproductions (cont.)

Solid mahogany canopy bed from Lloyd Buxton

Retail: $6,305.00   Discounted price: $3,105.00
Savings at American Reproductions: $3,200.00 = 51% off retail

Solid mahogany chest on chest from Lloyd Buxton

Retail: $7,665.00   Discounted price: $3,775.00
Savings at American Reproductions: $3,890.00 = 51% off retail

Lines carried (cont.):

Lloyd Buxton	Our House Designs	Southern Furniture	Winston Furniture
Lyon-Shaw Inc.	Paladin	Spring Air Mattress	Wisconsin
Madison Square	PAMA	Stuart	Woodard
Master Design Furniture	Peters Revington	Taylor King	
Magnussen Presidential	Progressive Furniture	Timmerman	
McKay Custom Products	Pulaski Furniture Corp.	Tom Seely Furniture	
Millennium	RER Furniture	Uwharrie Chair	
Mobel, Inc.Oakwood	River Forks Imports	Vaughan Furniture	
Interiors	Riverside Furniture Co.	William Sheppe	
Ohio Table Pad Co.	Sam Moore	Winners Only	

Amish Oak and Cherry

4370 Hickory Blvd.
Granite Falls, NC 28630

Phone:	(828) 396-5001	**Hours:**	M-Sat 9:00-5:00
Toll Free:	None	**E-mail:**	sales@amishoakandcherry.com
Fax:	(828) 396-5688	**Web site:**	www.amishoakandcherry.com

Amish Oak and Cherry is a great source for genuine Amish furniture in North Carolina. They work directly with Amish craftspeople to market their furniture to the general public. They have two locations: this one in Granite Falls, and one at the Hickory Furniture Mart about 15 minutes south in Hickory, NC.

The quality is top notch. Each piece is solid oak or solid cherry. They also use a 15 step catalyzed finish on each piece that makes it highly resistant to scratches, spills, and other damage. The finish looks great as well.

Their entire product line is casegoods only, no upholstery. Most of their stock is in bedrooms sets, dining room sets, and entertainment centers. Styles include Shaker, Mission, and traditional. You can check out their entire product line at their Web site, above.

They also have a very nice collection of home office furniture, including the only old fashioned rolltop desks I've ever seen that are designed for a modern computer!

Their prices are good, if you consider the quality you receive. Please see my review of their Hickory store for a specific example of the quality and price you can expect to find from this source.

In terms of quality and value for money, Amish Oak and Cherry is a great source. Their service is outstanding as well. I've never heard one single complaint about them.

Phone orders accepted:	Yes
Discount:	Factory direct prices to the public
Payment methods:	VISA, MC, Discover, personal checks
In-house financing available:	No
Deposits required:	20% deposit when order is placed, balance due when furniture is ready to be shipped
Catalog available:	No
Clearance center:	No
Delivery:	Full service in-home delivery and set-up. Customer pays freight company directly for shipping costs.

Directions: From I-40, take exit #123 and drive north on Hwy. 321 to Granite Falls. Amish Oak and Cherry is on the right side of the road.

Amish Oak and Cherry

Level 1
Hickory Furniture Mart
U. S. Hwy 70 SE
Hickory, NC 28602

Phone:	**(828) 261-4776**	**Hours:**	**M-Sat 9:00-6:00**
Toll Free:	**None**	**E-mail:**	**sales@amishoakandcherry.com**
Fax:	**(828) 261-4779**	**Web site:**	**www.amishoakandcherry.com**

Amish Oak and Cherry is a great source for genuine Amish furniture in North Carolina. They work directly with Amish craftspeople to market Amish-made furniture to the general public. They have two locations: this one at the Hickory Furniture Mart, and another showroom about 15 minutes north in Granite Falls, NC.

The quality is top notch. Each piece is solid oak or solid cherry. They also use a 15 step catalyzed finish on each piece that makes it highly resistant to scratches, spills, and other damage. The finish looks great as well.

Their entire product line is casegoods only, no upholstery. Most of their stock is in bedrooms sets, dining room sets, and entertainment centers. Styles include Shaker, Mission, and traditional. You can check out their entire product line at their Web site, above.

They also have a very nice collection of home office furniture, including the only old fashioned rolltop desks I've ever seen that are designed for a modern computer!

Their prices are good, if you consider the quality you receive. For instance, on a recent visit I found a very nice Mission dining room set in solid oak (pictured on the following page). The total retail for the set including the table, six chairs, and china hutch was $13,322.00. During their after-market sale, the price was discounted to $10,092.00. $10,000 is a great buy for a solid oak dining room set in this quality. This is the kind of set you can give your grandchildren some day.

However, you can get certainly similar styles in lesser quality for a better price around NC. They won't be built to the high standard of quality you'll find here, but they'll certainly be fine for most families. So, it just depends on what your budget is and what you're looking for.

In terms of quality and value for money, Amish Oak and Cherry is a great source. Their service is outstanding as well. I've never heard one single complaint about them.

Phone orders accepted:	**Yes**
Discount:	**Factory direct prices to the public**
Payment methods:	**VISA, MC, Discover, personal checks**
In-house financing available:	**No**
Deposits required:	**20% deposit when order is placed, balance due when furniture is ready to be shipped**
Catalog available:	**No**
Clearance center:	**No**
Delivery:	**Full service in-home delivery and set-up. Customer pays freight company directly for shipping costs.**

Directions: Amish Oak and Cherry is located inside the Hickory Furniture Mart. Please see *Hickory Furniture Mart* for complete directions.

Amish Oak and Cherry (cont.)

Solid oak dining room set from Amish Oak and Cherry

Retail: $13,322.00   Discounted price: $10,092.00
Savings at Amish Oak and Cherry: $3,230.00 = 25% off retail

Ashley Interiors (Braxton Culler Factory Outlet)

310 S. Elm St.
(inside the Braxton Culler Bldg.)
High Point, NC 27260

Phone:	**(336) 889-7573**	**Hours:**	**M-Sat 9:00-5:00**
Toll Free:	None		**Closed April and October**
Fax:	**(336) 889-7574**	**E-mail:**	None
		Web site:	**www.braxtonculler.com**

Ashley Interiors is a retailer of new furniture, but they also function as the Braxton Culler factory outlet. They will take orders by phone or in person for new furniture from Braxton Culler's current line at 50% off the manufacturer's suggested retail.

The showroom also has a limited selection of Braxton Culler floor samples and discontinued styles at 75% off retail. These can be purchased by phone if you know exactly what style you want and the outlet happens to have it on the sales floor.

This showroom is closed during April and October due to the bi-annual High Point International Home Furnishings Market, when retailers from all over the U. S. converge on High Point, NC, to see and purchase the latest furniture styles. However, just prior to closing for market, Ashley Interiors normally has a special sale where all items, including those from Braxton Culler's current line, are marked down to 75% off retail. These sales normally run for the entire months of March and September. Please check www.smartdecorating.com for the exact sale dates each spring and fall.

So, if you're planning a trip to the High Point area in March or September, you should definitely check out this outlet. If you specifically wish to purchase new Braxton Culler furniture, you should strongly consider waiting for the March or September sale and buying it here. I haven't seen any other source that can match Ashley Interiors' special sale prices on the Braxton Culler line.

Phone orders accepted:	Yes
Discount:	**50%-75% off mfrs. suggested retail**
Payment methods:	**VISA, MC, personal checks**
In-house financing available:	No
Deposits required:	**35% deposit when order is placed, balance due when furniture is ready to be shipped**
Catalog available:	No
Clearance center:	Not applicable
Delivery:	**Full service in-home delivery and set-up. Customer pays freight company directly for shipping costs.**

Directions: **From I-85, take exit #111 (Hwy. 311), and head northwest into High Point. Go several miles into downtown High Point. Just after you pass The Atrium furniture mall and Alan Ferguson associates on your left, turn left at the next light onto Russell Ave. Ashley Interiors, inside the Braxton Culler Bldg., is one block down on your right on the corner of Russell and Elm St.**

The Atrium

430 S. Main St.
High Point, NC 27260

Phone:	(336) 882-5599	**Hours:**	M-F 9:00-6:00, Sat 9:00-5:00
Toll Free:	None	**E-mail:**	info@atriumfurniture.com
Fax:	(336) 882-6950	**Web site:**	www.atriumfurniture.com

The Atrium Furniture Mall is a huge four-story building in downtown High Point which contains 21 furniture showrooms.

Please see the individual listings in this book for each gallery or outlet for details on payment, shipping, lines carried, etc:

A Land Of Furniture	(336) 882-3876
American Accents	(336) 885-7412
American Reproductions	(336) 889-8305
Decorators Choice	(336) 889-6115
Decorators Choice 3rd Level	(336) 889-8568
Far Eastern Furnishings	(336) 882-0180
French Furniture Outlet	(336) 883-3984
Georgian Lane	(336) 882-0414
Heirloom Traditions	(336) 882-5597
HomeLand Furniture USA	(336) 454-1955
Kagan's American Drew	(336) 885-8568
Kagan's Gallery 1st Level	(336) 885-1333
Kagan's Gallery 3rd Level	(336) 885-8300
Klaussner Home	(336) 884-0438
Leather & More	(336) 882-3042
LeatherLand USA	(336) 454-2215
Medallion Furniture	(336) 889-3432
Robert Bergelin Co.	(336) 889-2189
Room By Room	(336) 889-0423
Rooms To Grow	(336) 885-4705
Wood-Armfield	(336) 889-6522

The Atrium has two very good mall-wide sales in May and November, right after the bi-annual High Point International Home Furnishings Market. Many other factory outlets and showrooms in the High Point area have special sales during these months, too, so you may wish to plan any trips to High Point to take advantage of these extra discounts.

You may also wish to join one of my shopping tours, which visit the High Point area during the after-market sales. Complete details are at www.smartdecorating.com.

Directions: **The Atrium Furniture Mall is in downtown High Point, NC. From I-85, take exit #111 (Hwy. 311), and head northwest into High Point. After several miles, when you reach downtown High Point, Hwy. 311 will become S. Main St. The Atrium Furniture Mall is on the left hand side of the road, right next to Alan Ferguson Associates.**

The Atrium (cont.)

The Atrium Furniture Mall

Baker Odds & Ends (Factory Outlet)

267 East Altamonte Drive
Altamonte Springs, FL 32701

Phone:	**(407) 262-9179**	**Hours:**	**M-F 10:00-6:00, Sat 10:00-5:00**
Toll Free:	**None**		**Sun 12:00-5:00**
Fax:	**(407) 262-9181**	**E-mail:**	**None**
		Web site:	**www.kohlerinteriors.com**

Baker Odds & Ends in Altamonte Springs, FL, (a close suburb of Orlando) is the one of the three newest direct outlets to the public for Baker Furniture. Like the other Baker Odds & Ends stores, the outlet is fairly small, but it has some terrific bargains.

This outlet has a nice variety of upholstered pieces, beds, desks, armoires, chests, etc. Most pieces are floor samples from the various Baker wholesale showrooms in design centers all over the U. S.   There are a few seconds, but the vast majority of the stock here is in new first-quality condition. New pieces arrive every week. If you're going to be in the Orlando area, you should definitely check out this outlet.

Phone orders accepted:	**No**
Discount:	**60%-75% off mfrs. suggested retail**
Payment methods:	**VISA, MC, AMEX, Discover, personal checks**
In-house financing available:	**No**
Deposits required:	**Not applicable**
Catalog available:	**No**
Clearance center:	**Not applicable**
Delivery:	**Full service inside delivery and setup are available through several services. Please contact the outlet for more information.**

Directions: From I-4, take the Exit #38 (Hwy. 436), and go east. Baker Odds and Ends is at the first left, in the Marshall's Shopping Center. You'll see a Denny's restaurant on the corner.

Baker Odds & Ends (Factory Outlet)

765-J Woodlake Rd.
Kohler, WI 53044

Phone:	**(920) 458-2033**	**Hours:**	**M-F 10:00-6:00, Sat 10:00-5:00**
Toll Free:	**None**		**Sun 12:00-5:00**
Fax:	**(920) 458-3202**	**E-mail:**	**None**
		Web site:	**www.kohlerinteriors.com**

Baker Odds & Ends in Kohler, WI, was the first of Baker Furniture's new "Odds and Ends" outlets where they sell direct to the public. Baker is owned by the Kohler Co., which is based here. Kohler, WI, is a suburb of Sheboygan, WI, about one hour's drive north of Milwaukee on Interstate 43. The store is a bit small compared to most furniture factory outlets, but it does have some very good bargains.

On my last visit here, I found a very nice mahogany dining room set from Baker's Williamsburg Reproduction Collection (pictured on the following page). The table normally retails for $6,286.00, but the outlet price was only $2,995.00. The chairs normally retail for $2,091.00 each, but the outlet had them for only $795.00 apiece. The total discount was about 55% off Baker's normal retail price on this set. The set I found at the outlet was a floor sample in new first-quality condition.

The outlet has a good variety of upholstered pieces, beds, desks, armoires, chests, etc. Most pieces are floor samples from the various Baker wholesale showrooms in design centers around the U. S. Some are overruns from their manufacturing plants in nearby Holland, MI, and Grand Rapids, MI. There are a few seconds, but the vast majority of the stock here is in new first-quality condition. New pieces arrive every Wednesday. If you're going to be in the Milwaukee or Madison area, you should definitely consider taking a side trip to this outlet.

Phone orders accepted:	**No**
Discount:	**60%-75% off mfrs. suggested retail**
Payment methods:	**VISA, MC, AMEX, Discover, personal checks**
In-house financing available:	**No**
Deposits required:	**Not applicable**
Catalog available:	**No**
Clearance center:	**Not applicable**
Delivery:	**A separate company, Jim's Delivery, makes deliveries from this outlet to Chicago and various points in Indiana and Michigan. Please call (920) 565-3738 for more information. Other customers must make their own arrangements to take purchases home.**

Directions: **From I-43, take exit #126 (Hwy. 23) and head west into Kohler, WI. After about 2/3 of a mile, take the "Y" exit into the village of Kohler. You will see the Shops at Woodlake on your left. Baker Odds & Ends is near the center of the Shops at Woodlake strip mall.**

Baker Odds & Ends (Factory Outlet) (cont.)

Inside Baker Odds & Ends in Kohler, WI

Williamsburg Reproduction mahogany dining room set from Baker Furniture

Retail: $14,650.00   Discounted price: $6,175.00
Savings at Baker Odds & Ends: $8,475.00 = 58% off retail

Baker Odds & Ends (Factory Outlet)

4329 South Peoria Avenue
Tulsa, OK 74105

Phone:	(918) 746-0329	**Hours:**	M-F 10:00-6:00, Sat 10:00-5:00
Toll Free:	None		Sun 1:00-6:00
Fax:	(918) 746-0368	**E-mail:**	None
		Web site:	None

Baker Odds & Ends in Tulsa, OK, is the one of the three newest direct outlets to the public for Baker Furniture. Like the first Baker Odds & Ends stores in Kohler, WI, and St. Louis, MO, the outlet is fairly small, but it has some terrific bargains.

This outlet has a nice variety of upholstered pieces, beds, desks, armoires, chests, etc. Most pieces are floor samples from the various Baker wholesale showrooms in design centers all over the U. S. There are a few seconds, but the vast majority of the stock here is in new first-quality condition. New pieces arrive every week. If you're going to be in the Tulsa area, you should definitely check out this outlet.

Phone orders accepted:	**No**
Discount:	**60%-75% off mfrs. suggested retail**
Payment methods:	**VISA, MC, AMEX, Discover, personal checks**
In-house financing available:	**No**
Deposits required:	**Not applicable**
Catalog available:	**No**
Clearance center:	**Not applicable**
Delivery:	**Full service inside delivery and setup are available through several services. Please contact the outlet for more information**

Directions: From I-44, take the Peoria Ave. exit and go north on Peoria Ave. Go 7/10 of a mile, and then you'll see the outlet on the right hand side in a strip mall.

Baker Odds & Ends (Factory Outlet)

10027 Manchester Rd.
Warson Woods, MO 63122

Phone:	**(314) 909-7902**	**Hours:**	**M-F 10:00-8:00, Sat 10:00-5:00**
Toll Free:	**None**		**Sun 12:00-5:00**
Fax:	**None**	**E-mail:**	**None**
		Web site:	**None**

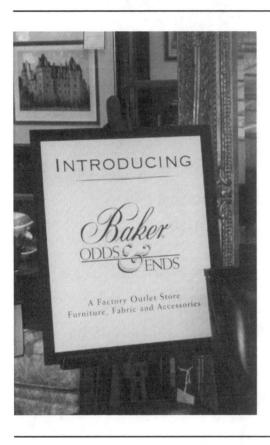

Baker Odds & Ends in the St. Louis area is one of the largest of Baker Furniture's direct outlets to the public.

On my most recent visit here, I found a beautiful mahogany highboy from Baker's Williamsburg Reproduction Collection (pictured on the following page) for 62% off retail. This piece normally retails for $26,140.00, but the outlet had one available for $9,995.00. It was a floor sample in new first-quality condition.

This outlet has a nice variety of upholstered pieces, beds, desks, armoires, chests, etc. Most pieces are floor samples from the various Baker wholesale showrooms in design centers all over the U. S. There are a few seconds, but the vast majority of the stock here is in new first-quality condition. New pieces arrive every week. If you're going to be in the St. Louis area, you should definitely check out this outlet.

Phone orders accepted:	**No**
Discount:	**60%-75% off mfrs. suggested retail**
Payment methods:	**VISA, MC, AMEX, Discover, personal checks**
In-house financing available:	**No**
Deposits required:	**Not applicable**
Catalog available:	**No**
Clearance center:	**Not applicable**
Delivery:	**Delivery in St. Louis area for a flat $75 fee per trip, regardless of the amount of furniture purchased. Out-of-town customers must make their own arrangements to take purchases home**

Directions: From the I-270 perimeter around St. Louis, take exit #9 (Manchester Rd.) and head east into St. Louis. Baker Odds & Ends is about 3 miles down on the right side of Manchester Rd.

Baker Odds & Ends (Factory Outlet) (cont.)

Baker Odds & Ends in St. Louis, MO (Warson Woods)

Williamsburg Reproduction mahogany highboy from Baker Furniture

Retail: $26,140.00   Discounted price: $9,995.00
Savings at Baker Odds & Ends: $16,145.00 = 62% off retail

Bassett Furniture Direct

Level 3
Hickory Furniture Mart
U. S. Hwy. 70 SE
Hickory, NC 28602

Phone:	**(828) 267-0670**	**Hours:**	**M-Sat 9:00-6:00**
Toll Free:	**None**	**E-mail:**	**None**
Fax:	**(828) 267-0843**	**Web site:**	**www.bassettfurniture.com**

Bassett Furniture Direct at the Hickory Furniture Mart is part of Bassett Furniture's new chain of outlets direct to the public. They have over 100 locations now all over the U. S., with more opening all the time. Please check their Web site, www.bassettfurniture.com, for locations, directions, and hours of each store.

Bassett Furniture Direct isn't a true factory outlet in the sense of being a place to liquidate floor samples, seconds, irregulars, and returns. Bassett's only true factory outlet is in Bassett, VA. Please see the separate listing in this book for more information on the Bassett Factory Outlet. Bassett Furniture Direct is exactly like a traditional furniture store except that it's owned by the manufacturer itself, much as Ethan Allen has done for years.

Bassett does discount its furniture here somewhat compared to most retailers who carry their products.. Most pieces are about 30% off retail. Designers and decorators receive an extra 10% off everything. However, I have found better discounts on Bassett furniture from various order-by-phone furniture discounters who still carry the line. By all means, check Bassett's prices at their own stores, but don't assume that they are the lowest prices out there on this brand. You can likely do better elsewhere.

On a recent trip to Bassett Furniture Direct, I found a good deal on a Mission Oak bedroom set from their Grove Park Collection (pictured on the following page). The bed, entertainment center, nightstand, chest, and mirror normally retail separately for $4,843.00, but you can order the same set through Bassett Furniture Direct for only $2,996.00, or about 38% off.

Be sure to pick up a catalog at the service counter when you visit the store or request one when you call. They sometimes have a $25.00 off gift certificate in the back which can be used on any purchase of $50.00 or more.

Phone orders accepted:	**Yes**
Discount:	**Approximately 30% off mfrs. suggested retail (Decorators and designers receive 40% off)**
Payment methods:	**VISA, MC, or personal check**
In-house financing available:	**Yes**
Deposits required:	**20% deposit when order is placed, balance due when furniture is ready to be shipped**
Catalog available:	**Yes**
Clearance center:	**No**
Delivery:	**Full service in-home delivery and set-up. Customer pays freight company directly for shipping costs.**

Directions: Please see www.bassettfurniture.com for directions to the store nearest you.

Bassett Furniture Direct (cont.)

Mission Oak bedroom set from Bassett Furniture

Retail: $4,843.00   Discounted price: $2,996.00
Savings at Bassett Furniture Direct: $1,847.00 = 38% off retail

Bassett Factory Outlet

3525 Fairystone Park Highway
Bassett, VA 24055

Phone:	**(276) 629-6446**	**Hours:**	**M-Sat 10:00-6:00**
Toll Free:	**None**	**E-mail:**	**None**
Fax:	**(276) 629-6307**	**Web site:**	**None**

This is Basset Furniture's only true factory outlet, near their factory in Bassett, VA. Bassett is a suburb of Martinsville, VA, which is about one hour north of High Point, NC. If you plan to be in the High Point area, you may wish to allow one day to travel to the factory outlets in and around Martinsville, VA. Between the factory outlets for Hooker, Lane, Bassett, and Stanley, there are some great deals there.

They've got a fairly even mix of upholstery and casegoods in this 60,000 square foot outlet. Do be aware that this outlet has a higher percentage of damaged merchandise than most, approximately 60%. Fortunately, even the damaged pieces have very slight flaws. Be sure to look each piece over very carefully before buying.

None of the pieces in stock had the original retail prices marked, which makes it more difficult to know exactly how much you're saving. In checking random items, I found that the discounts ran 60%-70% off retail.

They do have some good deals. For instance, on a recent visit I found a nice little entertainment cabinet for only $209.00 (pictured on the following page). The only damage I could find were two tiny scuff marks on the top which could be easily touched up invisibly with a touchup pen. I was unable to ascertain the original retail, as this piece has been discontinued. Still, $209.00 was certainly quite a bargain.

Every December, they have a big truck sale out back in which Bassett liquidates any furniture which has been damaged in transit from the factory to their company owned stores (Bassett Furniture Direct). In December 2003, they had 12 semi-trailer loads of furniture at their tent sale, so there's quite a bit to choose from.

From time to time throughout the year, the outlet will run a 20% off sale, on top of the discounts already marked. These sales do not follow any particular pattern. They only happen when the outlet is seriously over-stocked. Check out Web site, www.smartdecorating.com, for announcements of any upcoming factory outlet sales.

One major drawback at this outlet is the fact that they are not set up to arrange shipping. Customers shipping to the East Coast can make their own delivery arrangements through Hopkins Delivery Service. Before visiting this outlet, you should call them at (276) 647-5200 to be sure they do deliver to your area and get a freight estimate.

The best way to handle this would be to contact the shipping company or companies which are already handling any other outlet purchases you've made in NC and contract with them to pick up any purchases at the Bassett outlet and deliver them to you along with your other purchases.

Phone orders accepted:	**No**
Discount:	**60%-70% off mfrs. suggested retail**
Payment methods:	**VISA, MC, personal checks, cash**
In-house financing available:	**No**
Deposits required:	**Not applicable**
Catalog available:	**No**
Clearance center:	**Not applicable**
Delivery:	**East Coast only, through Hopkins Delivery Service (276-647-5200)**

Directions: **From I-40 in Greensboro, NC, take the Hwy. 68/Airport exit (#210), and head north on Hwy. 68. After about 30 minutes, turn onto Hwy. 220 toward Martinsville/Roanoke. After another 30 minutes, take the VA Hwy. 57 West/Fairystone Park Hwy. exit and drive toward Bassett. After about 4 miles, you'll see the Bassett Factory Outlet on your left.**

Bassett Factory Outlet

Entertainment chest from Bassett Furniture

Retail: Not available   Discounted price: $209.00
Savings at Bassett Factory Outlet = Estimated 60% off retail

Benchcraft Factory Outlet

703 Coley Rd.
Tupelo, MS 38803

Phone:	**(662) 841-1329**		**Hours:**	**M-Sat 9:30-5:30**
Toll Free:	**None**		**E-mail:**	**None**
Fax:	**(662) 844-9063**		**Web site:**	**None**

This is Benchcraft's only true factory outlet, near their factory in Tupelo. They have a good selection of upholstered furniture, primarily recliners and leather sofas. The quality is medium-end, and most of the items in stock are in new first-quality condition. There are a few seconds in-stock, but they were very well marked and kept in a separate room in the back of the outlet.

On my last visit here, I found a very nice first-quality leather sofa (pictured on the following page). The retail on this sofa is normally $1,172.00, but the outlet had several for only $384.00.

If you're looking for good deals on medium-quality upholstery, this outlet is definitely worth a visit.

Phone orders accepted:	**No**
Discount:	**50%-75% off mfrs. suggested retail**
Payment methods:	**Personal checks. No credit cards.**
In-house financing available:	**Yes**
Deposits required:	**Not applicable**
Catalog available:	**No**
Clearance center:	**Not applicable**
Delivery:	**No delivery available. Customer's must make their own arrangements to take furniture home**

Directions: From Hwy. 78, take the Belden exit. You don't have a choice of which way to turn. The exit will automatically put you in the right direction. Go to the 2nd traffic light and turn right (you'll see a Shell station on the corner) onto Coley Rd. The Benchcraft Factory Outlet is on the right side of the road, just past the Tupelo Furniture Market.

Benchcraft Factory Outlet (cont.)

Benchcraft Factory Outlet

Leather sofa from Benchcraft

Retail: $1,172.00   Discounted price: $384.00
Savings at the Benchcraft Factory Outlet: $788.00 = 67% off retail

Bernhardt Factory Outlet

Manufacturer-Owned Factory Outlets
4916 Hickory Blvd
Hickory, NC 28601

Phone:	(828) 313-0795	**Hours:**	M-Sat 9:00-6:00
Toll Free:	None	**E-mail:**	None
Fax:	(828) 313-0796	**Web site:**	www.bernhardtfurniture.com

This is Bernhardt's only factory outlet nationwide. It's on the north side of Hickory, not far from their factory. The outlet itself is fairly large and has a good selection of upholstery and case goods.

Virtually all of the furniture in stock is first-quality, although there are a few seconds and irregulars. Make sure you look each piece over very carefully because, unlike most outlets, Bernhardt does not use special coded tags to mark pieces that have flaws or damage.

This is a particularly good outlet to visit if you're looking for high-end contemporary furniture, which can be hard to find at U. S. factory outlets. They had a nice selection of contemporary upholstery and case goods, in addition to many more traditional styles.

Bernhardt has made arrangements with a local refinisher to correct any flaws or damage for $50.00-$150.00, depending on the specific job that needs to be done. Work is normally competed in 1-2 weeks, but it can take as long as a month during periods of heavy demand.

On a recent visit here, I found a great bargain on an armoire (pictured on the following page). It was a discontinued style in first-quality condition. This item normally retailed for $7,200.00, but the outlet had this one in stock for only $3,121.00. A matching bedroom set was also available at similar savings.

This brand new outlet building also houses factory owned outlets for Broyhill, Kincaid, and La-Z-Boy. One nice added touch in the Bernhardt outlet is their play area for children.

If you're in the Hickory area, this outlet should definitely be on your "must-visit" list.

Phone orders accepted:	No
Discount:	55%-70% off mfrs. suggested retail
Payment methods:	VISA, MC, Discover, personal checks.
In-house financing available:	No
Deposits required:	Not applicable
Catalog available:	Not applicable
Clearance center:	Not applicable
Delivery:	Full service in-home delivery and set-up. Customer pays freight company directly for shipping costs.

Directions: From I-40, take exit #123 (Hwy. 321) and head north through Hickory. The outlet will be on the right, approximately 6 miles north of I-40.

Bernhardt Factory Outlet (cont.)

Bernhardt Factory Outlet at the Manufacturer Owned Furniture Outlets in Hickory, NC

Armoire by Bernhardt Furniture

Retail: $7,200.00   Discounted price: $3,121.00
Savings at the Bernhardt Factory Outlet: $4,079.00 = 57% off retail

Better Homes Discount Furniture

248 1st Ave. NW
Hickory, NC 28601

Phone:	(828) 328-8302	**Hours:**	M-F 9:00-5:30, Sat 9:00-5:00
Toll Free:	None	**E-mail:**	betterhomesfurniture@earthlink.net
Fax:	(828) 327-6088	**Web site:**	www.bhdf.com

Better Homes Discount Furniture has been in business since 1917. They carry a nice selection of traditional furniture from high quality brands. They also have a long reputation for excellent customer service.

If you plan to order by phone, definitely compare their prices. If traveling to Hickory in person, do call to see if they have floor samples, market samples, or discontinued pieces available during your visit. They offer some very good deals on these items. They'll also sell any item off the floor, which can help you avoid shipping delays.

Lines carried:

Aico	DMI	Kingsdown	Sam Moore
American Drew	England Corsair	Kroehler	Schnadig
Barn Door	Fairfield	La-Z-Boy	Shamrock
Bassett Mirror Company	Fashion Bed	Lea	South Sea Rattan
Benchcraft	Flexsteel	Legacy Classics	Standard
Berkline	Hammary	Liberty	Stoneville
Bermex	Harbor Home	Ligo	Stylecraft Lamps
Best Chair	Hekman	Magnussen Presidential	Sumter Cabinet
Broyhill	Hickory Hill	Morgan Stewart	Universal
Bruards	Hooker	Ohio Table Pad	Vaughan
Casapelle Leather	Howard Miller	Platinum	Vaughan Bassett
Chromcraft	Jackson Furniture	Pulaski	Webb
Clayton Marcus	Jami L. Designs	Relax-R	Winners Only
Cochrane	Keller	Richardson Bros.	
Craftique	Kimball	Riverside	
Davis Int'l	King Hickory	Rowe	

Phone orders accepted:	Yes
Discount:	50%-70% off mfrs. suggested retail
Payment methods:	Personal checks and cash
In-house financing available:	Yes, 90 days no interest
Deposits required:	25% deposit when order is placed, balance due when furniture is ready to be shipped
Catalog available:	No
Clearance center:	No
Delivery:	Full service in-home delivery and set-up. Customer pays freight company directly for shipping costs.

Directions: From I-40, take exit #125 (Lenoir-Rhyne Rd.), and head north for one and a half miles. Turn left onto Tate Blvd. SE. Go to the first red light, and turn right onto Hwy. 127 SE. Go to the first red light, and turn left onto 1st Ave. NE. Go to the second red light, and you'll see Better Homes on your right.

Black's Furniture Company

2800 Westchester Dr.
High Point, NC 27262

575 chair
350 ottoman
126 shipping
Paul

Phone:	**(336) 886-5011**	**Hours:**	**M-F 8:00-5:00, Sat 9:00-5:00**
Toll Free:	**None**	**E-mail:**	**blacks@highpoint.net**
Fax:	**(336) 886-4734**	**Web site:**	**www.blacksfurniture.com**

Black's Furniture in High Point has a very nice store with a good selection of very high-end furniture from brands such as Hickory White, Baker, Century, Thomasville, Hooker, Lexington, and others.

Most of the furniture in-stock is new first-quality, and they charge the same price whether you buy in person or over the phone. Most brands are discounted 40%-55% off retail.

They advertise that their clearance center in the back basement is only open on the last Saturday of every month, but I've always found that you can pretty much waltz right in whenever you want. Just look for the brick-walled stairs in the far right rear corner of the store.

If you're planning to visit High Point in person, your time would be better spent at other factory outlets and clearance centers in the area that have a better selection of floor samples and discontinued styles at bigger discounts. However, if you plan to order your furniture over the phone, you should definitely give this source a call. They have excellent bargains on many lines.

Lines carried:

A. A. Laun	Barcalounger	Bucks County	Classic Gallery
Aico	Bassett Mirror Co.	Butler Table	Classic Leather
American Drew	Benicia Foundry Beds	C. R. Laine	Clayton Marcus
Andrew Pearson	Bevan Funnell	Capel Rugs	Cochrane
Athol	Bob Timberlake	Cambridge Lamps	Cooper Classics
Ardley Hall	Bradington Young	Carsons	Corsican Brass Co.
Arte de Mexico	Braxton Culler	Cebu	Cox
Artistica	Broyhill	Charleston Forge	Craftique

Phone orders accepted:	**Yes**
Discount:	**40%-55% off mfrs. suggested retail**
Payment methods:	**VISA, MC, Discover, and personal checks.**
In-house financing available:	**No**
Deposits required:	**1/3 deposit when order is placed, balance due when furniture is ready to be shipped**
Catalog available:	**No**
Clearance center:	**Yes**
Delivery:	**Full service in-home delivery and set-up. Customer pays freight company directly for shipping costs.**

Directions: **From I-85, take exit #111 (Hwy. 311), and head northwest into High Point. After several miles, when you reach downtown High Point, Hwy. 311 will become S. Main St. Go through High Point until you come to Westchester Ave. on the north side of town. Turn left on Westchester. Black's Furniture is a few miles down on the right.**

Black's Furnitu

Paul Linton
Black's Furn.
1 (336) 886-5011

Black's Furniture Company

Lines carried (cont.):

Crystal Clear	Hart Industries	Nora Fenton	Stanford
Creative Metal & Wood	High Point Furniture	North Bay Collections	Statesville Chair
Crystal Clear	Hooker	Now Seating	Stein World
Currey & Co.	Howard Miller Clocks	Null	Swaim
Decorative Crafts	Jasper	OFS	Tapestries Ltd.
Denny Lamps	Johnston Casuals	Ohio Table Pads	Thayer Coggin
Dimplex	JSI	Parker Southern	Theodore Alexander
Dinaire	Lane	Pearson	Thomasville
Elliotts Design	Lea	Powell Company	Tropitone
Elvis Presley Furniture	Leathercraft	Pulaski	Uttermost
Emerson et Cie	Lexington	Quoizel	Uwharrie Chair
EXL Designs Upholstery	Lloyd/Flanders	Riverside	Vaughan Bassett
Fairfield Chair	Madison Square	Robin Bruce	Webb
Florita Nova	Mario Lamps	Rowe	Wellington Hall
Frederick Cooper	Mayline	Sam Moore	Wesley Hall
Friedman Mirrors	McKay Table Pads	Sarreid	Wesley Allen
Gat Creek	Miller Desk	Sedgefield	Woodard
Global	Minoff Lamps	Serta Mattress	World Design Center
Great City Traders	Moosehead	Shady Lady	
Habersham Plantation	Murray Feiss	Sherrill Occasional	
Hammary	Nichols & Stone	Southern Reproductions	

Blowing Rock Furniture Company

3428 Hickory Blvd. N.
Hwy. 321
Hudson, NC 28638

Phone:	**(828) 396-3186**	**Hours:**	**M-F 9:00-6:00, Sat 8:30-6:00**
Toll Free:	**None**	**E-mail:**	**info@blowingrockfurniture.com**
Fax:	**(828) 396-6031**	**Web site:**	**www.blowingrockfurniture.com**

Blowing Rock Furniture Co. closed in July 2002 after a rash of complaints. Their former location is now occupied by Cross Creek Furniture, which is not affiliated with Blowing Rock in any way.

One of Blowing Rock's partners was able to refund all customer deposits at his own expense. There should not be any customers at this point with unresolved business here. If you have any questions regarding a past problem with this store, please contact the North Carolina Attorney General's office.

Bombay Company Factory Outlet

Multiple locations nationwide

Phone:	**Varies by location**	**Hours:**	**Varies by location**
Toll Free:	**(800) 829-7789**	**E-mail:**	**Please visit Web site**
Fax:	**None**	**Web site:**	**www.bombaycompany.com**

The Bombay Company has recently opened dozens of "factory outlets" in factory outlet shopping centers nationwide. Unfortunately, their outlets don't have much in the way of selection or savings. They are not at all comparable to the factory outlets run by major furniture brand name manufacturers in North Carolina.

The selection at the outlets I have visited is fairly poor. The outlets are small, usually 1000-2000 square feet. The biggest disappointment, though, is the pricing.

On my recent visit to the Bombay Outlet in Dawsonville, GA, I found a full-size "Savannah Metal Bed" in stock for $279.00 (pictured on the following page). The outlet also had a display of The Bombay Company's current catalog with a price on the full-size "Savannah Metal Bed" of $279.00.

When I asked the manager to explain why this item, and indeed most of the items in the store, weren't priced one cent below their catalog prices for new merchandise, he admitted that the Bombay Outlet isn't really a factory outlet. With a few exceptions, the prices aren't any cheaper than their catalog or their full-priced stores at the mall. This kind of misuse of the word "outlet" is what give the real factory outlets a bad name.

The "outlets" do have a very few overstock items priced at discounts of about 20% off the original price, but other than that, this is just a retail store. Driving to a Bombay Outlet is a complete waste of time. Just call their 800 number for a catalog and save yourself the trip.

Or, better yet, visit a real furniture factory outlet (such as the ones for Henredon, Thomasville, and Drexel Heritage), and get much better quality furniture for the same money.

Phone orders accepted:	**Yes**
Discount:	**None-50% off mfrs. suggested retail**
Payment methods:	**VISA, MC, AMEX, Discover, personal checks.**
In-house financing available:	**Yes, through their Bombay Co. credit card.**
Deposits required:	**Not applicable**
Catalog available:	**Yes**
Clearance center:	**Not applicable**
Delivery:	**Common carrier only.**

Directions: Varies by location. Please visit www.bombaycompany.com or call (800) 829-7789 or for complete directions to the Bombay Company Factory Outlet in your area.

Bombay Company Factory Outlet (cont.)

Bombay Outlet in Dawsonville, GA

"Savannah Metal Bed" at the Bombay Outlet

Retail: $279.00   Discounted price: $279.00
Savings at the Bombay Outlet: $0

Bonita Furniture Galleries

210 13th St. SW and Hwy. 321
Hickory, NC 28603

Phone:	**(828) 324-1992**	**Hours:**	**M-Sat 9:00-5:00**
Toll Free:	**None**	**E-mail:**	**None**
Fax:	**(828) 324-7972**	**Web site:**	**www.bonitagalleries.com**

    Bonita Furniture Galleries has a very high-end store in Hickory with large galleries for Bernhardt and other high end lines. Discounts here generally run about 40%-50% off the manufacturer's retail price, with the exception of Bernhardt which has lesser discounts mandated by the manufacturer.

    There are some floor samples and discontinued items on the sales floor, marked down to about 65%-75% off retail.

    Bonita has a very good reputation for customer service, as well. I have never heard a single complaint about them from my readers.

    They do have good deals on many lines. Anyone ordering furniture by phone should call this source to compare prices. If you plan to visit the Hickory area in person, you should definitely stop in to see their deals on floor samples.

Phone orders accepted:	**Yes**
Discount:	**40%-50% off mfrs. suggested retail**
Payment methods:	**Personal checks. No credit cards.**
In-house financing available:	**No**
Deposits required:	**50% deposit when order is placed, balance due when furniture is ready to be shipped**
Catalog available:	**No**
Clearance center:	**No**
Delivery:	**Full service in-home delivery and set-up. Customer pays freight company directly for shipping costs.**

Directions: From I-40, take exit #123 and go one mile north on Hwy. 321. Bonita Furniture Galleries is on the right side of the road.

Bonita Furniture Galleries (cont.)

Lines carried:

American Drew
Athol
Barcalounger
Bassett
Bernhardt
Bob Timberlake
Bradington Young
Broyhill
Carson's
Casa Bique
Charleston Forge
Clayton Marcus
Clyde Pearson
Craftique
Elliott's Designs
Fairfield
Fine Art Lamps
Fitz & Floyd
Frederick Cooper
Great City Traders
Guildmaster
Hammary
Hekman
Henry Link
Hooker
Howard Miller Clocks
Johnston Casuals
Keller
King Hickory
La-Z-Boy
Leathercraft
Lexington
Null
Pennsylvania House
Pulaski
Rex
Sadek
Sam Moore
Sarreid
Sedgefield Collection
Serta
Shuford
Southwood Reproductions
Stanley
Statton
Sumter Cabinet
Superior
Toyo
Universal

Velco Bedspreads
Virginia Metalcrafters
Wesley Allen
Wildwood
Woodard

Boyles Clearance Center

2125 Sardis Rd.
Charlotte, NC 28277

Phone:	(704) 846-8470	**Hours:**	Sat 10-6, Sun 1-6
Toll Free:	None	**E-mail:**	None
Fax:	None	**Web site:**	www.boyles.com

This is the newest clearance center for Boyles, which is one of the top furniture discounters in North Carolina. Most of the furniture in stock is very high-end and in new first-quality condition. Most pieces are floor samples, discontinued styles, and a few customer returns. The clearance center is fairly large, and has a good assortment of upholstery and case goods, all at deep discounts.

On a recent visit here, I found a beautiful mahogany armoire from Jeffco in perfect first-quality condition. It had been marked down to $4,999.00 from the original retail of $19,042.00. That's a savings of almost 75% off the price you'd pay for the same furniture through a local retail store.

If you're traveling to the Hickory, NC, area in person to shop for high-end furniture, you will probably pass through Charlotte, especially if you arrive by plane. If so, definitely check out this clearance center.

Lines carried:

American Drew	Councill-Craftsmen	Jeffco	Pulaski
Baker	Cox	Karges	Sam Moore
Bernhardt	Drexel-Heritage	Kincaid	Sherrill
Benicia Foundry	Hancock & Moore	Kingsdown	Southwood Reproductions
Bevan Funnell	Harden	La Barge	Stanley
Bob Timberlake	Hekman	Lane	Theodore Alexander
Bradington Young	Henkel-Harris	Lexington	Thomasville
Cape Craftsman	Henredon	Madison Square	Wellington Hall
Carvers Guild	Hickory Chair	Maitland-Smith	Wesley Allen
Casa Stradivari	Hickory White	Marge Carson	Whittemore-Sherrill
Century	Hooker	Pennsylvania House	Winston
Charleston Forge	Jasper	Precedent	Woodard

Phone orders accepted:	**No**
Discount:	**40%-75% off mfrs. suggested retail**
Payment methods:	**VISA, MC, personal checks**
In-house financing available:	**No**
Deposits required:	**Not applicable**
Catalog available:	**Not applicable**
Clearance center:	**Not applicable**
Delivery:	**Full service in-home delivery and set-up. Customer pays freight company directly for shipping costs.**

Directions: **From I-85, take exit 36, and go south on I-277 to the "Independence Blvd." exit. Go south on Independence Blvd for 5 miles. You'll see Sardis Rd. on your right (by the Chili's restaurant). Turn right on Sardis, and the clearance center will be 1/2 mile down on your right.**

Boyles Clearance Center (cont.)

Boyles Clearance Center

Jeffco mahogany armoire

Retail: $19,042.00   Discounted price: $4,999.00
Savings at Boyles Clearance Center: $14,043.00 = 74% off retail

Boyles Clearance Center

739 Old Lenoir Rd.
Hickory, NC 28601

Phone:	(828) 326-1700	**Hours:**	M-F 9:00-6:00, Sat 9:00-5:00
Toll Free:	None	**E-mail:**	None
Fax:	(828) 328-5183	**Web site:**	www.boyles.com

This is the original clearance center for all 12 Boyles stores, including Hendrick's in Mocksville, plus Boyles' huge telephone sales operation. Recently, Boyles has added a new clearance center in Charlotte.

Most of the furniture in stock is very high-end and in new first-quality condition. Most are floor samples, discontinued styles, and a few customer returns. The clearance center itself is huge, one of the largest clearance centers of its type in North Carolina. There's an even mix of upholstery and case goods here.

They have some terrific deals. On a recent visit here, I found a Councill-Craftsmen mahogany drum table (pictured on the following page) that normally retails for $3,830.00 marked down to $1,474.00, over 60% off. This particular piece was a floor sample in new first-quality condition.

If you're traveling to the Hickory, NC, area in person to shop for high-end furniture, you should definitely check out Boyles' clearance center. This one is a "must-visit".

Lines carried:

American Drew	Councill-Craftsmen	Jeffco	Pulaski
Baker	Cox	Karges	Sam Moore
Bernhardt	Drexel-Heritage	Kincaid	Sherrill
Benicia Foundry	Hancock & Moore	Kingsdown	Southwood Reproductions
Bevan Funnell	Harden	La Barge	Stanley
Bob Timberlake	Hekman	Lane	Theodore Alexander
Bradington Young	Henkel-Harris	Lexington	Thomasville
Cape Craftsman	Henredon	Madison Square	Wellington Hall
Carvers Guild	Hickory Chair	Maitland-Smith	Wesley Allen
Casa Stradivari	Hickory White	Marge Carson	Whittemore-Sherrill
Century	Hooker	Pennsylvania House	Winston
Charleston Forge	Jasper	Precedent	Woodard

Phone orders accepted:	No
Discount:	40%-60% off mfrs. suggested retail
Payment methods:	VISA, MC, personal checks
In-house financing available:	No
Deposits required:	Not applicable
Catalog available:	Not applicable
Clearance center:	Not applicable
Delivery:	Full service in-home delivery and set-up. Customer pays freight company directly for shipping costs.

Directions: From I-40, take exit #123 and head north on Hwy. 321. After about ten miles, turn right onto Old Lenoir Rd. The clearance center is on the right, behind Boyles Country Shop.

Boyles Clearance Center (cont.)

Boyles Clearance Center

Councill-Craftsmen mahogany drum table

Retail: $3,830.00   Discounted price: $1,474.00
Savings at Boyles Clearance Center: $2,356.00 = 62% off retail

Boyles Country Shop

739 Old Lenoir Rd.
Hickory, NC 28601

Phone:	(828) 326-1700	**Hours:**	M-F 9:00-6:00, Sat 9:00-5:00
Toll Free:	None	**E-mail:**	None
Fax:	(828) 328-5183	**Web site:**	www.boyles.com

The "Country Shop" is Boyles' original furniture store in Hickory, NC. Of course, now Boyles has 11 more locations, and they've become one of the biggest furniture discounters in North Carolina.

Like the other Boyles locations, this store has an extensive high-end gallery. All of the furniture in stock is new first-quality. The discounts range from 30%-50% off retail depending on the brand. All of Boyles' floor samples and discontinued items are sent to their clearance center, located right behind the "Country Shop".

One significant advantage to buying from Boyles is that, unlike most discounters, they will allow you to make your final payment for your furniture on delivery instead of requiring that you pay the rest of your bill before the furniture is shipped to your home. They have a great reputation for service.

Lines carried:

Acquisitions	Designmaster	Ital Art	Pulaski
Ambiance Imports	Fine Art Lamps	Jeffco	Ralph Lauren
American Drew	Fine Furniture Designs	Jessica Charles	Royal Patina
Artex	Fremarc	John Richard	Sam Moore
Artistica	Glass Arts	Karges	Sherrill
Baker	Guy Chaddock	Kingsdown	Sligh
Bernhardt	Habersham	La Barge	Southampton
Benicia Foundry	Hancock & Moore	Lane	Southwood Reproductions
Bob Timberlake	Harden	Lexington	Stanley
Bradington Young	Hekman	Madison Square	Theodore Alexander
Brown Jordan	Henkel-Harris	Maitland-Smith	Timberwood Trading
Casa Stradivari	Henredon	Milling Road	Venture By Lane
Century	Hickory Chair	Motioncraft	Wesley Allen
Charleston Forge	Hickory White	Nichols & Stone	Whittemore-Sherrill
Classic Imports	Hooker	Parlance	Winston
Councill-Craftsmen	Howard Miller	Platt	Woodard
Cox	Hunt Country	Precedent	Wright Table

Phone orders accepted:	Yes
Discount:	**30%-50% off mfrs. suggested retail**
Payment methods:	**VISA, MC, personal checks**
In-house financing available:	No
Deposits required:	**1/3 deposit when order is placed, balance due when furniture is delivered to your home**
Catalog available:	No
Clearance center:	**Yes -- See *Boyles Clearance Center***
Delivery:	**Full service in-home delivery and set-up. Customer pays freight company directly for shipping costs.**

Directions: From I-40, take exit #123 and go north on Hwy. 321. After about 10 miles, turn right onto Old Lenoir Rd. The Country Shop is on the right.

Boyles Distinctive Furniture

616 Greensboro Rd.
High Point, NC 27261

Phone:	**(336) 884-8088**	**Hours:**	**M-W 8:30-5:30, Sat 8:30-5:30**
Toll Free:	**None**		**Th-F 8:30-8:30**
Fax:	**None**	**E-mail:**	**None**
		Web site:	**www.boyles.com**

Boyles Distinctive Furniture is the only Boyles location in High Point proper. There is also a much bigger Boyles store a few miles away in Jamestown, NC.

Like the other Boyles locations, this store has an extensive high-end gallery. All of the furniture in stock is new first-quality. The discounts range from 30%-50% off retail depending on the brand. All of Boyles' floor samples and discontinued items are sent to their clearance center, located right behind the "Country Shop" in Hickory, NC.

One significant advantage to buying from Boyles is that, unlike most discounters, they will allow you to make your final payment for your furniture on delivery instead of requiring that you pay the rest of your bill before the furniture is shipped to your home. This is some extra security, and it's worth taking into account when you're deciding where to shop. They have a great reputation for service.

If you're buying furniture by phone, you should compare prices with this source.

Lines carried:

Artistica	Habersham	Karges	Sligh
Bernhardt	Hancock & Moore	Kingsdown	Stanley
Bob Timberlake	Hekman	La Barge	Taylor King
Bradington Young	Henkel-Harris	Lane	Theodore Alexander
Casa Stradivari	Henkel-Moore	Lane/Venture	Tommy Bahama
Century	Hickory White	Lexington	Wesley Allen
Charleston Forge	Hooker	Maitland-Smith	Wright Table Co.
Councill-Craftsmen	Ital Art	Marge Carson	
Fine Furniture Designs	Jasper	Nichols & Stone	
Fremarc	Jessica Charles	Oscar de la Renta	

Phone orders accepted:	**Yes**
Discount:	**30%-50% off mfrs. suggested retail**
Payment methods:	**VISA, MC, personal checks**
In-house financing available:	**No**
Deposits required:	**1/3 deposit when order is placed, balance due when furniture is delivered to your home**
Catalog available:	**No**
Clearance center:	**Yes -- See *Boyles Clearance Center***
Delivery:	**Full service in-home delivery and set-up. Customer pays freight company directly.**

**Directions: From I-85, take exit #111, and head north on Hwy. 311 into High Point
Turn right on Greensboro Rd. Boyles is a few miles down on the right.**

Boyles Distinctive Furniture

5700 Riverdale Dr.
Jamestown, NC 27282

Phone:	**(336) 812-2200**	**Hours:**	**M-W 8:30-5:30, Sat 8:30-5:30**
Toll Free:	None		**Th-F 8:30-8:30**
Fax:	None	**E-mail:**	None
		Web site:	**www.boyles.com**

This is Boyles' flagship store, perched on a hill right above I-85 on the outskirts of High Point, NC. Boyles also has 11 more locations, and they've become one of the biggest furniture discounters in North Carolina.

Like the other Boyles locations, this store has an extensive high-end gallery. All of the furniture in stock is new first-quality. The discounts range from 30%-50% off retail depending on the brand. All of Boyles' floor samples and discontinued items are sent to their clearance center, located right behind the "Country Shop".

One significant advantage to buying from Boyles is that, unlike most discounters, they will allow you to make your final payment for your furniture on delivery instead of requiring that you pay the rest of your bill before the furniture is shipped to your home. This is some extra security, and it's worth taking into account when you're deciding where to shop. They have a great reputation for service.

If you're buying furniture by phone, you should compare prices with this source.

Lines carried:

Acquisitions Antiques	Harden	Kindel	Royal Patina
Baker	Henkel-Harris	Kingsdown	Sherrill
Bernhardt	Henkel-Moore	Maitland-Smith	Southampton
Brown Jordan	Henredon	Marge Carson	Southwood
Casa Stradivari	Hickory Chair	Martha Stewart	Theodore Alexander
Design Master	Hooker	by Bernhardt	Thomasville
Fine Furniture Designs	Isenhour	Milling Road	Whittemore-Sherrill
Guy Chaddock	Jeffco	Motioncraft	Ziba Oriental Rugs
Habersham	Jessica Charles	Precedent	
Hancock & Moore	Karges	Ralph Lauren	

Phone orders accepted:	**Yes**
Discount:	**30%-50% off mfrs. suggested retail**
Payment methods:	**VISA, MC, personal checks**
In-house financing available:	**No**
Deposits required:	**1/3 deposit when order is placed, balance due when furniture is delivered to your home**
Catalog available:	**No**
Clearance center:	**Yes -- See *Boyles Clearance Center***
Delivery:	**Full service in-home delivery and set-up. Customer pays freight company directly for shipping costs.**

Directions: From I-85, take exit #118, and go west on Riverdale Rd. You'll see Boyles right in front of you. It's easily visible from the interstate.

Boyles Distinctive Furniture (cont.)

Boyles Distinctive Furniture in Jamestown, NC

Boyles Furniture

I-40, Exit #174
182 Farmington Rd.
Mocksville, NC 27028

Phone:	**(336) 998-7712**	**Hours:**	**M-F 9:00-6:00, Sat 9:00-5:00**
Toll Free:	**(888) 316-3351**	**E-mail:**	**None**
Fax:	**(336) 998-9598**	**Web site:**	**www.boyles.com**

Boyles Furniture in Mocksville (formerly Hendricks Furniture Galleries) is part of the Boyles conglomerate. Boyles also has 11 more locations, and they've become one of the biggest furniture discounters in North Carolina. Little has changed here other than the name on the sign. This store continues to be owned and operated by Boyles, as it has for many years. They continue to have a very good reputation for service.

Like the other Boyles locations, this store has an extensive high-end gallery. All of the furniture in stock is new first-quality. The discounts range from 30%-50% off retail. All of this store's floor samples and discontinued items are sent to Boyles' clearance center in Hickory, NC, located right behind Boyles' Country Shop.

On a recent visit, I found a great deal on an "Embassy Row" bedroom set by Bernhardt (pictured on the following page). This set (bed, dresser, bachelor's chest, and master chest) normally retails for $16,020.00, but it was marked down to $7,059.00, 56% off. The extra discount was due to their annual January "winter sale", when most items are marked 55%-60% off retail.

One big advantage to buying from Boyles is that, unlike most discounters, they will allow you to make your final payment for your furniture on delivery instead of requiring that you pay the rest of your bill before the furniture is shipped to your home.

If you're buying furniture by phone, you should compare prices with this source. If you're traveling to the Hickory or Charlotte areas in person to shop, you should definitely check out Boyles' clearance centers.

Phone orders accepted:	**Yes**
Discount:	**30%-50% off mfrs. suggested retail**
Payment methods:	**VISA, MC, personal checks**
In-house financing available:	**No**
Deposits required:	**1/3 deposit when order is placed, balance due when furniture is delivered to your home**
Catalog available:	**No**
Clearance center:	**Yes -- See *Boyles Clearance Center***
Delivery:	**Full service in-home delivery and set-up. Customer pays freight company directly for shipping costs.**

Directions: From I-40, take exit #174 (Farmington Rd.). You'll see Boyles right next to the expressway exit.

Boyles Furniture (cont.)

Boyles Furniture in Mocksville

Embassy Row bedroom set from Bernhardt Furniture

Retail: $16,020.00   Discounted price: $7,059.00
Savings at Boyles Furniture: $8,961.00 = 56% off retail

Boyles Furniture (cont.)

Lines carried:

American Drew
Artistica
Baker
Bernhardt
Bob Timberlake
Bradington Young
Brown Jordan
Broyhill
Canadel
Century
Charleston Forge
Councill-Craftsmen
Drexel-Heritage
Fine Furniture Design
Fremarc
Habersham
Hancock & Moore
Harden
Hekman
Henkel-Harris
Henredon
Hickory Chair
Hickory White
Hooker
Isenhour
Jeffco
Kingsdown
Lane
Lane/Venture
Lexington
Maitland-Smith
Martha Stewart by Bernhardt
Milling Road
Motioncraft
Nichols & Stone
Precedent
Ralph Lauren
Sherrill
Sligh
Southwood Reproductions
Stanley
Theodore Alexander
Thomasville
Whittemore-Sherrill

Boyles Galleries

Level 4
Hickory Furniture Mart
2220 Hwy. 70 SE
Hickory, NC 28602

Phone:	**(828) 326-1740**	**Hours:**	**M-Sat 9:00-6:00**
Toll Free:	**None**	**E-mail:**	**None**
Fax:	**(828) 326-1097**	**Web site:**	**www.boyles.com**

This Boyles' gallery takes up about one-fourth of the fourth level of the Hickory Furniture Mart. Boyles also has 11 more locations, and they've become one of the biggest furniture discounters in North Carolina.

Like the other Boyles locations, this store has extensive galleries for many very high-end brands such as Baker and Councill-Craftsmen. All of the furniture in stock is new first-quality. The discounts run about 30%-50% off retail, depending on the particular brand.

One significant advantage to buying from Boyles is that, unlike most discounters, they will allow you to make your final payment for your furniture on delivery instead of requiring that you pay the rest of your bill before the furniture is shipped to your home. This is some extra security, and it's worth taking into account when you're deciding where to shop. They have a great reputation for service.

Lines carried:

Ambiance Imports	Cox	Jessica Charles	Port Royal
Artex	Designmaster	John Richard	Sligh
Artistica	Elements By Grapevine	Karges	Southampton
Baker	Fine Art Lamps	Kindel	Southwood Reproductions
Baroque Masters	Frederick Cooper	Kingsdown	Stanley
Benicia Foundry	Fremarc	La Barge	Taylor King
Bradburn Gallery	Friedman Brothers	Lloyd Buxton	Theodore Alexander
Bradington Young	Henkel-Harris	Maitland-Smith	Waterford
Brown Jordan	Henkel Moore	Majestic Mirror	Wright Table
Cape Craftsman	Hickory Chair	McGuire	Winston
Casa Stradivari	Howard Miller	Milling Road	
Chelsea House	Hunt Country	Motioncraft	
Councill-Craftsmen	Isenhour	Platt	

Phone orders accepted:	**Yes**
Discount:	**30%-50% off mfrs. suggested retail**
Payment methods:	**VISA, MC, personal checks**
In-house financing available:	**No**
Deposits required:	**1/3 deposit when order is placed, balance due when furniture is delivered to your home**
Catalog available:	**No**
Clearance center:	**Yes -- See *Boyles Clearance Center***
Delivery:	**Full service in-home delivery and set-up. Customer pays freight company directly for shipping costs.**

Directions: Please see *Hickory Furniture Mart* for complete directions.

Boyles Shoppes

Level 1 & 2
Hickory Furniture Mart
2220 Hwy. 70 SE
Hickory, NC 28602

Phone:	**(828) 326-1060**	**Hours:**	**M-Sat 9:00-6:00**
Toll Free:	**None**	**E-mail:**	**None**
Fax:	**(828) 326-1097**	**Web site:**	**www.boyles.com**

This is one of Boyles' four showrooms at the Hickory Furniture Mart. This one has large galleries for Bernhardt, Drexel Heritage, and French Heritage. Boyles also has 11 more locations, and they've become one of the biggest furniture discounters in North Carolina.

Like the other Boyles locations, this store is high-end. All of the furniture in stock is new first-quality. The discount runs about 50% off retail. All of Boyles' floor samples and discontinued items are sent to their clearance center, located right behind the "Country Shop".

One significant advantage to buying from Boyles is that, unlike most discounters, they will allow you to make your final payment for your furniture on delivery instead of requiring that you pay the rest of your bill before the furniture is shipped to your home. This is some extra security, and it's worth taking into account when you're deciding where to shop. They are also very well established, and they have a good reputation with their customers.

If you're traveling to the Hickory, NC, area in person to shop, you should also definitely check out Boyles' clearance center.

Lines carried:

Artex	Frederick Cooper	Lexington	Royal Patina
Bernhardt	French Heritage	Lillian August	Timberwood
Cisco Brothers	Friedman Brothers	Martha Stewart	Wesley Allen
Drexel Heritage	John Richard	Old Biscayne Designs	Wildwood
Fine Art Lamps	Kingsdown	Quoizel	

Phone orders accepted:	**Yes**
Discount:	**30%-50% off mfrs. suggested retail**
Payment methods:	**VISA, MC, personal checks**
In-house financing available:	**No**
Deposits required:	**1/3 deposit when order is placed, balance due when furniture is delivered to your home**
Catalog available:	**No**
Clearance center:	**Yes -- See *Boyles Clearance Center***
Delivery:	**Full service in-home delivery and set-up. Customer pays freight company directly for shipping costs.**

Directions: Please see *Hickory Furniture Mart* for complete directions.

Boyles Showcase

Level 2 & 3
Hickory Furniture Mart
2220 Hwy. 70 SE
Hickory, NC 28602

Phone:	**(828) 326-1735**	**Hours:**	**M-Sat 9:00-6:00**
Toll Free:	**None**	**E-mail:**	**None**
Fax:	**(828) 326-1758**	**Web site:**	**www.boyles.com**

Boyles' Showcase Gallery is huge, taking up about one-fourth of the second and third floors of the Hickory Furniture Mart. Boyles also has 11 more locations, and they've become one of the biggest furniture discounters in North Carolina.

Like the other Boyles locations, this store has extensive galleries for many very high-end brands. All of the furniture in stock is new first-quality. The discounts run about 30%-50% off retail, depending on the particular brand.

One significant advantage to buying from Boyles is that, unlike most discounters, they will allow you to make your final payment for your furniture on delivery instead of requiring that you pay the rest of your bill before the furniture is shipped to your home. This is some extra security, and it's worth taking into account when you're deciding where to shop. They have a great reputation for service.

If you're buying furniture by phone, you should compare prices with this source.

Lines carried:

Acquisitions	Ellis	Hickory White	Ralph Lauren
Ambiance Imports	Fine Art Lamps	Hooker	Sam Moore
Artex	Fine Furniture Designs	Howard Miller	Sealy
Baroque Masters	Frederick Cooper	Ital Art	Sherrill
Bernhardt	Friedman Brothers	Jeffco	Venture By Lane
Brown Jordan	Glass Arts	John Richard	Whittemore-Sherrill
C. S. Designs	Gloster	Kingsdown	Wildwood
Cape Craftsman	Guy Chaddock	La Barge	Winston
Casa Stradivari	Habersham	Lane	Woodard
Century	Hancock & Moore	Maitland-Smith	Wright Table
Christian Aubry	Harden	Marge Carson	Ziba Oriental Rugs
Classic Imports	Hart Associates	Nichols & Stone	
Cox	Henredon	Precedent	

Phone orders accepted:	**Yes**
Discount:	**30%-50% off mfrs. suggested retail**
Payment methods:	**VISA, MC, personal checks**
In-house financing available:	**No**
Deposits required:	**1/3 deposit when order is placed, balance due when furniture is delivered to your home**
Catalog available:	**No**
Clearance center:	**Yes -- See *Boyles Clearance Center***
Delivery:	**Full service in-home delivery and set-up. Customer pays freight company directly.**

Directions: Please see *Hickory Furniture Mart* for complete directions.

Boyles Thomasville Gallery

Level 4
Hickory Furniture Mart
2220 Hwy. 70 SE
Hickory, NC 28602

Phone:	**(828) 326-1709**	**Hours:**	**M-Sat 9:00-6:00**
Toll Free:	**None**	**E-mail:**	**None**
Fax:	**(828) 326-8766**	**Web site:**	**www.boyles.com**

This is Boyles' main Thomasville gallery. Boyles also has 11 more locations, and they've become one of the biggest furniture discounters in North Carolina.

Like the other Boyles locations, this store is high-end. All of the furniture in stock is new first-quality. The discount runs about 50% off retail. All of Boyles' floor samples and discontinued items are sent to their clearance center, located right behind the "Country Shop".

One significant advantage to buying from Boyles is that, unlike most discounters, they will allow you to make your final payment for your furniture on delivery instead of requiring that you pay the rest of your bill before the furniture is shipped to your home. This is some extra security, and it's worth taking into account when you're deciding where to shop. They are also very well established, and they have a good reputation with their customers.

If you're buying Thomasville by phone, you should compare prices with this source.

Phone orders accepted:	**Yes**
Discount:	**50% off mfrs. suggested retail**
Payment methods:	**VISA, MC, personal checks**
In-house financing available:	**No**
Deposits required:	**1/3 deposit when order is placed, balance due when furniture is delivered to your home**
Catalog available:	**No**
Clearance center:	**Yes -- See *Boyles Clearance Center***
Delivery:	**Full service in-home delivery and set-up. Customer pays freight company directly for shipping costs.**

Directions: Please see *Hickory Furniture Mart* for complete directions.

Brass Bed Shoppe

12421 Cedar Rd.
Cleveland Heights, OH 44106

Phone:	**(216) 371-0400**	**Hours:**	**M-Sat 10:00-6:00**
Toll Free:	**None**	**E-mail:**	**None**
Fax:	**(216) 292-0026**	**Web site:**	**www.brassbedshoppe.com**

The Brass Bed Shoppe is a true factory outlet. They manufacture their own line of brass and iron beds and sell them at about 50% off retail. The quality is very good, and they have a nice selection of traditional styles.

Unfortunately, they've been accumulating complaints recently with the BBB, at least one of which is still unresolved. Until all complaints are resolved, I must recommend that consumers not buy from this source.

Lines carried:	**All major national brands. Please call for product information.**
Phone orders accepted:	**Yes**
Discount:	**50% off mfrs. suggested retail**
Payment methods:	**VISA, MC, personal checks**
In-house financing available:	**Layaway program available**
Deposits required:	**50% deposit when order is placed, balance due when furniture is ready to be shipped**
Catalog available:	**Yes**
Clearance center:	**No**
Delivery:	**All orders are shipped by common carrier. Customer must unpack and assemble beds. Customer pays freight charges directly to driver.**

Directions: **From I-271, take exit #32, and go west 6 miles on Cedar Rd. The Brass Bed Shoppe is on the right side of the road across from Firestone Tire.**

Broyhill Factory Outlet

Manufacturer-Owned Factory Outlets
4930 Hickory Blvd
Hickory, NC 28601

Phone:	**(828) 758-8899**	**Hours:**	**M-Sat 9:00-6:00, Sun 1:00-5:00**
Toll Free:	**None**	**E-mail:**	**None**
Fax:	**(828) 396-6860**	**Web site:**	**None**

This is Broyhill's only true factory outlet. Broyhill has just moved into it's new 40,000 square foot outlet on the north side of Hickory. It's considerably larger than their old outlet in Lenoir, and it's certainly more convenient to other furniture shopping in Hickory.

The stock at this outlet is an even mix of case goods and upholstery. Most of the furniture in stock are floor samples and discontinued items in new, first-quality condition, although they do have a few seconds. The quality is generally about medium. They also have a nice selection of accessories along one wall at very deep discounts.

On a recent visit here, I found a good deal on a new "Empire" poster bed (pictured on the following page). The retail on this bed is $1,489.97, but this bed at the outlet was marked down to only $798.97, over 46% off the original retail. Most of the items in the outlet were marked down about 45% to 60% off retail.

If you travel to Hickory, you'll definitely want to visit this outlet center, which also houses outlets for Kincaid, La-Z-Boy, and Bernhardt.

Phone orders accepted:	**No**
Discount:	**45%-60% off mfrs. suggested retail**
Payment methods:	**VISA, MC, personal checks**
In-house financing available:	**No**
Deposits required:	**Not applicable**
Catalog available:	**Not applicable**
Clearance center:	**Not applicable**
Delivery:	**Full service in-home delivery and set-up. Customer pays freight company directly for shipping costs.**

Directions: From I-40, take exit #123 (Hwy. 321) and head north through Hickory. The outlet will be on the right, approximately 6 miles north of I-40.

Broyhill Factory Outlet (cont.)

Broyhill Factory Outlet at the Manufacturer Owned Furniture Outlets in Lenoir, NC

"Empire" poster bed from Broyhill

Retail: $1,489.97   Discounted price: $798.97
Savings at the Broyhill Factory Outlet: $691.00 = 46% off retail

Broyhill Showcase Gallery

Level 4
Hickory Furniture Mart
U. S. Hwy. 70 SE
Hickory, NC 28602

Phone:	**(828) 322-4440**	**Hours:**	**M-Sat 9:00-6:00**
Toll Free:	**None**	**E-mail:**	**hparksales@hickorypark.com**
Fax:	**(828) 267-0821**	**Web site:**	**www.hickorypark.com**

The Broyhill Showcase Gallery in the Hickory Furniture Mart is not a true factory outlet, but they are a legitimate deep discounter for this brand. This gallery was taken over by Hickory Park Furniture in 2002. Hickory Park has a generally good reputation for service.

The Hickory Furniture Mart showroom carries all kinds of traditional styles: bedroom furniture, living room furniture, upholstery, etc. However, they don't sell off the floor. All furniture must be special ordered. Broyhill is the only brand carried by this source. They will special order any Broyhill piece you find at a local furniture retailer.

Their discounts are fine, about 40% to 50% off of retail. Most of the pieces on the floor were priced at about 50% off retail. For example, on my last visit here, I found a living room group that normally retailed for $2,729.00 marked down to $1,330.00 (pictured on the next page). Like all of the other furniture here, this price was for brand new furniture in first quality condition.

This is certainly a good source to check out for new Broyhill products from their current lines. For better bargains on floor samples and discontinued styles, check out Broyhill's factory-owned factory outlet further north on Hwy. 321 in Hickory, NC.

Phone orders accepted:	**Yes**
Discount:	**40%-50% off mfrs. suggested retail**
Payment methods:	**VISA, MC, personal checks**
In-house financing available:	**No**
Deposits required:	**30% deposit when order is placed, balance due when furniture is ready to be shipped**
Catalog available:	**No**
Clearance center:	**No**
Delivery:	**Full service in-home delivery and set-up. Customer pays freight company directly for shipping costs.**

Directions: Please see *Hickory Furniture Mart* for complete directions.

Broyhill Showcase Gallery (cont.)

Living room group from Broyhill

Retail: $2,729.00   Discounted price: $1,330.00
Savings at the Broyhill Showcase Gallery: $1,399.00 = 51% off retail

Bulluck Furniture Company

124 S. Main Street
Rocky Mount, NC 27804

Phone:	**(252) 446-1138**	**Hours:**	**M-F 9:00-5:30, Sat 9:00-5:00**
Toll Free:	**None**	**E-mail:**	**None**
Fax:	**(252) 977-7870**	**Web site:**	**www.bulluckfurniture.com**

Bulluck Furniture has been in business since 1900, and they have a lovely showroom in Rocky Mount, NC, about an hour's drive east of Raleigh on Hwy. 64. They have good deals by phone on all the lines below.

They also have a huge weekend decorative accessory sale from late January to early March. Check their Web site above for exact dates and times.

Lines carried:

Allibert	Garcia	Lane/Venture	St. Timothy
Amotek/USA	Gregson	Lexington	Stanley
Barcalounger	Habersham Plantation	Link Taylor	Stanton-Cooper
Bevan Funnell	Hancock & Moore	Lloyd/Flanders	Statton
Bradington Young	Henkel-Harris	Lone Star Leather	Statesville Chair
Carolina Mirror	Henry Link	Madison Square	Stewart
Carvers Guild	Hickory Chair	Maitland Smith	Telescope
Casa Bique	High Point Furniture	McGuire	Tomlin
Colonial Traditions	Hooker	Meadowcraft	Tradition House
Councill-Craftsmen	Howard Miller Clocks	Michael Thomas	Tramswall
Craftique	Hyundai Furniture	National Mt. Airy	Trosby
Cramer	Jamestown Sterling	Nichols & Stone	Vogue Rattan
Creative Metal	Jasper	O'Asian	Wellington Hall
Dixie	Jasper Desk	Pleion	Wesley Hall
Ello	J. B. Ross	Pompeii	Wicker World
Fairington	Jeffco	Royal Patina	Winston
Ficks Reed	Jofco	Schott	Woodfield
Finkel	John Boos	Shelby Williams	Woodmark Chair
Fremarc	John Richard	Southampton	Wright Table
Friedman Bros. Mirrors	Lane	Southwood Reproductions	Young Hinkle

Phone orders accepted:	**Yes**
Discount:	**30%-50% off mfrs. suggested retail**
Payment methods:	**VISA, MC, personal checks**
In-house financing available:	**No**
Deposits required:	**50% deposit when order is placed, balance due when furniture is ready to be shipped**
Catalog available:	**No**
Clearance center:	**No**
Delivery:	**Full service in-home delivery and set-up. Customer pays freight company directly for shipping costs.**

Directions: From I-85, take exit #138, and head a few miles east into Rocky Mount, NC. You'll see signs for Bulluck Furniture as you enter town.

Cannon Village

Between Oak Ave. and Main St.
Kannapolis, NC 28081

Phone:	**(704) 938-3200**	**Hours:**	**M-F 9-5, Sat 10-6, Sun 1-6**
Toll Free:	**(800) 438-6111**	**E-mail:**	**Sales@cannonvillage.com**
Fax:	**(704) 938-2990**	**Web site:**	**www.cannonvillage.com**

Cannon Village has a variety of reputable furniture discounters, and one furniture clearance center. Unfortunately, all the factory outlets that used to be here have closed.

Transit Damage Freight operates a clearance center here with some fairly good bargains. Please see their listing in this book for more detailed information.

K-Town Furniture, Carolina Interiors, and Village Furniture House all have good discounts on brand name furniture and good reputations for service. Please see the individual listings for each store in this book for further information.

If you plan to be in Charlotte, you may wish to drive the half-hour to Kannapolis to see what is offered here. If you are planning a trip to NC in general, you'll be best served to concentrate on Hickory and/or High Point. Kannapolis is over an hour's drive from each city, and offers only a fraction of the bargains and selection available in either Hickory or High Point.

Directions: From I-85, take exit #63, and follow the signs to Cannon Village.

Carolina Discount Furniture

4382 Hickory Blvd.
Granite Falls, NC 28630

Phone:	**(828) 396-2347**	**Hours:**	**M-F 9:00-5:00, Sat 9:00-6:00**
Toll Free:	**None**	**E-mail:**	**None**
Fax:	**(828) 396-6746**	**Web site:**	**None**

Carolina Discount Furniture is a large warehouse type store with a good selection of the brands listed below in stock. Their discounts run around 30%-50% off retail. There are no discontinued items or floor samples in stock. All in stock furniture is new and is sold at exactly the same price whether you shop in person or by phone.

Unlike many other furniture discounters, this source is not able to order any lines other than those listed below. They say that by concentrating on only a few brands, they can buy in sufficient volume to get the very best price and service for their customers.

So, if you're interested in any of the brands listed below, give this source a call to compare prices.

Lines carried:

Action Lane	Douglas	Null	Universal
Brooks	England Corsair	Pulaski	Vaughan
Broyhill	Lea	Riverside	Vaughan-Bassett

Phone orders accepted:	**Yes**
Discount:	**30%-50% off mfrs. suggested retail**
Payment methods:	**VISA, MC, personal checks**
In-house financing available:	**No**
Deposits required:	**50% deposit when order is placed, balance due when furniture is ready to be shipped**
Catalog available:	**No**
Clearance center:	**No**
Delivery:	**Full service in-home delivery and set-up. Customer pays freight company directly for shipping costs.**

Directions: From I-40, take exit #123 and drive north on Hwy. 321 to Granite Falls. Carolina Discount Furniture is on the right side of the road.

Carolina Furniture Of Williamsburg

5425 Richmond Rd.
Williamsburg, VA 23188

Phone:	**(757) 565-3000**	**Hours:**	**M-Thurs & Sat 9:00-6:00**
Toll Free:	**(800) 582-8916 (VA only)**		**Fri 9:00-9:00, Sun 1:00-6:00**
Fax:	**(757) 565-4476**	**E-mail:**	**furnish@carolina-furniture.com**
		Web site:	**www.carolina-furniture.com**

Carolina Furniture Of Williamsburg is located only 3 miles from Colonial Williamsburg, just 30 miles north of Norfolk, VA. They have a very nice selection of high end lines, including a large Pennsylvania House gallery.

They don't have a clearance center or any floor samples or discontinued pieces on display. For this reason, there is no monetary advantage to visiting in person. They do have great deals on many lines sold over the phone, though. So, if you're planning to order your furniture by phone, definitely give this source a call to compare their prices.

Please note that this company is in no way affiliated with Carolina Furniture at www.carolinafurniture.com, which was closed down by the attorney general of NC in 2003 for defrauding customers. Carolina Furniture of Williamsburg is a completely different company with an excellent reputation for service.

Phone orders accepted:	**Yes**
Discount:	**30%-60% off mfrs. suggested retail**
Payment methods:	**VISA, MC, AMEX, Discover, personal checks**
In-house financing available:	**No**
Deposits required:	**50% deposit when order is placed, balance due when furniture is ready to be shipped**
Catalog available:	**No**
Clearance center:	**No**
Delivery:	**Full service in-home delivery and set-up. Customer pays freight company directly for shipping costs.**

Directions: Carolina Furniture Of Williamsburg is located 3 miles west of Colonial Williamsburg on State Route 60.

Carolina Furniture Of Williamsburg (cont.)

Lines carried:

Aladdin Light Lift
Alfonso Marina
American Mirror
Angelo Brothers
Arroyo
Artistic Frame
Artistic Lighting
Artistica
Ashlen Chairs
Athol
Aura International Rugs
Bailey & Griffin
Baker
Baldwin Brass
Ball & Ball
Barcalounger
Barlow Tyne
Basta Sole
Bausman
Bernhardt
Bevan Funnell
Bexley Heath
Bradington-Young
Brubaker
Bruce Post
Butler
Candella Lighting
Capel Rugs
Carlton McLendon
Carolina Mirror
Casa Stradivari
Century
Chapman
Charleston Forge
Chatham Furniture
Chelsea House
Clarence House
Classic Leather
Colonial Furniture
Conover Chair
Cooper Classics
Councill-Craftsmen
Country Swedish
Country Traditions
Cox
Craftique
CTH Sherrill
Custom Comfort
Custom Craft

De Nunzio
Decorative Crafts
Designmaster
E. J. Victor
Eastern Shore Trading Co.
Edrich Mills Wood Shop
Eldred Wheeler
Ello
Emerson et Cie
Fairfield Chair
Ficks Reed
Flat Rock Furniture
Framburg
Frederick Cooper
French Heritage
Friedman Mirrors
Froelich
Furniture Guild
G. L. Sawyer
Gat Creek
George Kovacs
Giemme
Great City Traders
Guild Master
Habersham Plantation
Hale Of Vermont
Hancock & Moore
Harounian Rugs
Harden
Heirloom
Hekman
Hen Feathers
Henkel-Harris
Henkel-Moore
Henredon
Hickory Chair
Hitchcock
Hooker
House Of Troy
Howard Miller
Hubbardton Forge
Isenhour
J. R. Bird
Jessica Charles
Joal
John Boos
Johnston Casuals
Kaiser-Kuhn
Kalanik

Kalco
Karastan
Karges
Kincaid
Kingsley Bate
Koch & Lowy
La Barge
Lane
Livex Lighting
Leisters Furniture
Lexington
Lloyd Braxton
Lloyd/Flanders
Lt. Moses Willard
Lyon Shaw
Madison Square
Maitland Smith
Marge Carson
Marshall James
Martha Stewart
McLean Lighting Works
Metal Specialties
Michael Thomas
Miles Talbot
Milling Road
Mirror Fair
Moosehead
Motioncraft
Murray Feiss
NDI
Nichols & Stone
Northeast Lantern
Nulco
Old Biscayne Designs
Old World Pewter
Payne Street Imports
Pande Cameron
Peacock Alley
Pearson
Pennsylvania House
Quoizel
Ralph Lauren
River Bend Chair
Richardson Brothers
Riverside Furniture
Robert Allen
Romweber
Ron Fisher
Royal Patina

Saloom
Sam Moore
Sanderson
Sarreid
Scalamandre
Schumacher
Scott Thomas
Sedgefield
Sherrill
Simmons
Sligh
Southampton
Southwood
Speer
Stanley
Stakmore
Statton
Superior
Swaim
Telescope
Thayer Coggin
Tomlinson
Tom Seely
Trading Company
Trica
Tropitone
Uwharrie
Vermont Precision
Vermont Tubbs
Virginia House
Virginia
    Metalcrafters
Vitalie
Waterford Lighting
Waverly
Weiman
Weiss & Biheller
Wellington Hall
Wesley Allen
Westgate
Wildwood Lamps
Woodard
Woodwright Co.
World Imports
Wright Table Co.
Yorkshire House

Carolina Interiors

115 Oak Ave.
Kannapolis, NC 28081

Phone:	**(704) 933-2261**	**Hours:**	**M-Sat 9:00-6:00**
Toll Free:	**None**	**E-mail:**	**sales@carolinainteriors.com**
Fax:	**(704) 932-0434**	**Web site:**	**www.carolinainteriors.com**

Carolina Interiors in Cannon Village has a very nice store with a good selection of high-end furniture. Most of the furniture in stock is new first-quality, and priced at about 40%-50% off retail. There are a few floor samples and discontinued styles scattered around priced at 50%-70% off retail. They will also sell by phone, and they claim to save you 30%-60% off retail on special order furniture. Also, the staff here tends to announce very quickly that all prices are negotiable, so be sure to haggle.

On a recent visit here, I found a very good deal on a Hekman triple-arch bookcase (pictured on the following page). The retail on this piece is normally $7,518.00, but this one was marked down to only $3,799.00. This piece was brand-new and in first-quality condition.

They frequently have outlet pieces in stock from Maitland-Smith as well, at up to 60% off. There used to be a factory outlet for Maitland-Smith at Cannon Village, but Carolina Interiors has been liquidating these pieces since the outlet closed.

If you are ordering furniture by phone, definitely give this source a call. They have a very good reputation for customer service, and they will haggle. I have found that they will try hard to outdo any competitor's prices. Let them!

Phone orders accepted:	Yes
Discount:	**30%-60% off mfrs. suggested retail**
Payment methods:	**Personal checks. No credit cards.**
In-house financing available:	**No**
Deposits required:	**1/3 deposit when order is placed, balance due when furniture is ready to be shipped**
Catalog available:	**No**
Clearance center:	**No**
Delivery:	**Full service in-home delivery and set-up. Customer pays freight company directly for shipping costs.**

Directions: From I-85, take exit #63, and follow the signs to Cannon Village.

Carolina Interiors (cont.)

Carolina Interiors

Triple-arch bookcase from Hekman

Retail: $7,518.00   Discounted price: $3,799.00
Savings at Carolina Interiors: $3,719.00 = 50% off retail

Carolina Interiors (cont.)

Lines carried:

Accessories Abroad
Alexvale
American Drew
Artistica
As You Like It
Athol
Austin
Baker
Baldwin Brass
Barcalounger
Bashian Carpets
Bassett
Berkline
Bevan Funnell
Blacksmith Shop
Bradington Young
Braxton Culler
Broyhill
Butler Specialty
Carolina Mirror
CTH/Sherrill
Carsons
Casa Bique
Casa Stradivari
Century
Chapman Lamps
Charleston Forge
Chelsea House/Port Royal
Chromcraft
Classic Leather
Clayton Marcus
Collezione Europa
Colonial
Councill Craftsmen
Cox
Craftique
Craftwork Guild
C. R. Laine Upholstery
Custom Shoppe
Davis & Davis Carpets
Decorative Crafts
Designmaster
Dinaire
Distinction Leather
Ello
Fairfield
Fashion Bed Group
Ficks Reed
Flexsteel

Florita Nova
Frederick Cooper
Fremarc
French Heritage
Friedman Bros.
Great City Traders
Guildmaster
Habersham Plantation
Hammary
Hancock & Moore
Hart Lamps
Heirloom
Hekman
Henry Link Wicker
Hickory Chair
Hickory Frye
High Point Desk
Highland House
Hooker
House Parts
Howard Miller Clocks
Hyundai Furniture
J. Royale
Jasper Cabinet
Jessica Charles
John Boos
John Richard
Johnston Casuals
Karges
Keller
Kessler
Key City
Kimball
Kincaid
King Hickory
Kingsdown
Kingsley-Bate
Klaussner
La Barge
Lane
Lea
Leathercraft
Lexington
Lloyd/Flanders
Lyon Shaw
Madison Square
Maitland-Smith
Marbro Lamps
Masland Carpet

McGuire
McKinley Leather
Michael Thomas
Moosehead
Motioncraft
Nichols & Stone
Old Hickory Tannery
Pande Cameron
Paoli
Park Place
Paul Robert
Pearson
Pennsylvania House
Pompeii
Pulaski
Richardson Bros.
Ridgeway Clocks
Riverside
Rowe
Royal Patina
Sam Moore
Samuel Bent
Salem Square
Saloom
Sarreid
Sedgefield Lamps
Shuford
Sligh Desk/Clocks
Southampton
Southern Furniture
    Reproductions
Southern Of Conover
Southwood Reproductions
Speer Lamps
Stanford
Stanley
Stanton Cooper
Statesville Chair
Statton
Stein World
Stoneleigh
Swaim
Taylorsville
Thayer Coggin
Theodore Alexander
Tianjin Philadelphia
    Carpets
Touchstone
Tradition House

Universal
Vanguard
Vaughan Bassett
Venture/Lane
Vermont Tubbs
Virginia House
Virginia Metalcrafters
Waterford Lamps
Wellington Hall
Wesley Allen
Wesley Hall
Wildwood Lamps
William Alan
Winston
Woodard
Woodmark
Yorkshire House

Carolina Patio Warehouse

58 Largo Dr.
Stamford, CT 06907

Phone:	**(203) 975-9939**	**Hours:**	**M-Sat 9:00-6:00**
Toll Free:	**(800) 672-8466**	**E-mail:**	**None**
Fax:	**(203) 975-8144**	**Web sites:**	**www.carolinapatio.com**
			www.patio.com

Carolina Patio Warehouse isn't actually based in North Carolina. It was operated for many years by R & R Pool & Patio in Stamford, CT. It was purchased a couple of years ago by Patio.com, which owns twelve patio stores in Virginia, Connecticut, New York, Maryland, Massachusetts, and Pennsylvania.

Carolina Patio Warehouse/Patio.com has a written guarantee promising to beat any competitors prices on wicker, rattan, and outdoor furniture. They also carry poolside furniture and umbrellas.

Their prices are generally about 30%-60% below the manufacturer's suggested retail. They have a fairly extensive online catalog. Their shipping runs about 9% of the purchase price with a minimum shipping charge of $65.00 on truck shipments, and $25 on UPS shipments. They only ship to the continental U. S. and Canada.

Lines carried:

Atlantic Bench	Galtech	Pawley's Island	Triconfort
Basta Sole	Homecrest	Polywood	Tropitone
Beka	Kettler	Prairie Leisure	Tye-Sil Patio
Casual Creations	Kingsley Bate	Samsonite Aluminum	Veneman
Colonial Castings	Lane Venture	Scanply	Windsor Design
Coppa	Lyon Shaw	Summer Classics	Windward Classics
Cushion Factory	Outdoor Classics	Telescope	Zip

Phone orders accepted:	**Yes**
Discount:	**30%-60% off mfrs. suggested retail**
Payment methods:	**VISA, MC, DISC, AMEX, personal checks**
In-house financing available:	**No**
Deposits required:	**50% deposit when order is placed, balance due when furniture is ready to be shipped**
Catalog available:	**Yes**
Clearance center:	**No**
Delivery:	**Full service in-home delivery and set-up. Customer pays freight company directly for shipping costs.**

Directions: Please see Patio.com for a complete list of directions to all 12 stores.

Catawba Furniture Mall

377 US Highway 70 SW
Hickory, NC 28602

Phone:	**(828) 324-9701**	**Hours:**	**M-Sat 10:00-7:00**
Toll Free:	**(800) 789-0686**	**E-mail:**	**info@catawbafurniture.com**
Fax:	**None**	**Web site:**	**www.catawbafurniture.com**

The Catawba Furniture Mall has over 8 acres of furniture showrooms on two floors. It's well worth a stop if you're shopping in High Point. It's also just a few miles from the Hickory Furniture Mart, so if you travel to one, you really should take a little time to see the other.

The main attraction at the Catawba Furniture Mall is their new Designer's Outlet on the second floor. They have some quite good bargains. Please see this store's listing in this book for further information.

The Catawba Furniture Mall also offers occasional hotel discounts to Hickory shoppers through the Park Inn in Hickory, which is owned by the same company. Their "Furniture Shoppers Package" is offered four times each year during their big sale weekends, typically during February, May, August, and November. It includes discounted hotel rates, free breakfast and lunch, and a coupon worth $50 off a purchase of $500 or more. Please note that shoppers must register with the mall at least one week prior to their visit to receive the freebies and coupons. Call or check their Web site for details.

Please note that one of the stores in the Catawba Furniture Mall, Ashley Furniture, is not a deep discounter or factory outlet. It is just like any other Ashley Furniture store you would find around the U. S. The other stores in the mall all offer good bargains. Please see their individual listings in this book for more details.

About Last Nite	(828) 324-2830
Designer's Choice Furniture	(828) 327-3419
Designer's Choice Galleries	(828) 327-4617
Designer's Outlet	(828) 267-7253
Heritage Home	(828) 327-0697
Kathy Ireland Home Collection	(828) 327-2363
Klaussner Home	(828) 327-0501
Studio 70	(828) 322-2800

Directions: **The Catawba Furniture Mall is in Hickory, NC. From I-40, take exit #123-B and turn right. The mall will be about half a mile down on your right.**

Cayton Furniture

4525 Hwy. 264 W.
Washington, NC 27889

Phone:	**(252) 946-4121**	**Hours:**	**M-F 9:00-5:00**
Toll Free:	**(800) 849-8286**	**E-mail:**	**caytonfurniture@coastalnet.com**
Fax:	**(252) 975-6225**	**Web site:**	**www.caytonfurniture.com**

Cayton Furniture has been discounting furniture by phone for over 40 years. They can special order nearly any line, with the exception of some of the most high-end manufacturers.

Unfortunately, Cayton Furniture has been accumulating many complaints at the BBB during the past three years, including some which are unresolved. I have also been contacted by readers with complaints against this company. Until these problems are resolved, I must recommend that consumers not shop here.

Phone orders accepted:	**Yes**
Discount:	**40%-50% off mfrs. suggested retail**
Payment methods:	**VISA, MC, personal checks**
In-house financing available:	**Yes**
Deposits required:	**50% deposit when order is placed, balance due when furniture is ready to be shipped**
Catalog available:	**No**
Clearance center:	**No**
Delivery:	**Full service in-home delivery and set-up. Customer pays freight company directly for shipping costs.**

Directions: From I-95, take exit #121 (Hwy. 264), and take Hwy. 264 east about one hour to Washington, NC. Cayton Furniture is on Hwy. 264 in downtown Washington.

Cedar Rock Home Furnishings

3483 Hickory Blvd., Hwy. 321 S.
Hudson, NC 28638

Phone:	**(828) 396-2361**	**Hours:**	**M-Sat 9:00-6:00**
Toll Free:	**None**	**E-mail:**	**info@cedarrockfurniture.com**
Fax:	**(828) 396-7800**	**Web site:**	**www.cedarrockfurniture.com**

Cedar Rock Home Furnishings is located just a few miles north of Hickory, NC. They have a very nice selection of high end lines, including Lexington, Broyhill, Stanley, and Hooker. They've been in business for nearly 20 years, and they have a good reputation for customer service.

Every April and October, they run a market sample sale. Most pieces are an additional 30% off their regular prices. So, if you're visiting Hickory during those months, you may wish to stop in. Please check our Web site at www.smartdecorating.com for a current list of sale dates.

Phone orders accepted:	Yes
Discount:	**30%-50% off mfrs. suggested retail**
Payment methods:	**VISA, MC, Discover, personal checks**
In-house financing available:	No
Deposits required:	**50% deposit when order is placed, balance due when furniture is ready to be shipped**
Catalog available:	No
Clearance center:	No
Delivery:	**Full service in-home delivery and set-up. Customer pays freight company directly for shipping costs.**

**Directions: From I-40, take exit #123 and drive north on Hwy. 321 to Hudson, NC.
Cedar Rock Home Furnishings is on the right side of the road.**

Cedar Rock Home Furnishings (cont.)

Lines carried:

Action Lane
American Drew
American Of High Point
American Of Martinsville
As You Like It
Ashworth Art
Barcalounger
Bard
Barn Door
Bassett
Bassett Mirror
Bellecraft Upholstery
Benicia Foundry
Berkline
Bevan Funnell
Brasscrafters
Braxton Culler
Brent Jacobs
Brentwood Furniture
Builtright Chair
Cambridge Chair
Carlton McLendon
Carolina Furniture Works
Carolina Mirror
Carter
Charleston Forge
Chatham
Chromecraft
Clayton Marcus
C. M. Leather
CMI
Coaster Co.
Colonial Braided Rugs
Conover Chair
Craftique
Craftmaster
Crawford
Crescent
Crown Arts
CTH Sherrill
Decorative Crafts
Denny Lamps
Dillon
D. R. Kincaid
Eddie Bauer by Lane
Eddy West
Edward Art
Ello
Excel. Office-Contract

Fairfield Chair
Fairmont Designs
Fashion Bed Group
Fortune Rattan Imports
Furniture Traditions
Glass Arts
Goodwin Weavers
H. A. DeNunzio
            Oil Paintings
Hammary
Hampton Hall
Hanover Heirlooms
Harris
Hekman
Hickory Classics
Hickory Hill
Hickory Leather
Hickory Springs
Home Impressions
Howard Miller
J. Royale
John Boyd Designs
Kessler
King Hickory
Klaussner
Lane
Lane/Venture
Lea
Leather Classics
Legacy
Leisters
Little Miss Liberty
Lyon Shaw
Madison Square
Master Design
Med Lift
Mobel
Morgan Stewart
Nichols & Stone
Nordwinds
Northwestern
Null
Ohio Table Pads
Omnia Leather
Origo
Palliser
Parker Southern
Paul Roberts
Pelican Reef

Penns Creek
Peters-Revington
Pinnacle
Polcor Bedding
Primo
Pulaski
Quoizel
Regency Leather
Relax-R
Reprocrafters
Ridgeway Clocks
Riverside
Rockford
Rowe
Royal Patina
Salem House
Sam Moore
Sarreid
Schnadig
Schweiger
Sealy Upholstery
Sentry Rugs
Simmons Baby/Juvenile
Steinworld
Story & Clark Pianos
Superior Furniture
Temple
Therapedic Bedding
Timeless Bedding
Town Square
Tradewinds
Ultimate Accents
Universal
Uttermost
Uwharrie Chair
Universal
Vaughan
Vaughan-Bassett
Venture
Vineyard
Virginia House
Virginia Metalcrafters
Wayborn
Weather Master
Wellington Hall
Wesley Allen
Williamsburg by Lane
Willow Creek
Winston

Woodmark

Century Factory Outlet

Level 4
Hickory Furniture Mart
U. S. Hwy. 70 SE
Hickory, NC 28602

Phone:	(828) 324-2442	**Hours:**	M-Sat 9:00-6:00
Toll Free:	None	**E-mail:**	info@hollingate.com
Fax:	(828) 464-9964	**Web site:**	www.hickoryfurniture.com

   The Century Factory Outlet is a part of the Hollin Gate space at the Hickory Furniture Mart. This showroom also serves as the factory outlet for Councill-Craftsmen. This location is the only factory outlet for these three brands.
   This location is about half-stocked with antiques and accessories, with the other half of the showroom devoted to discontinued styles and floor samples from the above-mentioned three brands. The discounts on the outlet furniture generally runs a straight 60% off across the board. Virtually all of the furniture here is in new first-quality condition.
   Usuually, the sales staff immediately volunteers to customers that they can come down even further from the price marked, so be sure to haggle. They also runs periodic sales, usually giving another 10%-20% off the marked discount. These sales normally run in January, March, May, and September.
   The outlet has an excellent selection. Most of the pieces are traditional, but there are usually a few contemporary styles.
   On a recent visit here, I found a Century leather sofa (pictured on the following page) that normally retails for $5,040.00 marked down to $2,016.00, a discount of 60% off the normal retail price. This particular piece was a floor sample in first-quality condition.
   If you're traveling to Hickory, this outlet is a "must-visit"!

Phone orders accepted:	No
Discount:	60% off mfrs. suggested retail
Payment methods:	VISA, MC, personal checks
In-house financing available:	No
Deposits required:	Not applicable
Catalog available:	Not applicable
Clearance center:	Not applicable
Delivery:	Full service in-home delivery and set-up. Customer pays freight company directly for shipping costs.

Directions: Please see *Hickory Furniture Mart* for complete directions.

Century Factory Outlet (cont.)

Leather sofa from Century Furniture

Retail: $5,040.00   Discounted price: $2,016.00
Savings at the Century Factory Outlet: $3,024.00 = 60% off retail

Charleston Forge Factory Outlet

368 NC Hwy. 105 Extension
Boone, NC 28607

Phone:	**(828) 262-0096**	**Hours:**	**M-Sat 10:00-5:30**
Toll Free:	**None**	**E-mail:**	**None**
Fax:	**None**	**Web site:**	**None**

This is the new outlet for Charleston Forge. Unfortunately, there isn't much to it. Most of the stock is new patio furniture from various manufacturers.

The few Charleston Forge outlet pieces in stock are 58% off, and in new condition. The store also sells Woodard patio furniture at 35% off. All other lines are retail.

In my opinion, this "outlet" just isn't worth the one hour trip through the mountains it takes to get to it from any major interstate. It was very disappointing. It isn't factory owned, so the name "outlet" is misleading. It is primarily a retail patio furniture shop with a few outlet pieces sprinkled in.

If you are in Boone anyway, by all means check this outlet out. Otherwise, it really isn't worth the trip.

Phone orders accepted:	**No**
Discount:	**Mostly retail, Woodard 35% off, CF 58% off**
Payment methods:	**VISA, MC, Discover, personal checks**
In-house financing available:	**No**
Deposits required:	**Not applicable**
Catalog available:	**Not applicable**
Clearance center:	**Not applicable**
Delivery:	**Full service in-home delivery and set-up. Customer pays freight company directly for shipping costs.**

Directions: From Hickory, NC, go north on Hwy. 321 to Blowing Rock. Hwy. 321 will become 221 N. Continue into Boone. Turn right on Hwy. 105 (there's an Exxon at the corner). Store is past the 1st light on the left.

Classic Furniture

2052 Highway U.S. 321 South
Lenoir, NC 28645

Phone:	**(828) 726-8880**	**Hours:**	**M-Sat 9:30-6:00**
Toll Free:	**None**	**E-mail:**	**info@classicfurnitureltd.com**
Fax:	**(828) 728-6454**	**Web site:**	**www.classicfurnitureltd.com**

Classic Furniture advertises a line of custom casegoods to the public. They advertise on their Web site that they also offer "deep discounts on solid furniture from more than a hundred name brand manufacturers".

Unfortunately, they do not identify the extent of the "deep discounts" on their site or the specific manufacturers they offer, nor will they provide this information to me on request.

I can tell you that their record with the local BBB is very poor, and they have multiple unanswered complaints on their record with the BBB. I have asked Classic Furniture to keep me posted on any efforts to resolve the complaints on their record. Until they are resolved, I must recommend that consumers not buy from this source.

Phone orders accepted:	**Yes**
Discount:	**Factory direct to public**
Payment methods:	**Cash, personal checks, money**
In-house financing available:	**No**
Deposits required:	**50% deposit when order is placed, balance due when furniture is ready to be shipped**
Catalog available:	**Yes, online**
Clearance center:	**No**
Delivery:	**Full service in-home delivery and set-up. Customer pays freight company directly for shipping costs.**

Directions: From I-40, take exit #123 and drive north on Hwy. 321 to Lenoir. Classic Furniture is on the left side of the road.

Clayton-Marcus Factory Outlet

Level 4
Hickory Furniture Mart
U. S. Hwy. 70 SE
Hickory, NC 28602

Phone:	**(828) 327-0244**	**Hours:**	**M-Sat 9:00-6:00**	
Toll Free:	**None**	**E-mail:**	**moutlet@charterinternet.com**	
Fax:	**(828) 327-4544**	**Web site:**	**www.hickoryfurniture.com**	

The Clayton-Marcus outlet has just moved from Triplett's Furniture Fashions to a new showroom in the Hickory Furniture Mart. The outlet is now operated by Manufacturer's Outlet, a very reputable company with a long-standing reputation for service. Manufacturer's Outlet also operates the factory outlets for Hickory White and Theodore Alexander at the Hickory Furniture Mart.

The stock is made up of floor samples, discontinued styles, and customer returns. All of the furniture here is upholstery: sofas and occasional chairs. The discounts run from 50%-70% off retail. Virtually all of the furniture here is in new first-quality condition.

This factory outlet also features Simex, Leathertrend, Sofa Trend, and Mirador. In addition to furniture, they also have a line of European oil paintings at good prices and some Asian antique pieces.

They also participate in the regular mall-wide sales run by the Hickory Furniture Mart in February, May, July, and November. Please check out Web site at www.smartdecorating.com for upcoming sale dates.

Phone orders accepted:	**No**
Discount:	**50%-70% off mfrs. suggested retail**
Payment methods:	**VISA, MC, personal checks**
In-house financing available:	**Yes**
Deposits required:	**Not applicable**
Catalog available:	**Not applicable**
Clearance center:	**Not applicable**
Delivery:	**Full service in-home delivery and set-up. Customer pays freight company directly for shipping costs.**

Directions: Please see *Hickory Furniture Mart* for complete directions.

Coffey Furniture

Hwy. 321, Poovey Dr.
Granite Falls, NC 28630

Phone:	**(828) 396-2900**	**Hours:**	**M-Sat 9:00-5:00**
Toll Free:	**None**	**E-mail:**	**None**
Fax:	**(828) 396-3050**	**Web site:**	**None**

Coffey Furniture specializes in purchasing market samples from the various wholesale trade shows and reselling them to the public. They have three huge warehouses filled with all kinds of case goods and upholstery. They will also special order new furniture from many lines.

Nothing is marked at a discount; everything is just one flat price. This can make it confusing for an amateur furniture shopper to make sure their getting the best deal without the original manufacturer's retail as a reference point. The prices I have observed here seem to run approximately 30% to 60% off retail. There are some very good deals here mixed in with some other not-so-good deals.

This is a good place for an experienced furniture shopper to visit. Others may find it confusing. Those who don't have a good basic knowledge of what furniture is worth should stick with other sources.

Lines carried:

Action by Lane	Crawford	J. B. Ross	Pulaski
American Drew	Denny Lamps	Kimball Victorian	Ridgeway Clocks
Athens	Dining Ala Carte	Lane	Royale Komfort
Bassett	Dresher	Lane/Venture	Bedding
Bassett Baby/Juvenile	Fairfield Chair	Lea	Seay
Berkshire	Fashion Bed Group	Liberty	Spring Air Bedding
Blacksmith Shop	Flexsteel	Link Taylor	Temple Upholstery
Cal-Style	Goodwin Weavers	Lloyd/Flanders	U. S. Furniture Industry
Century Rugs	Hickory Hill	Morganton Chair	Universal
Chatham County	Hickory Mark	Ohio Table Pad	Vanguard Pictures
Chromecraft	Holiday House Sleepers	Parker Southern	Wesley Allen
Clayton Marcus	Howard Miller Clocks	Peters Revington	
Cochrane	Hyundai Furniture	Philip Reinisch Co.	

Phone orders accepted:	**Yes**
Discount:	**30%-60% off mfrs. suggested retail**
Payment methods:	**VISA, MC, personal checks**
In-house financing available:	**No**
Deposits required:	**50% deposit when order is placed, balance due when furniture is ready to be shipped**
Catalog available:	**No**
Clearance center:	**No**
Delivery:	**Full service in-home delivery and set-up. Customer pays freight company directly for shipping costs.**

Directions: From I-40, take exit #123 and drive north on Hwy. 321 to Granite Falls. Coffey Furniture is on the left at the end of Poovey Dr.

Coffey Furniture (cont.)

Coffey Furniture

Colfax Furniture

3501 McCuiston Ct.
I-85 at Holden Rd.
Greensboro, NC 27407

Phone:	(336) 855-0498	**Hours:**	M-F 10:00-9:00, Sat 10:00-6:00,
Toll Free:	None		Sun 12:00-6:00
Fax:	None	**E-mail:**	None
		Web site:	None

Colfax Furniture specializes in purchasing market samples from the various wholesale trade shows and reselling them to the public. They have an enormous warehouse filled with all kinds of case goods and upholstery, including a wide selection of recliners. Most of the furniture here is medium-quality. I saw very few high-end brands.

Nothing is marked at a discount; everything is just one flat price. This can make it confusing for an amateur furniture shopper to make sure their getting the best deal without the original manufacturer's retail as a reference point. The prices I have observed here seem to run approximately 30% to 70% off retail. There are some very good deals here mixed in with some other not-so-good deals.

This is a good place for an experienced furniture shopper to visit. Others may find it confusing. Those who don't have a good basic knowledge of what furniture is worth should stick with other sources.

Phone orders accepted:	No
Discount:	30%-70% off mfrs. suggested retail
Payment methods:	VISA, MC, personal checks
In-house financing available:	Yes
Deposits required:	Not applicable
Catalog available:	Not applicable
Clearance center:	Not applicable
Delivery:	Full service in-home delivery and set-up. Customer pays freight company directly for shipping costs.

Directions: From I-85, take exit #121 (Holden Rd.). Colfax Furniture is right off the interstate on the frontage road.

Corner Hutch Furniture

210 Signal Hill Dr.
Statesville, NC 28687

Phone:	**(704) 873-1773**	**Hours:**	**M-F 9:00-5:30, Sat 10:00-4:00**
Toll Free:	**None**	**E-mail:**	**info@cornerhutchfurniture.com**
Fax:	**(704) 873-1637**	**Web site:**	**www.cornerhutchfurniture.com**

Corner Hutch Furniture has closed its showroom in Statesville and shut down their Web site, but they continue to take orders by phone from their business office.

Consumers should be aware that Corner Hutch has a poor record with the BBB due to unanswered complaints. Until these complaints are resolved, I must recommend that my readers not buy from this company.

Lines carried:

American Drew	Distinction Leather	Kingsdown Bedding	Sarreid
Baldwin Brass	Fashion Bed Group	La Barge	Sedgefield
Barcalounger	Frederick Cooper Lamps	Lane	Serta
Boling Chair	Hancock & Moore	Lane/Venture	Southampton
Bradington Young	Friedman Bros. Mirrors	Lea	Southwood Reproduc-
Brown Jordan	Habersham Plantation	Lexington	tions
Broyhill	Hale Of Vermont	Lloyd/Flanders	Stanley
Builtright Chair	Hammary	Lyon Shaw	Stiffel Lamps
Carolina Mirror	Hekman	Madison Square	Superior
Cebu Imports	Henry Link Wicker	Maryland Classics	S. Bent
Chapman Lamps	Hickory Tavern	McKay Table Pads	Tradition House
Charleston Forge	Hickory White	Nichols & Stone	Tropitone
Chelsea House	Highland House	North Hickory Upholstery	Universal
Clark Casual	Hitchcock Chair	Ohio Table Pads	Virginia House
Cochrane	Hooker	Old Hickory Tannery	Virginia Metalcrafters
Colonial	Howard Miller Clocks	Pande Cameron Rugs	Wellington Hall
Conover Upholstery	Jasper	Park Place Upholstery	Wildwood Lamps
Corsican Beds	Kaiser Kuhn Lamps	Pulaski	Winston
Cox Upholstery	Keller	Richardson Bros.	Woodmark Chairs
Craftique	King Hickory Upholstery	Salem Square	

Phone orders accepted:	**Yes**
Discount:	**40%-50% off mfrs. suggested retail**
Payment methods:	**VISA, MC, personal checks**
In-house financing available:	**No**
Deposits required:	**50% deposit when order is placed, balance due when furniture is ready to be shipped**
Catalog available:	**No**
Clearance center:	**No**
Delivery:	**Full service in-home delivery and set-up. Customer pays freight company directly for shipping costs.**

Directions: From I-77, take the E. Broad St. exit and go east. Turn left on Signal Hill Dr. You'll see Corner Hutch Furniture on the right.

Councill-Craftsmen Factory Outlet

Level 4
Hickory Furniture Mart
U. S. Hwy. 70 SE
Hickory, NC 28602

Phone:	**(828) 324-2442**	**Hours:**	**M-Sat 9:00-6:00**
Toll Free:	**None**	**E-mail:**	**info@hollingate.com**
Fax:	**(828) 464-9964**	**Web site:**	**www.hickoryfurniture.com**

    The Councill-Craftsmen Factory Outlet is a part of the Hollin Gate space at the Hickory Furniture Mart. This showroom also serves as the factory outlet for Hickory Chair and Century. This location is the only factory outlet for these three brands.

    This location is about half-stocked with antiques and accessories, with the other half of the showroom devoted to discontinued styles and floor samples from the above-mentioned three brands. The discounts on the outlet furniture generally runs a straight 60% off across the board. Virtually all of the furniture here is in new first-quality condition.

    Usuually, the sales staff immediately volunteers to customers that they can come down even further from the price marked, so be sure to haggle. They also runs periodic sales, usually giving another 10%-20% off the marked discount. These sales normally run in January, March, May, and September.

    The outlet has an excellent selection. Most of the pieces are traditional, but there are usually a few contemporary styles. If you're traveling to Hickory, this outlet is a "must-visit"!

Phone orders accepted:	**No**
Discount:	**60% off mfrs. suggested retail**
Payment methods:	**VISA, MC, personal checks**
In-house financing available:	**No**
Deposits required:	**Not applicable**
Catalog available:	**Not applicable**
Clearance center:	**Not applicable**
Delivery:	**Full service in-home delivery and set-up. Customer pays freight company directly for shipping costs.**

Directions: Please see *Hickory Furniture Mart* for complete directions.

Cross Creek Furniture

3428 Hickory Blvd.
Hudson, NC 28638

Phone:	**(828) 396-7188**	**Hours:**	**M-F 9:00-5:00, Sat 9:00-6:00**
Toll Free:	None	**E-mail:**	None
Fax:	**(828) 396-5145**	**Web site:**	None

Cross Creek Furniture has recently opened in the old Blowing Rock Furniture building in Hudson, NC. Please note that Cross Creek Furniture is in no way affiliated with Blowing Rock, which closed after many complaints.

Unfortunately, Cross Creek is owned by the same people who own Smokey Mountain Furniture, which also has an unsatisfactory record with the BBB due to unanswered complaints. I have asked the owners to keep me posted on any efforts to answer these complaints. In the meantime, I must recommend that consumers not buy from this source.

Lines carried:

Cramco	Jetton	Ridgeway	Vaughan
Douglas	Kingsdown	Riverside	Vaughan-Bassett
Englander	Lane	Rowe	
Home Elegance	Master Design	Standard	
Jami L.	Pulaski	Universal	

Phone orders accepted:	**Yes**
Discount:	**40%-50% off mfrs. suggested retail**
Payment methods:	**Personal checks, cash**
In-house financing available:	**Yes**
Deposits required:	**50% deposit when order is placed, balance due when furniture is ready to be shipped**
Catalog available:	**No**
Clearance center:	**No**
Delivery:	**Full service in-home delivery and set-up. Customer pays freight company directly for shipping costs.**

Directions: From I-40, take exit #123 and drive north on Hwy. 321 to Hudson. Cross Creek Furniture is on the right side of the road.

Decorator's Choice

National Home Furnishings Center
1628 S. Main St.
High Point, NC 27261

Phone:	**(336) 889-9058**	**Hours:**	**M-Sat 9:00-6:00**
Toll Free:	**None**	**E-mail:**	**decchoice@aol.com**
Fax:	**(336) 889-8656**	**Web site:**	**None**

Decorator's Choice at the National Home Furnishings Center in High Point has some pretty good deals on special order furniture from a variety of lines, as well as on a small selection of showroom samples in new, first-quality condition. Their styles run from traditional to transitional. Their quality is very good. They also have a good reputation for customer service.

For example, on a recent visit I found a great deal on a hand-painted credenza. The retail price on this piece was $1,299.00. The price on this one showroom sample was only $590.00, a discount of 55% off the original retail price.

The showroom here at the National Home Furnishings Center is on the small side. For a greater selection, see Decorator's Choice's showrooms at the Atrium Furniture Mall in downtown High Point.

Lines carried:

Asiart	Greene Brothers	Null	Village Smith
Collezione Europa	Harris Marcus	Pastel	Visions Elite
Dinec	Magnussen	Trica	
DR Kincaid Chairs	Morgan Stewart	Vermont Precision	

Phone orders accepted:	**Yes**
Discount:	**40%-50% off mfrs. suggested retail**
Payment methods:	**VISA, MC, personal checks**
In-house financing available:	**No**
Deposits required:	**50% deposit when order is placed, balance due when furniture is ready to be shipped**
Catalog available:	**No**
Clearance center:	**No**
Delivery:	**Full service in-home delivery and set-up. Customer pays freight company directly for shipping costs.**

Directions: **From I-85, take exit #111 (Hwy. 311), and head northwest into High Point. After several miles, when you reach downtown High Point, Hwy. 311 will become S. Main St. The National Home Furnishings Center is on the left side of Main St.**

Decorator's Choice

Hand-painted credenza at Decorator's Choice

Retail: $1,299.00   Discounted price: $599.00
Savings at Decorator's Choice: $691.00 = 55% off retail

Decorator's Choice

The Atrium
430 S. Main St.
High Point, NC 27260

Phone:	**(336) 889-9058**	**Hours:**	**M-Sat 9:00-6:00**
Toll Free:	**None**	**E-mail:**	**decchoice@aol.com**
Fax:	**(336) 889-8656**	**Web site:**	**None**

Decorator's Choice at the Atrium Furniture Mall in High Point has some pretty good deals on special order furniture from a variety of lines, as well as on a small selection of showroom samples in new, first-quality condition. Their styles run from traditional to transitional. Their quality is very good. They also have a good reputation for customer service.

The first floor showroom carries a wide variety of furniture. The smaller showroom on the third floor carries mostly dining room sets and chairs.

Lines carried:

Asiart	Greene Brothers	Null	Village Smith
Collezione Europa	Harris Marcus	Pastel	Visions Elite
Dinec	Magnussen	Trica	
DR Kincaid Chairs	Morgan Stewart	Vermont Precision	

Phone orders accepted:	**Yes**
Discount:	**40%-50% off mfrs. suggested retail**
Payment methods:	**VISA, MC, personal checks**
In-house financing available:	**No**
Deposits required:	**50% deposit when order is placed, balance due when furniture is ready to be shipped**
Catalog available:	**No**
Clearance center:	**No**
Delivery:	**Full service in-home delivery and set-up. Customer pays freight company directly for shipping costs.**

Directions: Please see *The Atrium* for complete directions.

Designer's Choice Furniture

Catawba Furniture Mall
377 Hwy. 70 SW
Hickory, NC 28602

Phone:	**(828) 327-3419**	**Hours:**	**M-Sat 9:00-7:00**
Toll Free:	**None**	**E-mail:**	**info@catawbafurniture.com**
Fax:	**(828) 327-4036**	**Web site:**	**www.catawbafurniture.com**

Designer's Choice Furniture at the Catawba Furniture Mall is huge. With all of its combined galleries, it easily takes up over half of the entire mall. Discounts run 40-50% off retail. It's owned by the same company that owns the Catawba Furniture Mall, which has a good reputation for customer service.

All of the furniture at Designer's Choice is special order. If you see something you like, be sure to check upstairs at Designer's Outlet before buying. Designer's Outlet liquidates samples, overstock items, discontinued pieces, and customer returns for Designer's Choice. They have a nice variety of outlet pieces from the lines below at substantially greater savings: 50%-70% off retail. You may well find what you're looking for in stock at the outlet.

Please see the listing in this book for the Catawba Furniture Mall if you are planning a visit here. The Mall offers discounts on hotel rooms and coupons toward your furniture purchase during their big sale weekends four times each year.

Lines carried:

AICO	Clayton Marcus	Hollywoods	Pennsylvania Classics
American Drew	Clyde Pearson	Hooker	Regency House
APA	Craftmaster	J. Royale	Stratalounger
ARA	Cramco	Jasper Cabinet	Thomasville
Ardley Hall	Drexel Heritage	Klaussner	Vaughan Bassett
Broyhill	Hekman	Lane Venture	Virginia House
Catnapper	Hammary	Leatherworks	Wellington Hall
Charleston Forge	Highland House	Magnolia	Woodmark
Classico	Hitchcock	Orleans	

Phone orders accepted:	**Yes**
Discount:	**40%-50% off mfrs. suggested retail**
Payment methods:	**VISA, MC, personal checks**
In-house financing available:	**Yes, 90 days same as cash with 25% down pmt.**
Deposits required:	**50% deposit when order is placed, balance due when furniture is ready to be shipped**
Catalog available:	**No**
Clearance center:	**No**
Delivery:	**Full service in-home delivery and set-up. Customer pays freight company directly for shipping costs.**

Directions:	**The Catawba Furniture Mall is in Hickory, NC. From I-40, take exit #123-B and turn right. The mall will be about half a mile down on your right.**

Designer's Outlet

Catawba Furniture Mall
377 Hwy. 70 SW
Hickory, NC 28602

Phone:	**(828) 327-3419**	**Hours:**	**M-Sat 9:00-7:00**
Toll Free:	**None**	**E-mail:**	**info@catawbafurniture.com**
Fax:	**(828) 327-4036**	**Web site:**	**www.catawbafurniture.com**

Designer's Choice Outlet at the Catawba Furniture Mall occupies the entire second floor of the mall with over 70,000 square feet of outlet furniture at 50%-70% off retail. It's owned by the same company that owns the Catawba Furniture Mall, which has a good reputation for customer service.

They usually have pieces in stock from most or all of the brands below. In particular, they have a very large selection of Catnapper outlet pieces. Designer's Outlet is the only approved outlet for Catnapper. Catnapper has good quality motion furniture. If you're looking for outlet pieces by La-Z-Boy (which are scarce) or Barcalounger (which are nonexistent), you might consider Catnapper as an alternative.

I've found that the staff at this outlet will price match against their competitors. I've also found that they'll give you a break on price if you're buying a substantial amount of furniture. If you're buying at least $5,000.00 worth of furniture, ask for an extra 10% price break. Depending on how their sales are at the time you're shopping, you have a good chance of getting the extra discount.

Please see the listing in this book for the Catawba Furniture Mall if you are planning a visit here. The Mall offers discounts on hotel rooms and coupons toward your furniture purchase during their big sale weekends four times each year.

Lines carried:

AICO	Clayton Marcus	Hollywoods	Pennsylvania Classics
American Drew	Clyde Pearson	Hooker	Regency House
APA	Craftmaster	J. Royale	Stratalounger
ARA	Cramco	Jasper Cabinet	Thomasville
Ardley Hall	Drexel Heritage	Klaussner	Vaughan Bassett
Broyhill	Hekman	Lane Venture	Virginia House
Catnapper	Hammary	Leatherworks	Wellington Hall
Charleston Forge	Highland House	Magnolia	Woodmark
Classico	Hitchcock	Orleans	

Phone orders accepted:	**Yes**
Discount:	**40%-50% off mfrs. suggested retail**
Payment methods:	**VISA, MC, personal checks**
In-house financing available:	**Yes, 90 days same as cash with 25% down pmt.**
Deposits required:	**50% deposit when order is placed, balance due when furniture is ready to be shipped**
Catalog available:	**No**
Clearance center:	**No**
Delivery:	**Full service in-home delivery and set-up. Customer pays freight company directly for shipping costs.**

Directions: **The Catawba Furniture Mall is in Hickory, NC. From I-40, take exit #123-B and turn right. The mall is half a mile down on the right.**

Don Lamor

Level 4
Hickory Furniture Mart
U. S. Hwy. 70 SE
Hickory, NC 28602

Phone:	**(828) 324-1776**	**Hours:**	**M-Sat 9:00-6:00**
Toll Free:	**None**	**E-mail:**	**donlamor@twave.net**
Fax:	**(828) 324-1676**	**Web site:**	**www.donlamor.com**

The Don Lamor gallery in the Hickory Furniture Mart has a good selection of contemporary and traditional furniture, case goods and upholstery. They also have a huge rug showcase, also on the 4th floor at the Hickory Furniture Mart.

Don Lamor only sells new furniture. There aren't any floor samples or discontinued pieces on the sales floor, and they have no clearance center. Their discounts are pretty good, though: 40%-50% off retail.

They also have several nice lines that sell "knock-offs" of better known brands. Tom Seely Furniture, for instance, has high quality duplicates of many Lexington pieces, including some styles that are virtually identical to Lexington's very popular Bob Timberlake designs. If you're in the market for a highly advertised national brand, give this source a call to see what they may have to offer from a lesser known, but equally well-made, competitor. With some highly advertised national brands, too much of your money goes toward their ad campaigns.

If you're ordering furniture by phone, you should definitely call this source for a price comparison. They've been in business for many, many years, and they have an excellent reputation.

Lines carried:

Artitalia	Hickory House	Old Biscayne Beds	Southcone
Bauer Int'l.	Hurtado	Old Imports	Stanford
Brent Jacobs	John Richards	Old World Stone and Iron	Statesville Chair
California House	Leathercraft	Padma's Plantation	Swaim
Corsican	Lee Industries	Palecek	Thunderbird
Cox	L'Origine	Preston-Hill	Tom Seely
Craftique	Lorts	Restonic	Vanguard
Forms & Fixtures	Michael Weiss	Royal Craftsmen	Waterford Furniture
Gat Creek	Mikhail Darafeev	Rustic Integrity	
Giemme	Moosehead	Salem Square	
Francesco Molon	Noble	Simmons	

Phone orders accepted:	Yes
Discount:	**40%-50% off mfrs. suggested retail**
Payment methods:	**VISA, MC, personal checks**
In-house financing available:	No
Deposits required:	**50% deposit when order is placed, balance due when furniture is ready to be shipped**
Catalog available:	No
Clearance center:	No
Delivery:	**Full service in-home delivery and set-up. Customer pays freight company directly for shipping costs.**

Directions: Please see *Hickory Furniture Mart* for complete directions.

E. J. Victor Factory Outlet

116 S. Lindsay St.
High Point, NC 27260

Phone:	**(336) 889-5500**	**Hours:**	**M-F 9:00-5:00**
Toll Free:	**None**		**Closed April & October**
Fax:	**(336) 889-5705**	**E-mail:**	**None**
		Web site:	**None**

This is E. J. Victor's only factory outlet. This line is so high-end and exclusive that most people have never even heard of it. It's usually only carried by one or two very high-end stores in each state. They specialize in 18th and 19th century English reproductions. The furniture is very high-end, very high-quality, and frequently very ornate.

For what you get, however, the prices are actually quite good. As uptown as this furniture is, it won't break your bank account.

On a recent visit here, I found a great deal on a solid mahogany 18th century English reproduction king bed with walnut veneer (pictured on the following page). This bed normally retails for $6,500.00, but the floor sample I found at the outlet was priced at $1,995.00 -- 70% off retail! It was in perfect condition.

Like a few other High Point outlets, this showroom is closed during the months of April and October due to the High Point wholesale furniture markets.

The furniture here is so beautiful that it will absolutely knock you out. And it's affordable! Amazing! Run, don't walk, to this outlet if you plan to do any shopping in the High Point, NC, area.

Phone orders accepted:	**No**
Discount:	**65%-75% off mfrs. suggested retail**
Payment methods:	**Personal checks. No credit cards.**
In-house financing available:	**No**
Deposits required:	**Not applicable**
Catalog available:	**Not applicable**
Clearance center:	**Not applicable**
Delivery:	**Full service in-home delivery and set-up. Customer pays freight company directly for shipping costs.**

Directions: From I-85, take exit #111 (Hwy. 311), and head northwest into High Point. After several miles, when you reach downtown High Point, Hwy. 311 will become Main St. After you get through downtown High Point, turn left on English Rd. Two blocks down, turn left on Lindsay St. The E. J. Victor Factory Outlet is one-half mile down on the left.

E. J. Victor Factory Outlet (cont.)

E. J. Victor Factory Outlet

Solid mahogany 18th century reproduction bed from E. J. Victor

Retail: $6,500.00   Discounted price: $1,995.00
Savings at the E. J. Victor Factory Outlet: $4,505.00 = 70% off retail

Ellenburg's Furniture

I-40 & Stamey Farm Rd.
Statesville, NC 28687

Phone:	(704) 873-2900	**Hours:**	M-F 8:30-5:30, Sat 9:30-5:00
Toll Free:	(800) 841-1420	**E-mail:**	efurn@bellsouth.net
Fax:	(704) 873-6002	**Web site:**	www.ellenburgs.com

Ellenburg's Furniture is located in Statesville, about 30 miles east of Hickory, NC, on I-40. They have a good selection of medium to high-end lines, including Lexington, Harden, Universal, and Wellington Hall.

They also have a small selection of closeout pieces and floor samples available. They are displayed on their Web site, as well as at their store location.

There really is no reason to make an in-person visit to this store, especially as it is some distance from the larger factory outlet regions around Hickory and High Point, NC. If you're looking for special order furniture from any of the lines below, you definitely should check their Web site and give them a call.

Lines carried:

AP Generations	Clark Casual	Lane	Sedgefield Lamps
American Heritage	Classic Georgian	Lane/Venture	Shady Lady Lamps
Athol	Classic Rattan	Lazy Hill Farms	Silcast Statuary
Barn Door	Designer Wicker	Lea	South Sea Rattan
Bassett	Fashion Bed Group	Lexington	Stein World
Bassett Mirror	Ficks Reed	Link Taylor	Summer Classics
Benchcraft	Fortune Rattan	Lloyd Flanders	Tradewinds
Bevan Funnell	Heartwood	Lyon Shaw	Tyndall Creek
Bob Timberlake	Henry Link	Meadowcraft	Uwharrie Chair
Braxton Culler	Highland House	Mirage Rugs	Wellington Hall
Capel Rugs	Keller	Pulaski	Whitecraft
Capris	King Hickory	Regency House	Winners Only
Cebu Rattan	Kingsley Bate	Robert Abbey Lamps	Woodard
Charleston Forge	KNF Designs	Rowe Ironworks	Yesteryear Wicker

Phone orders accepted:	Yes
Discount:	40%-60% off mfrs. suggested retail
Payment methods:	VISA, MC, personal checks
In-house financing available:	No
Deposits required:	50% deposit when order is placed, balance due when furniture is ready to be shipped
Catalog available:	No
Clearance center:	No
Delivery:	Full service in-home delivery and set-up. Customer pays freight company directly for shipping costs.

Directions: From I-40, take the Stamey Farm Rd. exit and head south into Statesville. Ellenburg's Furniture is just off the interstate.

European Furniture Importers

2145 W. Grand Ave.
Chicago, IL 60612

Phone:	**(312) 243-1955**	**Hours:**	**M-Th 10:00-7:00, Fri & Sat 10:00-6:00, Sun 12:00-5:00**
Toll Free:	**(800) 283-1955**	**E-mail:**	**None**
Fax:	**(312) 633-9308**	**Web site:**	**None**

European Furniture Importers has been receiving complaints recently, some of which are unresolved. They also have an unsatisfactory record with the BBB. Until these issues are resolved, I must recommend that consumers not buy from this source.

Phone orders accepted:	**Yes**
Discount:	**20%-60% off mfrs. suggested retail**
Payment methods:	**VISA, MC, Discover, personal checks**
In-house financing available:	**No**
Deposits required:	**Full payment due with order**
Catalog available:	**Yes**
Clearance center:	**No**
Delivery:	**Full service in-home delivery and set-up. Customer pays freight company directly for shipping costs.**

Directions: **From I-290, take the Damen Ave exit, and go north to Grand Ave. Turn left, and go west on Grand Ave. European Furniture Importers is one block west on the left side of the street.**

Factory Direct
247 S. Main Street
High Point, NC 27260

Phone:	**(336) 882-1605**	**Hours:**	**M-F 10:00-6:00, Sat 10:00-5:00**
Toll Free:	**None**		**Closed March, April, Sept, Oct**
Fax:	**(336) 885-6242**	**E-mail:**	**None**
		Web site:	**None**

Factory Direct Furniture is the High Point wholesale showroom for Liberty Furniture, a medium-quality imported line of case goods. Their quality and style is most similar to Broyhill.

Their furniture is well-built, and they have a good reputation for service. They also offer good value for money. Their stock is primarily American-style bedroom furniture, dining room furniture, and entertainment centers.

For instance, on a recent visit I found this dining room set in their showroom which is very similar in style and quality to Broyhill's new Attic Heirlooms dining room set. This set by Liberty Furniture, however, is available directly from the manufacturer for only $1,329.00. That includes the table and six chairs. The matching hutch in the background sells for $878.00. That's quite a bargain!

As this is a wholesale showroom, it is closed to the public during March, April, September, and October for the International Home Furnishings Market in High Point. As a general rule, you really should not plan a trip to High Point during these months anyway. Wait until May and November when all the showrooms are open and many are running after-market sales.

If you're looking for good quality American-style casegoods, this is a source you definitely should check out.

Phone orders accepted:	**Yes**
Discount:	**50% off mfrs. suggested retail**
Payment methods:	**VISA, MC, Discover, personal checks**
In-house financing available:	**No**
Deposits required:	**50% deposit when order is placed, balance due when furniture is ready to be shipped**
Catalog available:	**Yes**
Clearance center:	**No**
Delivery:	**Full service in-home delivery and set-up. Customer pays freight company directly for shipping costs.**

Directions: **Factory Direct is in the Liberty Furniture showroom in downtown High Point, NC. From I-85, take exit #111 (Hwy. 311), and head northwest into High Point. After several miles, when you reach downtown High Point, Hwy. 311 will become Main St. Liberty Furniture will be on the far right corner at the intersection of N. Main St. and Green St.**

Factory Direct

Factory Direct, inside the Liberty Furniture showroom in downtown High Point

Dining room set from Liberty Furniture at Factory Direct

Retail: $.00   Discounted price: $1,329.00
Savings at Factory Direct: $.00 = % off retail

Far Eastern Furnishings

The Atrium
430 S. Main St.
High Point, NC 27260

Phone:	**(336) 882-0180**	**Hours:**	**M-F 9:00-6:00, Sat 9:00-5:00**
Toll Free:	**None**	**E-mail:**	**fareastfurn@atriumfurniture.com**
Fax:	**(336) 882-0190**	**Web site:**	**www.atriumfurniture.com**

Far Eastern Furnishings at the Atrium Furniture Mall in High Point is owned by FEFCO, a company which manufactures furniture in Asia and imports it to the U. S. They are factory direct to the public.

Their product line consists of casegoods for the bedroom, dining room, and living room in traditional Asian designs. The quality is good. All pieces are made of solid rosewood, ebony, or teak. Some pieces are intricately carved.

Their furniture does have that heavy, lacquered finish that so many Asian imports used to have. Most Asian companies selling furniture in the U. S. no longer use this finishing technique.

It is difficult to determine how their deals compare to other sources. Their products are very unique, and they sell only to the public at a set price. Overall, I would say they offer reasonable value for money.

From time to time, they do run sales in which they offer an extra 5%-10% off. These sales do not follow a set schedule.

If you're looking for furniture with a strong Asian look, this is a good source to contact.

Phone orders accepted:	**Yes**
Discount:	**Factory direct pricing to public**
Payment methods:	**VISA, MC, Discover, AMEX, personal checks**
In-house financing available:	**No**
Deposits required:	**1/3 deposit required on most orders, 1/2 deposit is required in special cases.**
Catalog available:	**No**
Clearance center:	**No**
Delivery:	**They only ship to the eastern half of the U. S., east of the Mississippi River. Please call for shipping details.**

Directions: **Please see *The Atrium* for complete directions.**

Farm House Furnishings ("The Red House")

1432 First Ave. SW & Hwy. 321 N
Hickory, NC 28602

Phone:	**(828) 324-4595**	**Hours:**	**M-Sat 9:00-6:00**
Toll Free:	**None**	**E-mail:**	**None**
Fax:	**None**	**Web site:**	**None**

Farm House Furnishings is located in a tiny red house in Hickory, NC. They have very little furniture on display due to space constraints, and it isn't discounted much, so there's no reason to go here in person.

They do have fairly good prices on the lines they carry, but not the best I've seen in the area. Still, if you plan to order furniture by phone, it's worth giving them a call to compare their prices.

Lines carried:

Amyx	Country Reproductions	Lea	SK Products
Athol	Fashion Bed Group	Martinsville Novelty	Southern Craftsmen's
Barfield Recliners	Heritage Haus	Murphy	Guild
Beechbrook	Hickory Leather	Oxford Leather	Timmerman
Black Forest Clocks	Hooker	Pine-tique	Top Notch Woodwork
Boling Chair	Howard Miller Clocks	Regency House	Universal
Builtright Chair	J. H. Carver	Relax-a-Cliner	Vaughan
Carolina Country	Johnston Benchworks	Riverside Bedding	Wesley Allen
Carolina Rockers	Kennedy Rockers	Rug Barn	
Carson Wind Chimes	Kevin-Christian	Sidex	

Phone orders accepted:	**Yes**
Discount:	**30%-50% off mfrs. suggested retail**
Payment methods:	**VISA, MC, personal checks**
In-house financing available:	**No**
Deposits required:	**50% deposit when order is placed, balance due when furniture is ready to be shipped**
Catalog available:	**No**
Clearance center:	**No**
Delivery:	**Full service in-home delivery and set-up. Customer pays freight company directly for shipping costs.**

Directions: From I-40, take exit #123 and drive north on Hwy. 321 to Hickory, NC. Farm House Furnishings is on the right side of the road, one block after you pass Hwy. 70.

Fran's Wicker & Rattan Furniture

295 Route 10 East
Succasunna, NJ 07876

Phone:	**(973) 584-2230**	**Hours:**	**Mon, Tues, & Fri 9:00-5:30**
Toll Free:	**(800) 372-6799**		**Wed & Thurs 9:00-8:30**
Fax:	**(973) 584-7446**		**Sat 9:30-6:00, Sun 12:00-5:00**
		E-mail:	**sales@franswicker.com**
		Web site:	**www.franswicker.com**

Fran's Wicker & Rattan has been discounting wicker for over 35 years. Most of their furniture and accessories are made in their own factories in China, Indonesia, and the Philippines. They have a huge catalog. They also have an enormous showroom just to the west of Newark -- over 100,000 square feet.

Fran's can also order many other brands of wicker and rattan at significant discounts. They will not give out a list of the specific brands they have access to, but they will give you a comparison price over the phone if you call with a specific brand and item number. I have found that they can order most national brands.

They also have a clearance center, which has a nice selection of discontinued styles and floor samples at up to 60% off retail. You can see their clearance items online at their Web site.

Unfortunately, Fran's Wicker & Rattan still as a poor record of customer service, as reported in the last edition of this book. They have cleaned up their BBB report since I wrote my last review of their store, but I continue to hear complaints about them constantly. Fran's has also not responded to my inquiries about what they are doing to improve their service. Until these problems are resolved, I must still recommend that consumers not shop here.

Lines carried:	**Please call for more information**
Phone orders accepted:	**Yes**
Discount:	**50% off mfrs. suggested retail**
Payment methods:	**VISA, MC, AMEX, Discover, checks**
In-house financing available:	**No**
Deposits required:	**Full amount due with order. Credit cards are not charged until merchandise is actually shipped.**
Catalog available:	**Yes**
Clearance center:	**No**
Delivery:	**Shipping costs are paid to Fran's with your order. Curbside delivery only by UPS or truck. In-home delivery and setup are available for an extra fee.**

Directions: From I-80, take exit #28. Follow the signs to Route 10. Take Route 10 east to the first red light. Fran's is on the corner.

Franklin Place

Level 3
Hickory Furniture Mart
U. S. Hwy. 70 SE
Hickory, NC 28602

Phone:	**(828) 322-5539**	**Hours:**	**M-Sat 9:00-6:00**
Toll Free:	**(800) 688-1168**	**E-mail:**	**franklinplace@bellsouth.net**
Fax:	**(828) 322-5539**	**Web site:**	**www.hickoryfurniture.com**

Franklin Place at the Hickory Furniture Mart has a very nice showroom with traditional furniture at good prices. They carry Pulaski, Victoria Collection, Cibola Bradburn, Oriental Accents, Decorative Crafts, and Tapestries LTD by special order. They also have a good reputation for customer service.

They are also the factory approved factory outlet for Cibola Leather. They've got some great deals on in stock outlet leather furniture ready to ship immediately, plus they can special order new Cibola Leather furniture at great prices.

For instance, on my most recent visit I found a great deal on a leather living room group (pictured on the following page). The sofa retailed for $5,397.00, could be special ordered every day for $2,399.00, and had an after-market sale price of $1,999.00 when I took this picture in November, 2003. The chair retailed for $2,847.00, could be special ordered every day for $1,199.00, and had an after-market sale price of $959.00. The ottoman retailed for $1,272,00, could be special ordered every day for $499.00, and had an after-market sale price of $399.00. That's an everyday savings of about 55%-60% off retail, and after-market sale savings of 63%-69% off retail.

Their after-market sales normally run the first full week of May and the first full week of November. These are generally the best two weeks of the year to visit any North Carolina factory outlet or discounter.

If you're looking for high-end leather in particular, you really should give this source a call. Cibola isn't as well-known a brand nationally as some others, but their quality is excellent.

Phone orders accepted:	Yes
Discount:	**50% off mfrs. suggested retail**
Payment methods:	**VISA, MC, personal checks**
In-house financing available:	**No**
Deposits required:	**Full amount due before shipment.**
Catalog available:	**No**
Clearance center:	**No**
Delivery:	**Full service in-home delivery and set-up. Customer pays freight company directly for shipping costs.**

Directions: Please see *Hickory Furniture Mart* for complete directions.

Franklin Place (cont.)

Leather sofa, chair, and ottoman from Cibola Leather at Franklin Place

Sofa:
Retail: $5,397.00   Discounted price: $1,999.00
Savings at Franklin Place: $3,398.00 = 63% off retail

Chair:
Retail: $2,847.00   Discounted price: $959.00
Savings at Franklin Place: $1,888.00 = 66% off retail

Ottoman:
Retail: $1,272.00   Discounted price: $399.00
Savings at Franklin Place: $873.00 = 69% off retail

French Furniture Outlet

The Atrium
430 S. Main St.
High Point, NC 27260

Phone:	**(336) 883-3984**	**Hours:**	**M-F 9:00-6:00, Sat 9:00-5:00**
Toll Free:	**None**	**E-mail:**	**frenchfurn@theatrium.com**
Fax:	**(336) 883-3985**	**Web site:**	**www.theatrium.com**

This outlet used to be called the "French Heritage Factory Outlet". It is still the only factory outlet for French Heritage, which specializes in French reproduction furniture. Now, the outlet also carries pieces by Mayland Court, another small North Carolina manufacturer. The quality of both lines is quite good.

The prices here range from 50%-75% off, and most of the furniture is in new first-quality condition.

Consumers should be aware that the outlet is only staffed intermittently. I have found it closed and unmanned several times in the last few months during their scheduled business hours. The owner has explained to me that she is dealing with severe family medical problems and cannot come into the store every day. If you plan to visit in person, you may wish to call ahead first.

Lines carried:

Country Club
Crosswinds Corner
De Bournais
French Heritage
Mayland Court
Richelieu

Phone orders accepted:	**No**
Discount:	**50%-75% off mfrs. suggested retail**
Payment methods:	**VISA, MC, personal checks**
In-house financing available:	**No**
Deposits required:	**Not applicable**
Catalog available:	**Not applicable**
Clearance center:	**Not applicable**
Delivery:	**Full service in-home delivery and set-up. Customer pays freight company directly for shipping costs.**

Directions: French Heritage is located inside the Atrium complex in downtown High Point. Please see *The Atrium* for complete directions.

Furniture Clearance Center

1107 Tate St.
High Point, NC 27260

Phone:	**(336) 882-1688**	**Hours:**	**M-Sat 9:00-5:00**
Toll Free:	**None**	**E-mail:**	**None**
Fax:	**(336) 882-8423**	**Web site:**	**None**

The Furniture Clearance Center in High Point, NC, serves as the clearance center for Utility Craft and Wood-Armfield, two major High Point furniture discounters. Please see the listings in this book for these two discounters for a listing of the lines you can expect to find here.

The stock here consists of floor samples, photography samples, discontinued styles, and customer returns. The discounts run about 50%-70% off retail, with most pieces marked at about 60% off. Virtually all of the furniture here is in first-quality condition.

This place is a gold mine for high end furniture. Most of the furniture is from very high-end lines, such as Hickory White, Century, Maitland Smith, Baker, etc.

On a recent visit here, I found a terrific deal on a Century dining room table (pictured on the following page). The retail on this piece is normally $6,860.00, but the clearance center had this one for only $2,625.00. It was in perfect condition.

From the outside, this place doesn't look like much. I'm sure most people (except the interior designers who are always here) drive right on past it. In reality, though, this is one of the very best sources in High Point for furniture that you can take home the same day. If you plan to visit High Point to buy high-end traditional furniture, this should be your first stop.

Phone orders accepted:	**No**
Discount:	**50%-70% off mfrs. suggested retail**
Payment methods:	**VISA, MC, AMEX, Discover, personal checks.**
In-house financing available:	**No**
Deposits required:	**Not applicable**
Catalog available:	**Not applicable**
Clearance center:	**Not applicable**
Delivery:	**Full service in-home delivery and set-up. Customer pays freight company directly for shipping costs.**

Directions: From I-85, take exit #111 (Hwy. 311), and head northwest into High Point. After several miles, when you reach downtown High Point, Hwy. 311 will become S. Main St. Shortly after you pass Business 85, turn right on Wheeler St. One block down, turn right again on Tate St. Furniture Clearance Center will be on your left.

Furniture Clearance Center - High Point (cont.)

Furniture Clearance Center

Dining room table from Century Furniture

Retail: $6,860.00   Discounted price: $2,625.00
Savings at Furniture Clearance Center: $4,235.00 = 62% off retail

Furniture Collections Of Carolina

3197 NC Hwy. 127 S.
Hickory, NC 28602

Phone:	**(828) 294-3593**	**Hours:**	**M-Sat 9:00-5:30**
Toll Free:	**None**	**E-mail:**	**info@furniturecollections.com**
Fax:	**(828) 294-4276**	**Web site:**	**www.furniturecollections.com**

   Furniture Collections Of Carolina has just gone out of business as of early 2004. The BBB is reporting many unresolved complaints against them. They recommend contacting the NC Attorney General at (919) 716-6000 if you have an unresolved problem with this company.

Furniture Express

4970 Riverside Dr.
Danville, VA 24541

Phone:	**(434) 822-0900**	**Hours:**	**M-Sat 9:00-5:00**
Toll Free:	**None**	**E-mail:**	**sales@furniture-express.net**
Fax:	**(434) 822-0195**	**Web site:**	**www.furniture-express.net**

Furniture Express is owned and operated by the Hinkle Group which also owns and operates A&H Wayside Furniture and American Reproductions at the Atrium Furniture Mall. They have a long-standing reputation for quality and service.

Their discounts range from 40%-50% off retail on a wide variety of medium to high end furniture brands. Most of their furniture is in the traditional style.

They also have a clearance center next door. Although they do have a large sign stating that this is a "factory outlet", it isn't. Furniture Express buys market samples and resells them here, which is not quite the same thing. Still, they do have some good bargains.

Consumers should be aware that Danville is about one hour's drive northeast of High Point, NC. Although they do have some good deals at their clearance center, I saw nothing there that wasn't also available all over High Point in far greater quantity and variety. Travelers who are pressed for time in planning their NC visit may want to just call this source to compare prices on their special order lines instead of visiting in person.

Lines carried:

Action Lane	Fairfield Chair	Maitland-Smith	Samuel Lawrence
American Drew	Harden	Milling Road	Stanley
Ashley	Hickory Chair	Motioncraft/Sherrill	Statton
Baker	Hickory White	Nichols and Stone	Taylor King
Bernhardt	John Richard	Oakwood Interiors	Theodore Alexander
Bradington Young	La Barge	Pennsylvania House	Thomasville
Century	Lane	Pulaski	Universal
Cibola	Legacy	Riverside	Winners Only
CTH Sherrill	Lloyd Buxton	Rowe	

Phone orders accepted:	**Yes**
Discount:	**40%-50% off mfrs. suggested retail**
Payment methods:	**VISA, MC, AMEX, Discover, personal checks**
In-house financing available:	**Yes**
Deposits required:	**50% deposit when order is placed, balance due when furniture is ready to be shipped**
Catalog available:	**No**
Clearance center:	**Yes**
Delivery:	**Full service in-home delivery and set-up. Customer pays freight company directly for shipping costs.**

Directions: From I-40, take exit #127 (US 29N/US 70E/US 220N), and go north to Reidsville, NC. Follow US 29 approximately one hour to Danville, VA. In Danville, merge onto Hwy. 58, which is also Riverside Dr. Furniture Express is on the left.

The Furniture Shoppe

3351 Hickory Blvd.
Hudson, NC 28638

Phone:	**(828) 396-1942**	**Hours:**	**M-Sat 9:00-5:00**
Toll Free:	**None**	**E-mail:**	**customerservice@furnitureshoppe.com**
Fax:	**(828) 396-2376**	**Web site:**	**www.furnitureshoppe.com**

   The Furniture Shoppe in Hudson, NC, just north of Hickory, has a very good selection of case goods, along with some upholstery and juvenile furniture.

   Their discounts on new furniture range from 45%-55% off retail, whether you shop in person or order by phone. They also have a 3,000 square foot clearance center in the back where they sell off floor samples, discontinued items, and customer returns. Discounts there range from 65%-75% off retail.

   This source has been in business for over twenty years, and they do a huge volume of phone sales. Their prices on many lines are quite good. If you plan to order furniture by phone, definitely call this source and give them a chance to bid on your business.

   If you plan to be in the Hickory, NC, area to shop for furniture, their clearance center is worth a look.

Lines carried:

Action By Lane	Fairfield Chair	Lane	Sam Moore
American Drew	Flexsteel	Lane/Venture	Serta
Bassett	Hammary	Lea	Shaw Rugs
Best Chair	Hooker	Mobel	Stanley
Braxton Culler	Keller	Pulaski	Universal
Clayton Marcus	Kimball	Riverside	Wesley Allen
Dinaire	Kincaid	Rowe	Winston

Phone orders accepted:	**Yes**
Discount:	**45%-55% off mfrs. suggested retail**
Payment methods:	**VISA, MC, Discover, personal checks**
In-house financing available:	**Yes**
Deposits required:	**50% deposit when order is placed, balance due when furniture is ready to be shipped**
Catalog available:	**No**
Clearance center:	**Yes**
Delivery:	**Full service in-home delivery and set-up. Customer pays freight company directly for shipping costs.**

Directions: From I-40, take exit #123 and drive north on Hwy. 321 to Hudson. The Furniture Shoppe is 12 miles from I-40 on the left.

The Furniture Shoppe (cont.)

The Furniture Shoppe

Furnitureland Express

2200 S. Main St
High Point, NC 27263

Phone:	**(336) 841-8599**	**Hours:**	**M-Sat 8:30-5:30**
Toll Free:	**None**	**E-mail:**	**johnmorton@furniturelandexpress.com**
Fax:	**(336) 841-5327**	**Web site:**	**www.furniturelandexpress.com**

Furnitureland Express is owned by Furnitureland South. This 40,000 square foot showroom stocks only furniture groupings that are in stock and ready for immediate shipment, thereby greatly reducing the usual 8-12 week wait time on special order furniture. Please contact them directly for the expected shipping time to your area.

Discounts on new furniture run 40%-50% off the manufacturer's retail. The quality of the lines they carry is quite good.

Furnitureland Express also has a huge 10,000 square foot clearance center right behind their main showroom which is well worth a visit. Discounts at the clearance center directly behind the main showroom can run as high as 60% off retail. The clearance center also has some excellent deals on decorative accessories.

For instance, on a recent visit to the clearance center I found this deal on a bedroom set from Wynwood (pictured on the following page). The headboard/wall unit, dresser, and mirror combined retails for $3,749.85. The price on a new ready-to ship set from Furnitureland Express is $2,185.00, a discount of 42% off retail. This one set in the clearance center, which was a floor sample in new condition, could be purchased for only $1,564.000, a 59% discount off retail.

Furnitureland South has also restored their former good reputation for customer service. Please see the main Furnitureland South listing in this book for all the details on the improvements in their service and delivery.

If you're traveling to High Point, the clearance center at Furnitureland Express, and at Furnitureland South itself, should be a "must visit" stop.

Lines carried:

Aico	Huntington House	Natuzzi	Spring Air
Broyhill	Lane	Pulaski	Vaughan
Brookwood	Leather Trend	Palliser	Vaughan-Bassett
CMI	Leisters	Ridgeway	Wynwood
Davis International	Magnussen	Serta	

Phone orders accepted:	**Yes**
Discount:	**40%-60% off mfrs. suggested retail**
Payment methods:	**Personal checks or cash. No credit cards.**
In-house financing available:	**Yes, via a Furnitureland South credit card**
Deposits required:	**33% deposit on in-stock items with balance due COD, full payment with order on special orders.**
Catalog available:	**Yes, online**
Clearance center:	**Yes, directly behind the main showroom**
Delivery:	**Full service in-home delivery and set-up. Customer pays freight company directly for shipping costs.**

Directions: From I-85, take exit #111 (Hwy. 311/Main St.), and turn west (away from downtown High Point). You'll see Furnitureland Express on your right just after you exit the interstate.

Furnitureland South

5635 Riverdale Dr.
Jamestown, NC 27282

Phone:	**(336) 841-4328**	**Hours:**	**M-W & Sat 8:30-5:30, Th-F 8:30-8:30**
Toll Free:	**None**	**E-mail:**	**sales@furniturelandsouth.com**
Fax:	**(336) 841-7026**	**Web site:**	**www.furniturelandsouth.com**

Furnitureland South is an enormous complex in Jamestown, NC, right on the outskirts of High Point. Just to give you an idea of how big the main building is (pictured on the following page), look at the top of the ball and claw foot on the faux highboy that decorates the front of the building. When I stand next to it, the top of the claw comes up to my waist. In addition to the main showroom, there is a catwalk to an additional two-story showroom building. This source also has two restaurants inside, so they're doing their best to keep you there for the day.

Furnitureland South is by far one of the biggest and best-established telephone discounters of furniture in North Carolina, rivaled only by Boyles and Rose Furniture. Most of their new furniture is offered at 40%-50% off retail.

The main showroom has a gallery devoted to their quick-ship program, which are identical to the offerings at the larger Furnitureland Express showroom in downtown High Point.

Furnitureland South also has a huge two-story clearance center right behind the main building. It has floor samples, customer returns, discontinued styles, and photography samples from all the lines sold by Furnitureland South at about 50%-70% off retail. Most of the stock here is in first-quality condition. Few pieces are damaged.

For instance, on a recent visit I found this beautiful Hekman secretary desk at the clearance center. It retails for $5,738.00, but you could get this one in first-quality condition for only $2,583.00, a savings of 55% off retail.

Over the last few years, as Furnitureland South experienced a period of extreme growth, their customer service suffered. In spring of 2003, they opened a huge new distribution center in an effort to improve their service.

I recently toured the distribution center, and I must say, I can't imagine how Furnitureland South could have made any greater effort to improve their service. This building is absolutely state of the art. All shipments from manufacturers are unpacked, inspected thoroughly for damage, bar coded for the end customer, and repacked for shipment. They've even made it possible for consumers to track their own orders and shipments through Furnitureland South's Web site. I have never seen such a well designed and operated furniture distribution facility.

I have received no complaints about Furnitureland South since early 2003. The BBB has also restored their satisfactory record. I now confidently recommend them as a source.

Phone orders accepted:	**Yes**
Discount:	**40%-70% off mfrs. suggested retail**
Payment methods:	**Personal checks or cash. No credit cards.**
In-house financing available:	**Yes, via a Furnitureland South credit card**
Deposits required:	**33% deposit on in-stock items with balance due COD, full payment with order on special orders.**
Catalog available:	**Yes, online**
Clearance center:	**Yes, directly behind the main showroom**
Delivery:	**Full service in-home delivery and set-up. Customer pays freight company directly for shipping costs.**

Directions: **From I-85, take exit #118, and turn west on Business 85. Furnitureland South will be about one mile down on your right at the Riverdale Rd. exit.**

Furnitureland South (cont.)

Furnitureland South

Secretary by Hekman at Furnitureland South's clearance center

Retail: $5,738.00   Discounted price: $2,583.00
Savings at Furnitureland South: $3,155.00 = 55% off retail

Furnitureland South (cont.)

Lines carried:

A. A. Laun
Action by Lane
Acacia Furniture
Accent Decor
Alexander Julian
All Continental
Allusions
Amanda Sutton
Ambiance Imports
Ambiance Lighting
American Bedding
American Drew
American Impressions
American Mirror
American of Martinsville
Amisco
Andrew Pearson
Anglo Oriental
Anichini
Ann Gish
Antiques & Interiors
Antler Art
Aquarius Mirrorworks
Arbek
Ardley Hall
Art & Commerce
Art Image
Art Up
Artagraph
Artisan House
Artisan's Design Guild
Artistica Metal Designs
Artitalia
Artmasters Collection
Artmax
Ashley Manor
Athol Table
Atlanta Glasscrafters
Aubergine Home Collection
Austin Sculpture
Austin's Farm Ent
Avantglide
Azzolin Bros. Importers
Baldwin
Banana Fish
Barcalounger
Bassett Mirror
Basta Sole by Tropitone
Bauer Lamps

Bean Station
Becker Designed
Bedtime
Bellino Fine Linens
Benchcraft
Benchcraft Rattan
Benicia
Bentley Churchill
Berco Tableworks
Berkline
Bernhardt
Bestar
Bevan Funnell
Bibi
Big Fish
Blacksmith Shop
Bob Timberlake
Bodrum Group
Bontempi
Boussac Fadini
Bradington Young
Braxton Culler
Brent Jacobs
Brown Jordan
Broyhill
Bush Industries
Butler Specialty
Cal-Bear
Cambridge Lamps
Canvas Company
Cape Craftsmen
Capris Furniture
Carey Moore Designs
Carolina Mirror
Carsons
Carvers Guild
Casa Bique
Casa Stradivari
Casey Collection
Cast Classics
Casual Lamps
Cebu Imports
Central Oriental
Century
CFI Manufacturing
Chapman
Charles Alan
Chicago Textiles
Child Craft

Christy USA
Chromecraft
CJC
Clark Casual
Classic Gallery
Classic Leather
Classic Rattan
Clayton Marcus
Cochrane
Coja Leather
Collections 85
Collezione Europa
Columbine Cody
Comfortaire
Company C
Con-Tab
Conover Chair
Corsican
Cox Manufacturing
Craft-Tex
Craftique
Craftwork Guild
Creations at Dallas
Creative Accents
Creative Concept
Creative Decor
Creative Fine Arts
Creative Ideas
Crystal Clear
Currey & Co.
CWL Designs
D & F Wicker & Rattan
Dalyn Rug Company
Dar-Ran
David Michael
Davis International
Daystom Furniture
Dayva International
Decorative Crafts
Deitz and Sons
Design Guild
Design Source
Design South Furniture
Designer's Attic
Design Systems
Designs By Robert Guenther
Deszign, Inc.
Dillon
Dimplex

Dinaire
Directional
Distinction Leather
Distinctive Designs
Distinctive Oils
DMI Custom
      Bedspreads
Drexel Heritage
Dunmore Furniture
Dura Hold
Duralee Fabrics
Dutalier
Eastern Accents
Eckadams/Vogel
      Peterson
Elements By Grapevine
Elite Manufacturing
Elliott's Designs
Ellis Home Furnishings
Ello
Emerson Et Cie
Emess Design Group
Englander
Espino
Euroreps
Evan Du Four
Evans Ceramics
Evans Frame Shop
Excelsior
Expressive
      Designs Rugs
Fabric To Frame
Fabrica International
Fairfield Chair
Fashion Bed Group
Ficks Reed
Fine Arts Ltd.
Fine Furniture Design
Flair Design
Flair International
Flexsteel
Floober Brothers
Floria Nova
Focus Rugs
Forma Design
Forms & Fixtures
Foster's Point
Francesco Molon
Frederick Cooper

Furnitureland South (cont.)

Lines carried (cont.):

Fremarc Designs
French Heritage
        Reproductions
Friedman Brothers
Furniture Values
Fusion Z
Galtech
Georgian Furnishings
Gianni
Giemme
Giorgio Collection
Gloster
Grace Manufacturing
Great City Traders
Great Impressions
Guardsman
Guildmaster
Gunlocke
H. Potter
H. K. H. International
Hamilton Collections
Hammary
Harris Furniture
        Reproductions
Harris Lamps
Hart Associates
Hedge Row Decorative
        Outdoors
Heirloom
Hekman
Henry Link Wicker
Hickory House
Hickory Springs
Hickory White
High Point Billiard Designs
High Point Furniture
Highland House
Hilda Flack Accessories
Historic Golf Prints
HollyWoods
Home Fires
Hooker
Howard Miller Clocks
Hubbardton Forge
Humane Trophies
Huntington House
Huppe
Hydra Designs
Hyundai Furniture

Idea Industries
Ideal Originals
Import Collection
Inmon Enterprises
Interactive Health
Isenhour Furniture
J. H. Craver & Son
Jackson of Danville
James R. Cooper
Jamestown Manor
Jasper Cabinet
Jaynor Furnishings
J. D. Store Equipment
JDI Group Cal-Style
Jensen Jarrah Leisure
John Boos & Co.
John Richard Collection
Johnston Benchworks
Johnston Casuals
Jon Elliott Upholstery
JSF Industries
JSP-LES Industries
Jubilee
K. Highsmith
Kaiser Kuhn Lighting
Karastan
Katha Diddel Home
        Collection
Keller
Kenroy International
Kessler
Key City
Kinder Harris
King Hickory
King Koil
Kingsley Bate
Koch & Lowy
Koch Originals
Koko Company
Kravet Fabrics
La Barge
Ladybug
Ladyslipper
Lambs & Ivy
Lane
Lane Action
Lane Venture
Latex Foam Products
Laurier Furniture

Le Blanc Linen Wash
Lea
Leathercraft
Leathertrend
Leeazanne
Leedo Furniture
Legacy
Leggett and Platt
Leisters Furniture
Leisure House
Lenox Lighting
Lexington
Limonta Home
Lloyd/Flanders
Lodi Down & Feather
Lorraine Headboards
Lorts
Lotus Arts
Lucia Cassa Textiles
Lux-Art Silks
Lyon Shaw
M. T. S. Besana-Carrara
Madison Square
Magnussen Presidential
Maharam
Maitland Smith
Mallin
Manchester Furniture
Mantua Manufacturing
Marbro
Marcella Fine Rugs
Mardan Publishing
Mario & Marielena
        Soft Home
Marlow
Marquis CLL
        Of Beverly Hills
Martha Stewart
        by Bernhardt
Marvel
Masland Carpets
Mastercraft Imports
Masterlooms Rugs
Masterpiece Accessories
Masterworks Decor
Meadowcraft
Mcr Corp.
Metropolitan Galleries
Mikhail Darafeev

Millender
Miller Desk
Minoff Lamps
Mirror Craft
Mohawk
Momeni
Montaage
Morgan Hill
Movi
MTS
Murobello
Murray Feiss
Mystic Valley Traders
N. C. Souther
Nan Wood Hall
        Fine Art
Natural Light
Natuzzi
Nautica Home
Nelson Garfield
Nichols & Stone
Norman Perry
North Bay Collections
Northern Fine Arts
Notables By Key City
Null
OFS
Ohio Table Pad
Oklahoma Importing
Old Hickory Furniture
Old Java
Old World Stone
        & Iron
Oldcastle Specialty
OLF Lamps Inc.
Orbit
Oriental Weavers
Original Plant Plant
Oscar de la Renta
        By Century
P & P Chair Co.
Pacific Coast Lighting
Palecek
Palmyra
Paper White
Paragon Pictures
Park Place
Parker Southern
Pastiche

Furnitureland South (cont.)

Lines carried (cont.):

Pavilion
Payne Street Imports
Peacock Alley
Pearson
Peel & Company
Pennsylvania House
Pentaura Limited
Perfect 45
Phoenix Galleries
Piage & Pieta Art Stone
Pieri Creations
Pine Creek Bedding
Plenty's Horn
Portfolio Textiles
Portobello International
Powell
Premier Bedding
Presidential Billiards
Preview
Privilege House
Protect-A-Bed
Pulaski
Quoizel
Raffia
Reliance Lamp Co.
Rembrandt Lamps
Remington Lamp
Ren-Wil
Renoir Designs
Reprocrafters
Reverie Dreamy Linens
Rex Furniture
Ridgeway Clocks
Ridgewood
Riverside
Robert Abbey Lamps
Robert Allen Fabrics
Rug Barn
Rug Market
Sagefield Leather
Salem Square
Saloom
Sam Moore
Samsonite
San Miguel Trading Co.
Sandicast
Sarreid
Savoir Faire
Savoy House

Scangift
Schnadig
Schweiger Industries
Sea Gull Lighting
Sealy
Second Avenue
Second Impressions
Sedgefield Lamps
Selva Style
Serta
Sferra Brothers
Shashi Cann
Shaw Industries
Shelby Williams
Sheres
Shuford
Sidney Arthur
Sierrarts
Signature Designer
    Rugs
Silk-Like
Silver Furniture
Simmons
Sligh Furniture
South Cone Trading Co.
Southport Furniture
Sovereign
Spring Air
St. Timothy
Stakmore
Stanley Furniture
Statesville Chair
Statton
Stein World
Steven Drew Int'l
Stevenson & Vestal
Stiffel Lamp
Stock Market
Stone Country Ironworks
Stone International
Stoneleigh
Stoneville
Stratford/Stratolounger
Strobel Technologies
Stroheim & Romann
Style Upholstering
Stylex
Summer Classics
Sumter Cabinet

Sunlite Casual Furniture
Sustainable Lifestyles
Swaim Classics
Swaim Designs
Swedish Blonde Corp.
Table Designs
Telescope
Temple
Tempur-pedic
Textillery
Thayer Coggin
Thief River Linens
Three Coins Imports
Timmerman
Tomlin Designs
Touchstone Fine Art
Toyo
Tozai Home
Tradition House
Triad Butcher Block Inc.
Triune
Tropitone
Trowbridge Gallery
Tucker Design
Two Day Design
Two's Company
Tyndall Creek Furniture
Tyne House of
    Lewes, England
Ultegra
Ultimate Accents
Union City Mirrors &
    Tables
Unique Lamp Creations
Unique Originals
Universal
University Loft Company
Urban Woods
Uttermost
Uwharrie Chair
Valspar
Van Teal
Vanguard
Vasco International
Vaughan
Vaughan Bassett
Veneman
Venture By Lane
Versteel

Victorian Classics
Vineyard
Vintage
Vintage Verandah
Virginia
    Metalcrafters
Vitafoam
    Feather Beds
Vitalie Mfg.
Vogel Peterson
Wade Furniture
Wara Tapestries
Waterford
    Furniture Makers
Watson
    Furniture Systems
Webb Furniture
Weiman
Wellington Hall
Wesley Allen
Westwood Lamps
Whitecraft
Whoa!
Wildcat Territory
Wildwood Lamps
Willow Creek
    Collection
Windsor
    Collections
Windsor Home
    Collection
Winners Only
Woodard
Woodlands
Woodmark
Zrike

Georgian Lane

Level 2
Hickory Furniture Mart
U. S. Hwy. 70 SE
Hickory, NC 28602

Phone:	Not established yet	**Hours:**	**M-Sat 9:00-6:00**
Toll Free:	None	**E-mail:**	**None**
Fax:	Not established yet	**Web site:**	**www.georgianlane.com**

Georgian Lane will open a new showroom in the Hickory Furniture Mart in March, 2004. At this printing in February 2004, their Hickory phone service was not yet operational. Please call the Hickory Furniture Mart's information desk at (800) 462-MART to get Georgian Lane's new phone number.

This showroom features solid mahogany furniture manufactured in Georgian Lane's own facility in the Philippines. This is their only outlet in the U. S.

Please note that the mahogany used in their furniture comes from Africa and the Philippines. This type of mahogany is inferior in quality to the Central American and South American mahogany used by most U. S. based manufacturers of mahogany furniture. In fact, Philippine "mahogany" really isn't mahogany at all. It's a totally different species of tree.

That said, the quality of Philippine mahogany furniture is reasonably good. Just be aware of exactly what you are getting. This will not be the same quality as your grandmother's heirloom mahogany furniture.

This company is so new that I really can't comment on their reliability.

Phone orders accepted:	**Yes**
Discount:	**Factory direct pricing to the public**
Payment methods:	**VISA, MC, AMEX, Discover, personal checks**
In-house financing available:	**No**
Deposits required:	**50% deposit when order is placed, balance due when furniture is ready to be shipped.**
Catalog available:	**Yes, limited catalog at Web site. Call for more detailed product information.**
Clearance center:	**No**
Delivery:	**Full service in-home delivery and set-up. Customer pays freight company directly for shipping costs.**

Directions: Please see *Hickory Furniture Mart* for complete directions.

Gibson Interiors

National Home Furnishings Center
1628 S. Main St.
High Point, NC 27260

Phone:	**(336) 883-4444**	**Hours:**	**M-Sat 9:00-6:00**
Toll Free:	**(800) 247-5460**	**E-mail:**	**gibsoninteriors@aol.com**
Fax:	**(336) 883-0417**	**Web site:**	**www.gibsoninteriors.com**

Gibson Interiors is part of the National Home Furnishings Center in High Point, which also houses Kagan's and Decorator's Choice. Their 5,000 square foot store carries about half its stock in furniture and the remaining half in accessories. If you are looking for unique accessories in particular, they're a good source.

Gibson Interiors has been in business for over 20 years. It's run by a husband, wife, and daughter team. They have a good reputation for customer service. They're also very pleasant to work with. Small family businesses can sometimes be more responsive to their customers than large companies.

Their regular stock runs 40%-50% off retail. In May and November, they purchase market samples from the wholesale showrooms which are offered at a better discount. They also show a selection of these market samples at their Web site.

On a recent visit, I found a great deal on a cute pub table set with two chairs (pictured on following page). The retail on this set is $540.00 (including the chairs), but you can special order is for $277.00. That's a discount of 49% off retail.

If you're visiting High Point to shop for unique occasional furniture and accessories, you should definitely stop by. Be sure to call them and compare pricing as well if you plan to order by phone.

Lines carried:

A.A. Importing Company	Artemide	Brett Austin Group	Coast Lamp
Accent Northwest	Artex	Cape Craftsman	Collector's Armoury
Accessories By Sherwood	The Ashton Company	Carolina Mirror	Collek
Alva Museum	Austin Sculpture	Castle Antiques	Cooper Classics
Reproductions	Baldwin Hardware	Chapman	Craft Tex
American Décor	Baroque Designs	Charles Sadek	Crystal Clear
Art And Frame Direct	Bernards	Classic Lamp Designs	Daddy's Trunk
The Art Gallery	Blue Ridge Designs	Clay Metal Stone	Dale Tiffany

Phone orders accepted:	**Yes**
Discount:	**40%-50% off retail**
Payment methods:	**VISA, MC, AMEX, Discover, personal checks**
In-house financing available:	**No**
Deposits required:	**30% deposit when order is placed, balance due when furniture is ready to be shipped.**
Catalog available:	**Yes, at their Web site**
Clearance center:	**No**
Delivery:	**Most items are small enough to ship by UPS**

Directions: From I-85, take exit #111 (Hwy. 311), and head northwest into High Point. After several miles, Hwy. 311 will become S. Main St. Gibson Interiors is on the left side of the road, inside the National Home Furnishings Center.

Gibson Interiors (cont.)

Pub table set at Gibson Interiors

Retail: $570.00   Discounted price: $277.00
Savings at Gibson Interiors: $293.00 = 49% off retail

Lines carried (cont.):

Decorative Crafts	JIJ Designs	Paragon	Toyo Trading
Demdaco	J. Edward Fine Art	Passport	Company
Denny Lamp	And Mirror	Philip Reinisch	Two Day Designs
Design Source, Ltd	Jay Willifred	Powell	Tyndale
Dezine	Jeremy's Place	Prestigeline	Ultimate Accents
Eastern Shore Trading Co.	Just Accents	Propac Images	Ultimate
Executive Imports	Ladybug	Quoizel	Manufacturing
Feather Light Lamp	Lampcrafters	Rembrandt	United Design
Fleur De Lis	Lt. Moses Willard	Remington Lamps	Upper Deck
Frederick Cooper	Mandalay Box Company	River Forks	Uttermost Company
Gallery	Manual Woodworkers	Rockford Furniture	Virginia Metalcrafters
Gatco	And Weavers	Rustic Crafts	Wayborn Furniture
H. A. Denunzio	Mario Industries	San Pacific	And Accessories
Hamilton Collections	Meyda	International	Wildwood Accents
High Cotton	Milano Designs	Sedgefield By Adams	Wildwood Lamps
H. K. H. International	Montaage	Seymour Mann	
Home Accents By Oai	Mud Pie	Silver Furniture	
House Of Troy	The Natural Light	Sterling Industries	
House Parts	Oklahoma Casting	Stylecraft Lamps	
Howard Miller	Pacific Rim Import	Tanner Collection	
Ital Art Designs	Painted Rain	Townsend Ceramics	

Gordon's Furniture Store

214 N. Center St.
Statesville, NC 28687

Phone:	**(704) 873-4329**	**Hours:**	**M-F 9:00-5:30, Sat 9:00-5:00**
Toll Free:	**None**	**E-mail:**	**lgordon@i-america.net**
Fax:	**(704) 873-4397**	**Web site:**	**www.gordonsfurniturestores.com**

Gordon's Furniture Store has occupied most of one city block in downtown Statesville, NC, since 1917. Their showroom is huge, and their discounts are quite good. They also have an excellent reputation for customer service.

On a recent trip here, I found a great deal on a queen-size solid cherry rice bed from Pennsylvania House (pictured on the following page). The retail on this bed is normally $2,267.00, but Gordon's will special-order it or sell you this one off the floor for only $1,133.50, exactly 50% off. This piece, like all of the other furniture on display, was new and in first-quality condition.

If you're ordering furniture by phone, you should definitely call Gordon's for a price comparison.

Phone orders accepted:	**Yes**
Discount:	**50%-55% off mfrs. suggested retail**
Payment methods:	**VISA, MC, personal checks**
In-house financing available:	**No**
Deposits required:	**30% deposit when order is placed, balance due when furniture is ready to be shipped.**
Catalog available:	**No**
Clearance center:	**No**
Delivery:	**Full service in-home delivery and set-up. Customer pays freight company directly for shipping costs.**

Directions: From I-40, take exit #150 (Hwy. 115) and head south. Hwy. 115 will become Center St. as you enter Statesville. Gordon's is downtown on the left.

Gordon's Furniture Store (cont.)

Gordon's Furniture Store

Solid cherry rice bed from Pennsylvania House

Retail: $2,267.00   Discounted price: $1,133.00
Savings at Gordon's Furniture Store: $1,134.00 = 50% off retail

Gordon's Furniture Stores

Lines carried:

Acacia
Alexander Julian
American Of Martinsville
American Drew
Arnold Palmer Collection
Bassett
Best Chairs
Blacksmith Shop
Bob Timberlake
Broyhill
Builtright Chair
Cabin Craft Carpet
Carolina Mirror
Chair Co.
Charleston Forge
Chatham County
China Traders Lamps
Chromecraft
Clayton-Marcus
Councill-Craftsmen
Custom Rugs
Denny Lamp
Distinction Leather
Ducks Unlimited
Fairfield Chair
Fashion Beds
Grace Iron Beds
Hammary
Hekman
Henry Link
Hooker
J-Royale
Kincaid
La-Z-Boy
Lane
Lea
Lexington
Ligo
Lloyd/Flanders
Lyon Shaw
Masland Carpet
Minoff Lamps
Nora Fenton
Ohio Table Pad
Pennsylvania House
Philadelphia Carpet
Pulaski
Riverside
SK Products

Sarreid
Sedgefield Lamp
Shaw Carpets
Simmons Bedding
Stanley
Stoneville
Stratolounger
Telescope
Universal
Vanguard Studios
Velco
Virginia House
Winston
WundaWeve

Green Front Furniture

316 N. Main St.
Farmville, VA 23901

Phone:	**(434) 392-5943**	**Hours:**	**M-F 10:00-5:30, Sat 9:00-6:15**
Toll Free:	**None**	**E-mail:**	**sales@greenfront.com**
Fax:	**None**	**Web site:**	**www.greenfront.com**

Green Front Furniture's main store and telephone sales operation is located in Farmville, VA, just west of Richmond. The store complex is huge, covering 4 city blocks. There are large galleries for Henredon, Sherrill, Henkel Harris, Statton, and Thomasville. They also carry many other medium to high-end lines of furniture and accessories.

The discounts on brand new first-quality furniture, whether bought in person or over the phone, run from 40%-50% off retail. There is also a clearance center on site which has even better deals.

If you're in the Richmond or Washington, DC, areas, it's worth a side trip to check out Green Front's clearance center. Otherwise, it's best to compare their prices over the phone. They do have very good deals on many lines.

The BBB has been receiving complaints on this company recently, and one complaint remains unresolved. Until this complaint is resolved, I must withdraw my former recommendation of this source.

Phone orders accepted:	**Yes**
Discount:	**40%-50% off mfrs. suggested retail**
Payment methods:	**VISA, MC, Discover, personal checks**
In-house financing available:	**No**
Deposits required:	**33% deposit when order is placed, balance due when furniture is ready to be shipped**
Catalog available:	**No**
Clearance center:	**Yes, on site**
Delivery:	**Full service in-home delivery and set-up. Customer pays freight company directly for shipping costs.**

Directions: From I-95, on the south side of Richmond, VA, take exit #62 and go west on Hwy. 288. Then, take Hwy. 360 west to Hwy. 307, and go west. Then, take Hwy. 307 to Hwy. 460, and continue west into downtown Farmville, VA. The three main Green Front buildings surround the intersection of Main St. and 2nd St. in downtown Farmville.

Green Front Furniture (cont.)

Lines carried:

Artistica
Barcalounger
Big Fish
Bradington Young
Brent Jacobs
Brown Street
Bucks County
Century
Charleston Forge
Chinese Imports
Cibola
Columbia
Congoleum
Crawford
CTH Occasional
Custom Shoppe
David Michael
Denny Lamps
Durham
E.J. Victor
Eastern Accents
Elite
English
Feathersound
Fleur de Lis
Formica
Frederick Cooper
Freidman Brothers
Giemme
Habersham
Hancock & Moore
Harbor Home
Harden
Hen Feathers
Henkel Harris
Henkel-Moore
Henredon
Henry Link
Hickory Chair
Highland House
Hooker
Huntington House
Indian Imports
Indonesian Imports
Jessica Charles
John Richard
Karndean Tile
Keller
King Hickory

Kingsley Bate
Lane/Venture
Leathercraft
Leatherworks
Leda
Legacy Linens
Leisters
Lexington
Lloyd Flanders
Madison Square
M. Grace Linens
Maitland-Smith
Majestic Mirrors
Malden
Marie Albert
Matelassee
McKay Table Pads
Meadowcraft
Michael Thomas
Miles Talbott
Mobel
Motioncraft
Mystic Valley Linens
Nichols & Stone
Olympia
Paragon Pictures
Pawley's Island
Pergo
Pinehurst
Possible Dreams
Precedent
Pride
Quoizel
Ragno Porcelain
Ralph Lauren
Robert Grace
Saloom
Sedgefield Lamps
Serta
Shadow Catchers
Shaw
Sherrill
Sligh
Somerset
Southampton
Southwood
Spanish Imports
Stanford
Statton

Sweet Dreams
Taylor King
Theodore Alexander
Timeworks
Toepperwein's
Tropitone
Tyndale
Tyndall Creek
Uwharrie
Vesterby
Wesley Allen
West Brothers
Whittemore-Sherrill
Wildwood
Woodard
Yorkshire House

Green Front Furniture

2004 Yonkers Road
Raleigh, NC 20166

Phone:	**(919) 754-9754**	**Hours:**	**M-Sat 10:00-6:00,**
Toll Free:	None		**Sun 1:00-5:00**
Fax:	**(919) 754-9464**	**E-mail:**	**sales@greenfront.com**
		Web site:	**www.greenfront.com**

This is Green Front Furniture's newest store. They have a very nice selection of medium to high-end lines, including Lexington, Hooker, Sherrill, and Maitland-Smith.

All of Green Front's floor samples and discontinued styles from their three stores and their phone sales service are all sent to their clearance center at their other location in Farmville, VA. For this reason, there is no monetary advantage to shopping at this location in person. All the furniture here is new, and you get the same price whether you buy in person or over the phone.

If you are near Farmville, VA, it's worth making a stop at their clearance center. Otherwise, most people would be better off saving the drive and just ordering from this source over the phone.

Green Front's Raleigh store has no BBB rating yet. The store hasn't been open long enough to rate their service. Green Front's Farmville location, however, has an unsatisfactory record with the BBB. Consumers ordering by phone from this source should ensure that their phone order will not be handled by the staff at the Farmville location.

Lines carried:	**Please see listings under *Green Front Furniture -- Farmville***
Phone orders accepted:	Yes
Discount:	**40%-50% off mfrs. suggested retail**
Payment methods:	**VISA, MC, Discover, personal checks**
In-house financing available:	No
Deposits required:	**33% deposit when order is placed, balance due when furniture is ready to be shipped**
Catalog available:	No
Clearance center:	**Yes, at Green Front's Farmville location**
Delivery:	**Full service in-home delivery and set-up. Customer pays freight company directly for shipping costs.**

Directions: **From the I-40, take the Raleigh-Chapel Hill Expy. (exit #289) toward Raleigh. After about 3 miles, merge onto I-440N/US-1N toward Wake Forest/Rocky Mount/Wilson. After about 7 miles, take the US-1/Capital Blvd/US-401 exit (exit #11) toward Wake Forest. Follow Capital Blvd. toward downtown. Almost immediately, take a left onto Yonkers Rd. You'll see Green Front's right after the turn.**

Green Front Furniture

1304-A Severn Way
Sterling, VA 20166

Phone:	(703) 406-0761	**Hours:**	M-Sat 10:00-6:00,
Toll Free:	None		Sun 12:00-5:00
Fax:	(703) 406-0763	**E-mail:**	sales@greenfront.com
		Web site:	www.greenfront.com

Green Front Furniture's Northern Virginia location is located in Sterling, VA, just a few miles west of Washington, DC. They have a very nice selection of medium to high-end lines, including Lexington, Hooker, Sherrill, and Maitland-Smith.

All of Green Front's floor samples and discontinued styles from their three stores and their phone sales service are all sent to their clearance center at their other location in Farmville, VA. For this reason, there is no monetary advantage to shopping at this location in person. All the furniture here is new, and you get the same price whether you buy in person or over the phone.

If you are near Farmville, VA, it's worth making a stop at their clearance center. Otherwise, most people would be better off saving the drive and just ordering from this source over the phone.

Green Front's Sterling location has a satisfactory record with the BBB. Only one complaint has been received in the last three years, and it has been resolved. Green Front's Farmville location, however, has an unsatisfactory record with the BBB. Consumers ordering by phone from this source should ensure that their phone order will be handled by the staff at Sterling, not Farmville.

Lines carried:	**Please see listings under *Green Front Furniture -- Farmville***
Phone orders accepted:	Yes
Discount:	40%-50% off mfrs. suggested retail
Payment methods:	VISA, MC, Discover, personal checks
In-house financing available:	No
Deposits required:	33% deposit when order is placed, balance due when furniture is ready to be shipped
Catalog available:	No
Clearance center:	Yes, at Green Front's Farmville location
Delivery:	Full service in-home delivery and set-up. Customer pays freight company directly for shipping costs.

Directions: From the I-495 perimeter around Washington, DC, take exit #12 and go west on the Dulles Toll Rd. Take exit #9B, and go left on 28N Sally Rd. After 4 miles, turn left on Severn Way. Green Front's is one block down on the right.

Grindstaff's Interiors

1007 W. Main St.
Forest City, NC 28043

Phone:	**(828) 245-4263**	**Hours:**	**M-Sat 9:00-6:00**
Toll Free:	**None**	**E-mail:**	**None**
Fax:	**(828) 245-7758**	**Web site:**	**None**

Grindstaff's Interiors is located in Forest City, NC, about an hour southwest of Hickory, NC. They have a very nice 80,000 square foot store with a good selection of high-end lines, including Bernhardt, Hekman, La Barge, Baker, Century, and Maitland Smith.

They don't have a clearance center or any floor samples or discontinued pieces on display. For this reason, there is no monetary advantage to visiting in person. They do have great deals on many lines sold over the phone, though. So, if you're planning to order your furniture by phone, definitely give this source a call to compare their prices.

Lines carried:

Baker	Frederick Cooper Lamps	Karges	Pennsylvania House
Baldwin	Friedman Brothers	Kincaid	Philadelphia
Bernhardt	Hancock Moore	La Barge	Sarreid
Bevan Funnell	Hekman	Lane	Serta
Bradington Young	Henkel Harris	Lexington	Southwood
Brown Jordan	Hickory Chair	Lloyd/Flanders	Reproductions
Casa Stradivari	Hitchcock Chair	Madison Square	Stanley
Century	Hon	Maitland Smith	Statton
Chapman	Hooker	Meadow Craft	Stiffel Lamps
Classic Leather	Jasper	Miller	Waterford
Councill-Craftsmen	Jeffco	National Mt. Airy	Wildwood
DMI	John Widdicomb	Pande Cameron	Woodard
Ekornes	Karastan	Pennsylvania Classics	Woodmark Originals

Phone orders accepted:	**Yes**
Discount:	**35%-50% off mfrs. suggested retail**
Payment methods:	**VISA, MC, Discover, personal checks**
In-house financing available:	**No**
Deposits required:	**50% deposit when order is placed, balance due when furniture is ready to be shipped**
Catalog available:	**No**
Clearance center:	**No**
Delivery:	**Full service in-home delivery and set-up. Customer pays freight company directly for shipping costs.**

Directions: From I-40, take the Hwy. 221 exit south (the exit is about one hour west of Hickory, NC). In downtown Forest City, turn left on Hwy. 74. Grindstaff's Interiors is one and a half blocks down on the right.

Hammary Furniture Factory Outlet

S. Hwy. 321-A
Saw Mills, NC 28645

Phone:	**(828) 726-3333**	**Hours:**	**Tues-F 10-6, Sat 9-3**
Toll Free:	**None**	**E-mail:**	**None**
Fax:	**None**	**Web site:**	**None**

Hammary Furniture's only factory-owned outlet, near their main factory just north of Hickory, NC.   Most of the stock here is wrought iron and case goods, primarily armoires and occasional tables. There are a few sofas and occasional chairs.

The furniture here is very nice quality and priced well. The discounts here are 20% off the usual wholesale price, which normally translates to 60%-70% off of retail.

On a recent visit to the Hammary Outlet, I found a good deal on an end table (pictured on the following page). It normally retails for $300.00, but this one was only $145.00.

If you're in the Lenoir/Hickory, NC, area looking for wrought iron tables, occasional tables, or armoires, this is a great place to check out.

Phone orders accepted:	**No**
Discount:	**60%-70% off mfrs. suggested retail**
Payment methods:	**Personal checks. No credit cards.**
In-house financing available:	**No**
Deposits required:	**Not applicable**
Catalog available:	**Not applicable**
Clearance center:	**Not applicable**
Delivery:	**Customer must make own arrangements to take furniture home.**

Directions: **From I-40, take exit #123, and drive north on Hwy. 321 to Hickory, NC. After you pass through Hickory, NC, you'll see Valley Chevrolet. At the next light (where there is a billboard for the Hammary Outlet), turn left on Mission Rd. At the turn, you'll see a sign for the city of Saw Mills. Go a few miles until Mission Rd. dead ends into Hwy. 321-A. Turn left on Hwy. 321-A, and you'll see the outlet about 1/4 mile down on the right, near one of Hammary Furniture's main manufacturing plants.**

Hammary Furniture Factory Outlet (cont.)

Hammary Furniture Factory Outlet

End table from Hammary Furniture

Retail: $300.00   Discounted price: $145.00
Savings at the Hammary Furniture Factory Outlet: $155.00 = 52% off retail

Harden Factory Outlet

Mill Pond Way
McConnellsville, NY 13401

Phone:	**(315) 245-1000**	**Hours:**	**M-Sat 10:00-5:00, Sun 1:00-5:00**
Toll Free:	**None**		**Closed first two weeks of July**
Fax:	**(315) 245-2884**	**E-mail:**	**None**
		Web site:	**None**

This is Harden Furniture's only factory outlet, located in the Harden factory itself in McConnellsville, NY, near Oneida Lake just east of Syracuse, NY. Actually, the outlet is what they call an "overpile" room, where they store photography samples, seconds, floor samples, discontinued styles, and overruns.

Most of the stock here is solid cherry case goods. This is a very high-quality traditional furniture line. The discounts here run from 50%-75% off retail.

Harden conducts business a bit differently from most outlets. If you come by to look through their overpile room, and you find something you like, they won't allow you to buy it on the spot. They tag it and ship it free of charge to the Harden dealer nearest you on the next Harden truck delivering furniture to that particular store. This can take up to a month. Then, when it arrives at your local Harden dealer, you'll be notified to come pick it up and pay the dealer for it directly. You do still pay the outlet price however.

If you plan to stop by this outlet, you may wish to plan your visit on a Wednesday morning. The Harden factory gives one-hour factory tours every Wednesday at 10:00. It's quite interesting, and it's free.

This is a good source. Harden has very high-quality gorgeous furniture, and the prices are quite good.

Phone orders accepted:	**No**
Discount:	**50%-75% off mfrs. suggested retail**
Payment methods:	**Personal checks. No credit cards.**
In-house financing available:	**No**
Deposits required:	**Not applicable**
Catalog available:	**Not applicable**
Clearance center:	**Not applicable**
Delivery:	**Furniture will be tagged and delivered free of charge via a Harden truck to the Harden dealer nearest the customer. The customer then picks up the furniture and pays for it at the local Harden dealer.**

Directions: From I-90, take exit #34, and go north on Hwy. 13. The Harden factory and outlet are just off Hwy. 13 in downtown McConnellsville.

Heirloom Traditions

Atrium Furniture Mall
430 S. Main St.
High Point, NC 27260

Phone:	**(336) 882-5597**	**Hours:**	**M-F 9:00-6:00, Sat 9:00-5:00**
Toll Free:	**None**	**E-mail:**	**heirloomtraditions@atriumfurniture.com**
Fax:	**(336) 882-5856**	**Web site:**	**www.atriumfurniture.com**

Heirloom Traditions opened their showroom in the Atrium Furniture Mall in August 2003. Their main line is Heirloom Traditions, imported by Global Furniture in Mooresville, NC.

Heirloom Traditions is a good quality line. All of their furniture is solid hardwood: mahogany, elm, birch, and cherry. Prices here run about 40%-50% off retail.

In addition to Heirloom Traditions, this showroom also carries a few other lines: Home Elegance, Goshen, Highland Designs, and Four Seasons Custom Upholstery. Most of the styles represented are traditional.

On a recent visit here, I found a great deal on a solid mahogany highboy (pictured on the following page). This piece normally retails for $1,469.00, but the outlet had this one for only $758.00. That's a savings of 49% off retail. This is a new piece, available by special order.

Heirloom Traditions doesn't have a Web site at present, but one is under construction which will feature photos of their line. In the meantime, consumers can call the showroom for photos of products available. The Atrium Furniture Mall's main Web site has a limited number of photos of furniture carried by this showroom.

If you're looking for good quality, traditional, solid wood furniture, you should certainly compare prices here.

Lines carried:

Four Seasons Custom Upholstery
Goshen
Highland Designs
Heirloom Traditions
Home Elegance

Phone orders accepted:	**Yes**
Discount:	**40%-50% off mfrs. suggested retail**
Payment methods:	**VISA, MC, AMEX, Discover, personal checks**
In-house financing available:	**No**
Deposits required:	**50% deposit when order is placed, balance due when furniture is ready to be shipped**
Catalog available:	**Yes**
Clearance center:	**No**
Delivery:	**Full service in-home delivery and set-up. Customer pays freight company directly for shipping costs.**

Directions: Please see *The Atrium* for complete directions.

Heirloom Traditions

Mahogany highboy at Heirloom Traditions

Retail: $1,469.00   Discounted price: $758.00
Savings at the Heirloom Traditionst: $711.00 = 49% off retail

Henredon Factory Clearance Center

Rte 3, Box 379
Henredon Rd.
Spruce Pine, NC 28777

Phone:	**(828) 765-1320**	**Hours:**	**M-Sat 9:00-4:30**
Toll Free:	**None**	**E-mail:**	**None**
Fax:	**None**	**Web site:**	**None**

The Henredon Factory Clearance Center in Spruce Pine is a huge warehouse with a nice selection of case goods. There are very few upholstered pieces in stock here, though. For Henredon upholstery, it's better to visit their other outlets in Hickory and High Point.

This outlet does have a great selection of case goods. There's one large room with dozens of occasional tables, another with beds and chests, and a third one with nothing but armoires. Don't forget to check the front loading dock for more beds. There's also a semi-hidden back room with more armoires.

On a recent visit here, I found a great deal on a solid ash burl veneer entertainment center (pictured on the following page). This piece normally retails for $9,500.00, but the outlet had this one for only $2,300.00. It was a photography sample with no damage.

The vast majority of the furniture at this outlet are discontinued styles, photography samples, floor samples, and a few seconds. The discounts range from 75% to 80% off retail. Nearly all of the pieces are in first quality condition.

Important note: The roads up to this outlet go essentially straight up a mountain. It takes nearly one hour of very challenging driving through the edge of the Smoky Mountains to reach this outlet from I-40. This is not a place you want to visit in bad weather or after dark. Also, this is not a good place for anyone to rent a truck or trailer and drive it up to the outlet to pick up their own furniture. Unless you are very experienced driving large vehicles on very bad roads, please let the outlet ship your furniture to you.

This outlet is wonderful, but very difficult to get to. Most people will be better off to visit the Henredon outlets in Hickory and High Point, which also have a terrific selection and great bargains. However, if you're in the Asheville area or on a vacation to the Smoky Mountains, and you feel up to the drive, by all means check out this outlet. It is definitely worth a visit.

Phone orders accepted:	**No**
Discount:	**75%-80% off mfrs. suggested retail**
Payment methods:	**VISA, MC, AMEX, Discover, personal checks**
In-house financing available:	**No**
Deposits required:	**Not applicable**
Catalog available:	**Not applicable**
Clearance center:	**Not applicable**
Delivery:	**Full service in-home delivery and set-up. Customer pays freight company directly for shipping costs.**

Directions: From I-40, take exit #86 (the Marion exit), and take Hwy. 221/226 north to Spruce Pine. There are many signs all along the way to Spruce Pine. Near the top of the mountain, you will come to a Shell station. Turn right at the station onto Hall Town Rd. Go 3-4 miles until you reach a dead end and turn right. Follow the Henredon signs to the outlet.

Henredon Factory Clearance Center (cont.)

Henredon Factory Clearance Center

Solid ash burl veneer entertainment center from Henredon

Retail: $9,500.00   Discounted price: $2,300.00
Savings at the Henredon Factory Clearance Center: $7,200.00 = 76% off retail

Henredon Factory Outlet

Level 1
Hickory Furniture Mart
U. S. Hwy. 70 SE
Hickory, NC 28602

Phone:	**(828) 322-7111**	**Hours:**	**M-Sat 9:00-6:00**
Toll Free:	**None**	**E-mail:**	**info@hickoryfurniture.com**
Fax:	**None**	**Web site:**	**www.hickoryfurniture.com**

The Henredon Factory Outlet at the Hickory Furniture Mart has a huge selection of Henredon case goods and upholstery. This is one of only three Henredon factory outlets.

Most of the pieces here are floor samples and discontinued items, although there are some seconds. Even the seconds have extremely small flaws, however. The discounts are very good: 65%-70% off retail.

On a recent visit, I found a wonderful deal on a solid mahogany bed (pictured on the following page). This queen mahogany bed normally retails for $7,485.00, but the outlet had this one for only $2,745.00, a discount of almost 65% off retail. This particular bed was a floor sample in first-quality condition.

This outlet normally has sales in February, May, and November, when all items are marked down an extra 10%-20%, so you may wish to consider this in making your travel plans to North Carolina. Many other outlets and showrooms have special sales in February, May, and November as well.

The outlet will not special order new Henredon furniture, but if you see a Henredon piece you like at a local furniture store, you can call the outlet to see if they might have a floor sample or a similar discontinued style. The outlet will take these types of orders by phone and have your furniture shipped to you.

Anyone considering purchasing Henredon furniture should definitely check this outlet out before they buy, preferably in person. This outlet is a "must-visit".

Phone orders accepted:	**Yes**
Discount:	**65%-70% off mfrs. suggested retail**
Payment methods:	**VISA, MC, personal checks**
In-house financing available:	**No**
Deposits required:	**Not applicable**
Catalog available:	**Not applicable**
Clearance center:	**Not applicable**
Delivery:	**Full service in-home delivery and set-up. Customer pays freight company directly for shipping costs.**

Directions: Please see *Hickory Furniture Mart* for complete directions.

Henredon Factory Outlet (cont.)

Carved solid mahogany bed from Henredon

Retail: $7,485.00   Discounted price: $2,745.00
Savings at the Henredon Factory Outlet: $4,740.00 = 63% off retail

Henredon Factory Outlet

641 West Ward Avenue
High Point, NC 28602

Phone:	(336) 888-2844	**Hours:**	M-F 10:00-5:00, Sat 10:00-3:00
Toll Free:	None	**E-mail:**	None
Fax:	(336) 885-5557	**Web site:**	None

The Henredon Factory Outlet in High Point has a huge selection of Henredon case goods and upholstery. Most of the pieces here are floor samples and discontinued items, although there are some seconds. Even the seconds have extremely small flaws, however. The discounts are very good: 60%-70% off retail.

On a recent visit, I found a wonderful deal on a solid mahogany armoire (pictured on the following page). This armoire normally retails for $13,785.00, but the outlet had this one for only $5,059.00, a discount of almost 65% off retail. This particular armoire was a floor sample with two slight flaws: a chip on the top surface (invisible unless you're on a ladder) and a small chip on the bottom back corner of the side (also virtually unnoticable). Please bear in mind that tiny flaws like this can easily be invisibly repaired with a simple touch-up marker.

The chair pictured next to the armoire was a great deal as well. It retailed for $3,450.00, but you could purchase this one for only $930.00, a savings of 73% off retail. The chair was an undamaged floor sample.

This outlet normally has after-market sales in May and November, when all items are marked down an extra 10%, so you may wish to consider this in making your travel plans to North Carolina. Many other outlets and showrooms have special sales in May and November as well. Please see www.smartdecorating.com for a list of upcoming sales.

Anyone considering purchasing Henredon furniture should definitely check this outlet out before they buy, preferably in person. This outlet is a "must-visit".

Phone orders accepted:	No
Discount:	60%-70% off mfrs. suggested retail
Payment methods:	VISA, MC, personal checks
In-house financing available:	No
Deposits required:	Not applicable
Catalog available:	Not applicable
Clearance center:	Not applicable
Delivery:	Full service in-home delivery and set-up. Customer pays freight company directly for shipping costs.

Directions: From I-85, take exit #111 (Hwy. 311), and head northwest into High Point. After several miles, take a left on West Ward Ave. The Henredon outlet is about a mile down on your left.

Henredon Factory Outlet (cont.)

Henredon Factory Outlet

Mahogany armoire from Henredon

Retail: $13,785.00   Discounted price: $5,059.00
Savings at the Henredon Factory Outlet: $8,726.00 = 65% off retail

Heritage Home

Catawba Furniture Mall
377 Hwy. 70 SW
Hickory, NC 28602

Phone:	**(828) 327-0697**	**Hours:**	**M-Sat 9:00-7:00**
Toll Free:	**None**	**E-mail:**	**info@catawbafurniture.com**
Fax:	**(828) 327-4036**	**Web site:**	**www.catawbafurniture.com**

The Heritage Home gallery at the Catawba Furniture Mall is owned and operated by Designer's Choice Furniture. Discounts run 40-50% off retail. Designer's Choice has a good reputation for customer service.

All of the furniture at Designer's Choice is special order. If you see something you like, be sure to check upstairs at Designer's Outlet before buying. Designer's Outlet liquidates samples, overstock items, discontinued pieces, and customer returns for Designer's Choice. They have a nice variety of outlet pieces from the lines below at substantially greater savings: 50%-70% off retail. You may well find what you're looking for in stock at the outlet.

Please see the listing in this book for the Catawba Furniture Mall if you are planning a visit here. The Mall offers discounts on hotel rooms and coupons toward your furniture purchase during their big sale weekends four times each year.

Phone orders accepted:	**Yes**
Discount:	**40%-50% off mfrs. suggested retail**
Payment methods:	**VISA, MC, personal checks**
In-house financing available:	**Yes, 90 days same as cash with 25% down pmt.**
Deposits required:	**50% deposit when order is placed, balance due when furniture is ready to be shipped**
Catalog available:	**No**
Clearance center:	**No**
Delivery:	**Full service in-home delivery and set-up. Customer pays freight company directly for shipping costs.**

Directions:	**The Catawba Furniture Mall is in Hickory, NC. From I-40, take exit #123-B and turn right. The mall will be about half a mile down on your right.**

Hickory Furniture Mart

U. S. Hwy. 70 SE
Hickory, NC 28602

Phone:	(828) 322-3510		**Hours:**	M-Sat 9:00-6:00
Toll Free:	(800) 462-MART		**E-mail:**	info@hickoryfurniture.com
Fax:	(828) 322-1132		**Web site:**	www.hickoryfurniture.com

The Hickory Furniture Mart has some excellent deals from legitimate discounters and true factory outlets. Please see the individual listings in this book for each discounter or outlet for details on payment, shipping, lines carried, etc:

Amish Oak and Cherry	(828) 261-4776
Bassett Furniture Direct	(828) 267-0670
Boyles Galleries	(828) 326-1740
Boyles Shoppes	(828) 326-1060
Boyles Showcase	(828) 326-1735
Boyles Thomasville Gallery	(828) 326-1709
Century Factory Outlet	(828) 324-2442
Clayton-Marcus Factory Outlet	(828) 327-0244
Don Lamor	(828) 324-1776
Franklin Place	(828) 322-5539
Henredon Factory Outlet	(828) 322-7111
Hickory Park Furniture Galleries	(828) 322-4440
Hickory White Factory Outlet	(828) 327-3766
Ironstone Galleries Factory Outlet	(828) 304-1094
Manufacturer's Outlet	(828) 327-0244
National Home Furnishing Center	(828) 324-7110
Nostalgia Furniture	(828) 325-4800
Pennsylvania House at the Mart	(828) 261-2026
Reflections Furniture	(828) 327-8485
Robert Bergelin Company	(828) 345-1500
Sity Slicker	(828) 325-0092
Southern Designs	(828) 328-8855
Southern Style	(828) 322-7000
The Wild Pear	(828) 326-9296
Zagaroli Classics	(828) 328-3373

Many discounters and outlets at the Mart have special sales in May and November, right after the bi-annual High Point International Home Furnishings Market, as well as in February and July when business is traditionally slow. Many other factory outlets and showrooms all over North Carolina have special sales during these months, too, so you may wish to plan any trips to take advantage of these extra discounts.

Directions: **From I-40, take exit #125. Head south on Hwy L-R (Lenoir-Rhyne). After about a mile, turn left onto Hwy. 70. You'll see the mart a couple of miles down on the right.**

Hickory Furniture Mart (cont.)

Hickory Furniture Mart

Hickory Park Furniture Galleries

Level 3
Hickory Furniture Mart
U. S. Hwy. 70 SE
Hickory, NC 28602

Phone:	**(828) 322-4440**	**Hours:**	**M-Sat 9:00-6:00**
Toll Free:	**None**	**E-mail:**	**hparksales@hickorypark.com**
Fax:	**(828) 267-0821**	**Web site:**	**www.hickorypark.com**

Although Hickory Park Furniture carries furniture for any room in the home, their specialty is upholstery. They have dedicated showrooms at the Hickory Furniture Mart for Flexsteel, Broyhill, Rowe, Temple, and La-Z-Boy youth furniture. They also have showrooms dedicated to home office furniture, outdoor furniture, and leather furniture. Their prices tend to run 40%-50% off retail.

For example, on a recent visit I found a Rowe sectional sofa at Hickory Park (pictured on the following page). The retail on this entire set is $4,815.00, but you can special order this set new for only $2,889.00, a discount of 40% off retail.

Their "Comfort Zone" showroom specializes in leather, upholstery, sectionals, and recliners. It also has some unique products, such as zero gravity recliners and massage chairs from Interactive Health.

Also, in July 2002, Hickory Park took over the Broyhill Showcase Gallery at the Hickory Furniture Mart from its former operators, Blowing Rock Furniture, after Blowing Rock closed. As a result, Hickory Park has now added Broyhill to their special order offerings.

Hickory Park has reliable service and good pricing. If you plan to special order any of the lines below by phone, though, you should definitely call them for a price quote.

Lines carried:

Action By Lane	Broyhill	Dinaire	High Point Desk
Alexvale	C. R. Laine	Dutailier	Holland Furniture
Artistica	Cebu	Ficks-Reed	Interactive Health
Barcalounger	Charleston Forge	Faith Walk	JSF Industries
Barn Door	Child Craft	Flat Rock	Jensen Jarrah
Beach Mfg.	Classic Leather	Flexsteel	Keller
Benchcraft	Color Shop	Hammary	Kincaid
Berkline	Crawford	Hekman	Kingsdown
Bermex	Creative Ideas	Hickory-Fry	KNF Designs

Phone orders accepted:	**Yes**
Discount:	**40%-50% off mfrs. suggested retail**
Payment methods:	**VISA, MC, personal checks**
In-house financing available:	**No**
Deposits required:	**30% deposit when order is placed, balance due when furniture is ready to be shipped**
Catalog available:	**No**
Clearance center:	**No**
Delivery:	**Full service in-home delivery and set-up. Customer pays freight company directly for shipping costs.**

Directions: Please see *Hickory Furniture Mart* for complete directions.

Hickory Park Furniture Galleries (cont.)

Rowe sectional sofa at Hickory Park

Retail: $4,815.00   Discounted price: $2,889.00
Savings at Hickory Park: $1,926.00 = 40% off retail

Lines carried (cont.):

Lane
La-Z-Boy
Lea
Leather Trend
Leather Mark
Legacy Furniture
Lloyd Flanders
Master Designs
McKay Table Pads
McKinley Leather
Old Hickory Tannery
Parker Southern
Pompeii
Reflections
Regency House

Riverside
Ron Fisher
Rowe
Sidney Arthur
Simmons
Spring Air
Stoneleigh
Style Upholstery
Temple Furniture
Timmerman
Whitaker
Winners Only
Woodard
Woodland

Hickory White Factory Outlet

2679 Ramada Rd.
Burlington, NC 2715

Phone:	**(336) 229-0831**	**Hours:**	**M-F 9:30-5:30, Sat 10:00-4:00**
Toll Free:	**None**	**E-mail:**	**None**
Fax:	**None**	**Web site:**	**None**

This is one of three Hickory White factory-owned factory outlets. The first floor has an extensive selection of case goods and upholstery. The smaller second floor has a nice selection of occasional chairs, ottomans, and odd sets of dining room chairs.

The stock here consists of floor samples, discontinued styles, overruns, customer returns, photography samples, and a few seconds. Virtually all of the furniture here is new and in first-quality condition. The discounts range from 60%-75% off retail, with most items marked about 65% off. Most of the furniture here is traditional, but there are a few contemporary pieces.

On my most recent visit here, I found a great deal on a white silk ottoman (pictured on the following page). This ottoman normally retails for $1,450.00, but this one was on sale for only $545.00. It was a floor sample in new first-quality condition.

This outlet is definitely a bit of a drive from the main outlet centers of Hickory and High Point, but if you're in the area, definitely check it out.

Phone orders accepted:	**No**
Discount:	**60%-75% off mfrs. suggested retail**
Payment methods:	**VISA, MC, personal checks**
In-house financing available:	**No**
Deposits required:	**Not applicable**
Catalog available:	**Not applicable**
Clearance center:	**Not applicable**
Delivery:	**Full service in-home delivery and set-up. Customer pays freight company directly for shipping costs.**

Directions: **From I-85, take exit #143, and go north on Hwy. 62. The Hickory White outlet is just off the interstate on the frontage road.**

Hickory White Factory Outlet (cont.)

Hickory White Factory Outlet in Burlington, NC

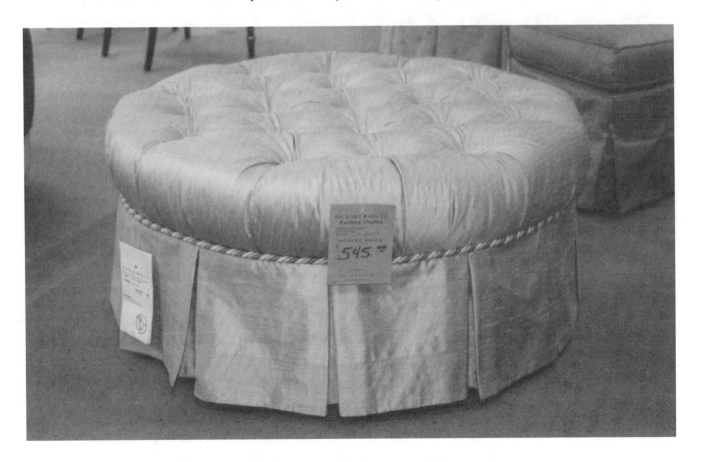

Silk ottoman from Hickory White

Retail: $1,450.00   Discounted price: $545.00
Savings at the Hickory White Factory Outlet: $905.00 = 62% off retail

Hickory White Factory Outlet

321 Pottery Factory Dr.
Commerce, GA 30529

Phone:	**(706) 336-8460**	**Hours:**	**M-F 9:00-9:00, Sun 12:00-6:00**
Toll Free:	**None**	**E-mail:**	**None**
Fax:	**(706) 336-8470**	**Web site:**	**None**

This is the newest Hickory White outlet, in Commerce, GA, about an hour north of Atlanta. Commerce is a major factory outlet center for clothing, china, etc., but this is the only furniture outlet in the area. This outlet also carries some outlet merchandise from Theodore Alexander, which is closely affiliated with Hickory White.

Most of the pieces here are floor samples and discontinued items, although there are some seconds. Even the seconds have extremely small flaws, however. The discounts are very good: 60%-70% off retail.

Phone orders accepted:	**No**
Discount:	**60%-70% off mfrs. suggested retail**
Payment methods:	**VISA, MC, personal checks**
In-house financing available:	**No**
Deposits required:	**Not applicable**
Catalog available:	**Not applicable**
Clearance center:	**Not applicable**
Delivery:	**Full service in-home delivery and set-up. Customer pays freight company directly for shipping costs.**

Directions: **From I-85, take Exit 149 (Commerce), and go toward the big Pottery Factory Outlet. You can't miss it. Turn right at the light as though you were going to the Pottery Outlet, then turn right at the stop sign. Continue around to the right, and you'll see the Hickory White outlet in the strip mall next to the Pottery Outlet.**

Hickory White Factory Outlet

Level 4
Hickory Furniture Mart
U. S. Hwy. 70 SE
Hickory, NC 28602

Phone:	**(828) 327-3766**	**Hours:**	**M-Sat 9:00-6:00**
Toll Free:	None	**E-mail:**	info@hickoryfurniture.com
Fax:	None	**Web site:**	www.hickoryfurniture.com

The Hickory White Factory Outlet at the Hickory Furniture Mart has a fair selection of upholstery and case goods. It's the smallest of the three Hickory White Factory Outlets, but it is the most conveniently located if you're planning a trip to North Carolina to see factory outlets for many brands.

Most of the pieces here are floor samples and discontinued items. The discounts are very good: 65%-70% off retail. They also have a very nice selection of accessories through their sister brand displayed at the same location: Theodore Alexander.

This outlet normally has sales in February, May, July, and November, when all items are marked down an extra 10%-20%, so you may wish to consider this in making your travel plans to North Carolina. Many other outlets and showrooms have special sales in February, May, and November as well.

Anyone considering purchasing Hickory White furniture should definitely check this outlet out before they buy. This outlet is a "must-visit".

Phone orders accepted:	Yes
Discount:	**65%-70% off mfrs. suggested retail**
Payment methods:	**VISA, MC, personal checks**
In-house financing available:	No
Deposits required:	**Not applicable**
Catalog available:	**Not applicable**
Clearance center:	**Not applicable**
Delivery:	**Full service in-home delivery and set-up. Customer pays freight company directly for shipping costs.**

Directions: Please see *Hickory Furniture Mart* for complete directions.

High Point Furniture Sales

2000 Baker Rd.
High Point, NC 27260

Phone:	**(336) 841-5664**	**Hours:**	**M-F 9:00-5:30, Sat 9:00-4:30**
Toll Free:	**(800) 334-1875**	**E-mail:**	**info@highpointfurnituresales.com**
Fax:	**(336) 885-7034**	**Web site:**	**www.highpointfurnituresales.com**

High Point Furniture Sales has a very nice store on the east side of High Point with large galleries for Thomasville and Lexington. They have good prices, 40-50% off retail on most of the brands they carry.

Please be advised that this showroom is temporarily closed due to a fire. They are remodeling, and expect to reopen in 2004. During the renovations, they are operating out of their clearance center on Brentwood St. in High Point.

They have no discontinued styles or floor samples on display, but they will give you an extra 5% off on any new furniture purchased off the sales floor if you ask. Of course, this is only helpful if you are a North Carolina resident. Residents of other states won't benefit from the extra discount because shopping in person rather than over the phone would obligate you to pay North Carolina sales tax.

Don't let the plain exterior fool you. This is a terrific source. Unless you're a North Carolina resident, there isn't any monetary advantage to shopping in person, but anyone considering buying furniture over the phone should definitely compare prices here. The staff is extremely helpful, and the discounts are very impressive on many lines.

Phone orders accepted:	**Yes**
Discount:	**40%-50% off mfrs. suggested retail**
Payment methods:	**Personal checks. No credit cards.**
In-house financing available:	**No**
Deposits required:	**25% deposit when order is placed, balance due when furniture is ready to be shipped**
Catalog available:	**No**
Clearance center:	**Yes -- See *High Point Furniture Sales Clearance***
Delivery:	**Full service in-home delivery and set-up. Customer pays freight company directly for shipping costs.**

Directions: From Business I-85, take the Baker Rd. exit, on the east side of High Point, NC. Go north on Baker Rd. High Point Furniture Sales is just off the interstate on the right side of the road.

High Point Furniture Sales (cont.)

Lines carried:

Action By Lane
American Drew
American Mirror
Andrew Pearson
Arnold Palmer Collection
Artistic Impressions
Austin Art
Balangier
Baldwin Brass
Baldwin Clocks
Barcalounger
Barn Door
Bauer Lamps
Benicia Beds
Berkline
Berkshire
Bob Timberlake
Bradington Young
Brass Craft Inc.
Braxton Culler
Brown Jordan
Broyhill
Cambridge Lamps
Cape Craftsman
Carlton McLendon
Carolina Mirror
Carsons
Carter Furniture
Casa Bique
Cebu
Charisma Chairs
Chatham County
Charter Table Co.
Chromcraft
Clark Casual
Classic Rattan
Clayton Marcus
Cochrane Furniture
Conover Chair
Cox Mfg.
Crawford Mfg.
Creations At Dallas
Crystal Clear Ind.
Dar Ran
Darafeau
Decorative Crafts
Design Masters
Dillon
Dinaire

Distinctive Designs
Dutailier
Ello
Excelsior
Fabricoate
Fairfield Chair
Fashion Bed Group
Ficks Reed
Fine Arts Lamps
Flexsteel
Floral Arts
Frederick Cooper Lamps
Friedman Brothers
Friendship Upholstery
Fitz & Floyd
Glass Arts
Grace
Great American
         Trading Co.
Great City Traders
Greene Brothers
Guildmaster
Halcyon
Hammary
Henry Link
Hickory Hill
High Point Furniture
Hollywoods
Hooker
Howard Miller Clocks
Huntington House
Hyundai Furniture
International Furniture
Jasper
Jeffco
Johnston Casuals
Keller
Key City
Kimball
Kincaid
Kinder Harris
Kingsdown
Lane
Lane/Venture
Laurier
Lea
Leisters
Lexington
Link Taylor

Lloyd/Flanders
Lyon Shaw
Marlow
Mary Dale Lamp
Master Design
Miller Desk
Mirror Craft
Mobel
Murray Feiss
Natural Light
Null Industries
Oriental Lacquer
Ohio Table Pad Co.
Palecek
Paragon
Park Place
Patrician
Peoplelounger
Peter Revington
Phillips Furniture
Pieri
Pinnacle
Plant Plant
Preview
Pulaski
Regency House
Remington Lamps
Rex Furniture
Richardson Brothers
Ridgeway
Riverside
Rowe Furniture
Rug Barn
Sam Moore
Samsonite
San Diego Design
Santee
Schnadig
Schweiger
Sealy Mattress
Sedgefield Lamps
Serta Mattress
Skillcraft
Shafer Seating
Sherrill
Signature Rugs
Stanley
Stiffel Lamps
Stratalounger

Stratford
Swaim Originals
Taylorsville
         Upholstery
Telescope
Thayer Coggin
Thomasville
Timeless Bedding
Toyo
Tropitone
Universal
U. S. Furniture
Uttermost Mirrors
Uwharrie Chair
Van Patten
Van Teal
Vanguard
Vaughan
Vaughan Bassett
Venture By Lane
Victorian Classics
Weiman
Wesley Allen
Winston
Woodard
Woodmark

High Point Furniture Sales Clearance

2035 Brentwood Street
High Point, NC 27260

Phone:	**(336) 841-5664**	**Hours:**	**M-F 9:00-5:30, Sat 9:00-4:30**
Toll Free:	**(800) 334-1875**	**E-mail:**	**info@highpointfurnituresales.com**
Fax:	**(336) 885-7034**	**Web site:**	**www.highpointfurnituresales.com**

High Point Furniture Sales Clearance is right up Business I-85 from their main showroom on Baker Rd., which is under renovation until sometime in 2004.

The clearance center has some quite good deals on a wide variety of the lines carried by the main showroom. Please see the listing in this book for *High Point Furniture Sales* for a full listing of the lines they carry. Most of the items at the clearance center are floor samples, discontinued styles, and customer returns. The majority are in new first-quality condition.

High Point Furniture Sales has an excellent reputation for customer service, and some very good bargains. If you are traveling to High Point in person to shop, this clearance center is well worth a visit.

Lines carried:	**Please see listings under *High Point Furniture Sales***
Phone orders accepted:	**No**
Discount:	**60%-70% off mfrs. suggested retail**
Payment methods:	**Personal checks. No credit cards.**
In-house financing available:	**No**
Deposits required:	**Not applicable**
Catalog available:	**Not applicable**
Clearance center:	**Not applicable**
Delivery:	**Full service in-home delivery and set-up. Customer pays freight company directly for shipping costs.**

Directions: From Business I-85, take the Brentwood St. exit and turn right (if you're facing north). High Point Furniture Sales Clearance is about 1/4 mile down on your left.

High Point Home Furnishings Center

1100 Trinity Ave.
High Point, NC 27260

Phone:	**(336) 887-7477**	**Hours:**	**M-Sat 10:00-5:00, Sun 12:00-4:00**
Toll Free:	**None**		**Closed April and October**
Fax:	**(336) 887-8874**	**E-mail:**	**showrooms@highpointcenter.com**
		Web site:	**www.highpointcenter.com**

The High Point Home Furnishings Center is owned by a Mexican furniture manufacturer of rustic furniture, Gonzalez and Associates. They also feature a number of other lines manufactured primarily in Mexico, Canada, and South America.

The quality is generally good. Styles are fairly basic. Catalogs of some of the lines featured can be viewed on their Web site.

Please note that this showroom is closed to the public during the International Home Furnishings Market, which takes place in late April and late October. Please see www.smartdecorating.com for the exact dates of upcoming markets.

With such a wide variety of manufacturers represented, there is also a wide variety of value here. Some pieces are good deals, others not so great. It would probably be best to compare pricing with this source after you've done a bit of shopping elsewhere and have a good idea what the kind of furniture you're interested in tends to cost.

Phone orders accepted:	**Yes**
Discount:	**40%-50% off mfrs. suggested retail**
Payment methods:	**VISA, MC, Discover, personal checks**
In-house financing available:	**Yes**
Deposits required:	**50% deposit when order is placed, balance due when furniture is ready to be shipped**
Catalog available:	**Yes, some lines can be viewed online**
Clearance center:	**No**
Delivery:	**Full service in-home delivery and set-up. Customer pays freight company directly for shipping costs.**

Directions: From Business I-85, take the Green St. exit near the southern edge of High Point. You'll see the High Point Home Furnishings center right off the interstate.

Hitchcock Chair Factory Outlet
Route 20
Riverton, CT 06065

Phone:	**(860) 379-4826**	**Hours:**	**M-Sat 9:30-6:00, Sun 12:00-6:00**
Toll Free:	**(888) 429-5354**	**E-mail:**	**None**
Fax:	**(860) 379-4185**	**Web site:**	**None**

The Hitchcock Chair Factory Outlet is located in the original house and factory owned by the company's original founder, Lambert Hitchcock. Aside from being very quaint and located in a gorgeous area of Connecticut, this outlet also has some terrific bargains.

The discounts here run from 40%-60% off retail. New furniture runs around 40% off, and discontinued styles and floor samples run from 50%-60% off. The outlet has a nice selection of case goods that covers just about every style Hitchcock Chair makes.

The outlet will allow you to order any new styles from the Hitchcock Chair line at about 40% off retail. They take orders over the phone, and they have a very nice full-color catalog.

On a recent visit here, I found a great deal on a solid cherry entertainment center (pictured on the following page). All three pieces together normally retail for $4,947.00, but this set was available at the outlet for only $2,997.00. This was a brand-new first-quality entertainment center directly from the factory. It could have been ordered by phone at the same price, 40% off retail.

This is a great outlet. It is a bit of a drive to get to, but it's in such a pretty area of the country. If you are ever in Northwest Connecticut, you really should consider visiting this outlet.

Phone orders accepted:	**Yes**
Discount:	**40%-60% off mfrs. suggested retail**
Payment methods:	**VISA, MC, personal checks.**
In-house financing available:	**No**
Deposits required:	**Not applicable**
Catalog available:	**Yes**
Clearance center:	**Not applicable**
Delivery:	**Full service in-home delivery and set-up. Customer pays freight company directly for shipping costs.**

Directions: From I-84, take exit #52, and go northwest on Hwy. 44. After about an hour, you'll run into Hwy. 8. Take Hwy. 8 north for a few miles, then turn east on Route 20 into downtown Riverton, CT. The Hitchcock Chair Factory Outlet is on Route 20 in the center of town.

Hitchcock Chair Factory Outlet (cont.)

Hitchcock Chair Factory Outlet

Solid cherry entertainment center from Hitchcock Chair

Retail: $4,947.00   Discounted price: $2,997.00
Savings at the Hitchcock Chair Factory Outlet: $1,950.00 = 40% off retail

Holton Furniture

805 Randolph St.
Thomasville, NC 27361

Phone:	**(336) 472-0400**	**Hours:**	**M-F 9:00-5:30, Sat 9:00-5:00**
Toll Free:	**None**	**E-mail:**	**holtonfurn@aol.com**
Fax:	**(336) 472-0415**	**Web site:**	**www.holtonfurniture.com**

Holton Furniture in Thomasville has a very upscale store with a large Thomasville gallery. They also carry many other high-end lines such as Hooker, Thayer Coggin, Flexsteel, Pennsylvania House, and Hickory Chair. Their discounts aren't quite as good as others in the High Point area, only 30% to 50% off retail. Due to manufacturer restrictions, Thomasville carries a lesser discount.

Phone orders accepted:	**Yes**
Discount:	**30%-50% off mfrs. suggested retail**
Payment methods:	**VISA, MC, AMEX, Discover, personal checks**
In-house financing available:	**Yes**
Deposits required:	**35% deposit when order is placed, balance due when furniture is ready to be shipped**
Catalog available:	**No**
Clearance center:	**No**
Delivery:	**Full service in-home delivery and set-up. Customer pays freight company directly for shipping costs.**

Directions: From I-85, take exit #103, and head one mile north on Hwy. 109, which will become Randolph St. Holton Furniture is about one mile from the interstate on the right side of the road.

Holton Furniture (cont.)

Lines carried:

Action By Lane
Alex Foster Chairs
Alexander Julian
American Drew
Arnold Palmer Collection
Athol Tables
Barcalounger
Bassett Mirror
Benchcraft
Benecia Beds
Bevan Funnell
Bob Timberlake
Bradington Young
British Traditions
Brown Jordan
Broyhill
Builtright
Butler
Carolina Mirror
Charleston Forge
Clayton Marcus
Classic Leather
Cochrane
Cotswold
Crawford
Craftique
Ducks Unlimited
Eddie Bauer Collection
Emerson
Faith Walk Designs
Fashion Bed Group
Fauld
Flexsteel
Grace Furniture
Hammary
Hekman
Henry Link Wicker
Hickory Chair
Hinkle Chair
Hooker
Howard Miller
Jasper
Jessica McClintock
John Richards
Kemp
Kessler
Kincaid
Kingsdown Mattress
Kingsley Bate

Lane
Lane/Venture
Lea
Laura Ashley
Legacy
Leisters
Lexington
Lloyd/Flanders
Mahdavis Rugs
Michael Thomas
Miles Talbot
Miller Desk
Miresco Rugs
Mobel
McKay Table Pad
Mystic Valley Traders
Nichols and Stone
Null
Ohio Table Pad
P & P Chair
Palmer Home Collection
Penns Creek
Pennsylvania House
Peters Revington
Pulaski
Riverside
Sam Moore
Serta Mattress
Sumter Cabinet
Tapestries Ltd.
Telescope
Thayer Coggin
Thomas Kinkade
Thomasville
Tropitone
Universal
Uwharrie Chair
Villageois
Wellington Hall
Winston
Younger Furniture

HomeLand Furniture

Atrium Furniture Mall
430 S. Main St.
High Point, NC 27260

Phone:	(336) 454-1955	**Hours:**	M-F 9:00-6:00, Sat 9:00-5:00
Toll Free:	None	**E-mail:**	info@homelandfurniture.com
Fax:	(336) 454-8926	**Web site:**	www.homelandfurniture.com

HomeLand Furniture is one of the newest showrooms at the Atrium Furniture Mall in High Point, NC. They have a good selection of medium quality traditional and transitional furniture. A partial catalog of their stock can be seen at their Web site above or at www.atriumfurniture.com. Their discounts run 40%-50% off retail.

Lines carried:

Calia
Eastman House
Magnussen
River's Edge
Riversforks
StratoLounger

Phone orders accepted:	Yes
Discount:	40%-50% off mfrs. suggested retail
Payment methods:	VISA, MC, AMEX, Discover, personal checks
In-house financing available:	Yes
Deposits required:	50% deposit when order is placed, balance due when furniture is ready to be shipped
Catalog available:	Yes, online
Clearance center:	No
Delivery:	Full service in-home delivery and set-up. Customer pays freight company directly for shipping costs.

Directions: Please see *The Atrium* for complete directions.

Homeway Furniture

121 W. Lebanon St.
Mount Airy, NC 27030

Phone:	**(336) 786-6151**	**Hours:**	**M-F 9:00-5:30, Sat 9:00-5:00**
Toll Free:	**(800) 334-9094**	**E-mail:**	**info@homewayfurniture.com**
Fax:	**(336) 786-1822**	**Web site:**	**www.homewayfurniture.com**

Homeway Furniture is located in Mt. Airy, NC, about an hour's drive north of High Point, NC. They have a very nice selection of high end lines, including Lexington, Hooker, and Hickory Chair.

They don't have a clearance center or any floor samples or discontinued pieces on display. For this reason, there is no monetary advantage to visiting in person. They do have great deals on many lines sold over the phone, though.

Unfortunately, Homeway Furniture has some unresolved complaints from customers. Until they are resolved, I must withdraw my former recommendation of this store.

Phone orders accepted:	**Yes**
Discount:	**40%-50% off mfrs. suggested retail**
Payment methods:	**Personal checks. No credit cards.**
In-house financing available:	**No**
Deposits required:	**50% deposit when order is placed, balance due when furniture is ready to be shipped**
Catalog available:	**No**
Clearance center:	**No**
Delivery:	**Full service in-home delivery and set-up. Customer pays freight company directly for shipping costs.**

Directions: From I-77, take exit #100, and go east on Hwy. 89. Go to the sixth stoplight, and turn north on Business 52. Go to the third stoplight, and turn left. Homeway Furniture will be on the left side of the road.

Hooker Furniture Factory Outlet

105 East Church Street
Martinsville, VA 24112

Phone:	**(276) 638-2040**	**Hours:**	**M-Sat 10:00-6:00**
Toll Free:	**None**	**E-mail:**	**hookeroutlet@hotmail.com**
Fax:	**(276) 632-2575**	**Web site:**	**www.hookerfurniture.com**

The Hooker Furniture Outlet in Martinsville, VA is about an hour's drive north of High Point, and worth every minute of the drive.

The majority of the stock at this outlet is new and in first-quality condition. Most pieces are 65% off retail. The staff is great to work with.

Unlike most factory outlets, this one will take phone orders. If there is a certain item you want from Hooker, just check Hooker's full online catalog at their site (above) and call the outlet to see if they have one in stock. If they do, they'll be happy to take your order over the phone and ship it.

Hooker is best known for their entertainment centers and armoires, which make up the majority of the stock here. You'll also find some nice marble-topped bathroom vanities.

On my most recent visit, I found a great deal on a beautiful hand painted wine cabinet (pictured on the following page). It retails for $1,850.00, but you could buy this one for only $650.00. That's a 65% discount.

The Hooker Furniture Outlet is owned and operated by Fred Martin Associates, which also owns and operates the Lane Factory Outlet, Martin Plaza, and The Showroom in Martinsville. They have a great reputation for service.

This is a great source. If you plan to visit High Point, you may wish to take a day to drive to the Martinsville, VA area, which has outlets for Hooker, Lane, Stanley, and Bassett, as well as a great clearance center (Martin Plaza). The bargains here are well worth the extra travel time.

Phone orders accepted:	**Yes**
Discount:	**65% off mfrs. suggested retail**
Payment methods:	**VISA, MC, AMEX, Discover, personal checks**
In-house financing available:	**No**
Deposits required:	**100% due with order. All items are in stock and ship immediately.**
Catalog available:	**No**
Clearance center:	**No**
Delivery:	**Full service in-home delivery and set-up. Customer pays freight company directly for shipping costs.**

Directions: **From I-40 in Greensboro, NC, take the Hwy. 68/Airport exit (#210), and head north on Hwy. 68. After about 30 minutes, turn onto Hwy. 220 toward Martinsville/Roanoke. After about another 20 minutes, you'll enter Martinsville. Be sure to stay on Business 220 through town, not on the 220 bypass which goes around Martinsville. About 10 miles after you get on Business 220, you'll come to Broad St. There's a green "John Deere" dealership sign on the corner. Broad St. will dead end into Church St. The Hooker Furniture Outlet will be directly in front of you.**

Hooker Furniture Factory Outlet (cont.)

Hooker Furniture Factory Outlet

Wine cabinet from Hooker Furniture

Retail: $1,850.00   Discounted price: $650.00
Savings at the Hooker Furniture Factory Outlet: $1,200.00 = 65% off retail

Hudson Discount Furniture

940 Highland Ave. NE
Hickory, NC 28601

Phone:	**(828) 322-4996**	**Hours:**	**M-Sat 8:30-5:00, closed Wed**
Toll Free:	**None**	**E-mail:**	**jehfurn@twave.net**
Fax:	**(828) 322-6953**	**Web site:**	**www.hudsonfurniture.com**

Hudson Discount Furniture has been discounting furniture for over 83 years. They have an excellent reputation. It's owned by the same family that owns and operates Lindy's Furniture and Better Homes Discount Furniture. They are very reputable and pleasant to work with.

They do occasionally have floor samples, seconds, and market samples available for sale below wholesale prices. They will also sell any item off the floor, which can help you avoid shipping delays. Their special order prices are among the best. Any customer who plans to order their furniture over the phone would do well to call this source and compare their prices.

Lines carried:

Aico	DMI	Kingsdown	Sam Moore
American Drew	England Corsair	Kroehler	Schnadig
Barn Door	Fairfield	La-Z-Boy	Shamrock
Bassett Mirror Company	Fashion Bed	Lea	South Sea Rattan
Benchcraft	Flexsteel	Legacy Classics	Standard
Berkline	Hammary	Liberty	Stoneville
Bermex	Harbor Home	Ligo	Stylecraft Lamps
Best Chair	Hekman	Magnussen Presidential	Sumter Cabinet
Broyhill	Hickory Hill	Morgan Stewart	Universal
Bruards	Hooker	Ohio Table Pad	Vaughan
Casapelle Leather	Howard Miller	Platinum	Vaughan Bassett
Chromcraft	Jackson Furniture	Pulaski	Webb
Clayton Marcus	Jami L. Designs	Relax-R	Winners Only
Cochrane	Keller	Richardson Bros.	
Craftique	Kimball	Riverside	
Davis Int'l	King Hickory	Rowe	

Phone orders accepted:	**Yes**
Discount:	**Up to 70% off mfrs. suggested retail**
Payment methods:	**VISA, MC, personal checks**
In-house financing available:	**Yes, 90 days no interest**
Deposits required:	**25% deposit when order is placed, balance due when furniture is ready to be shipped**
Catalog available:	**No**
Clearance center:	**No**
Delivery:	**Full service in-home delivery and set-up. Customer pays freight company directly for shipping costs.**

Directions: From I-40, take exit #125 and drive north on Lenoir-Rhyne Rd. to Hickory. The road will bear right and change name to Highland Ave. Hudson Furniture is a few miles down on the right side of the road.

Ironstone Galleries Factory Outlet

Level 2
Hickory Furniture Mart
U. S. Hwy. 70 SE
Hickory, NC 28602

Phone:	**(828) 304-1094**	**Hours:**	**M-Sat 9:00-6:00**
Toll Free:	**None**	**E-mail:**	**ironstone@ironstonegalleries.com**
Fax:	**(828) 261-0995**	**Web site:**	**www.ironstonegalleries.com**

This is the main factory outlet for Ironstone Galleries, a manufacturer of stone, metal, and glass furniture. They have very nice quality and a unique contemporary look. They have an extensive product catalog available on their new Web site, above. Their stock consists mostly of dining room sets, dinettes, bakers racks, barstools, beds, and occasional tables.

The normal discount on new special-order furniture is about 40% off retail. There are also some floor samples and discontinued styles in stock for about 50% off retail.

For example, on a recent visit here, I found a very nice leather-topped table with 4 chairs (pictured on the following page) that normally retails for $4,956.00 on sale for $2,691.00. I was able to further haggle the sales-woman down to $2,500.00 even on this set, a discount of just over 50% off retail.

I've found that they often have pieces very similar to those from better known lines, but at a much better price. For instance, recently two of my shopping tour members found a coffee table and end tables they liked at the Thomasville showroom at the Hickory Furniture Mart. I was able to show them tables from Ironstone Galleries that were almost identical, but only half of Thomasville's lowest discounted price. Again, sometimes with the heavily advertised national brands, you are to some extent paying for the name.

If you're in the Hickory area and you're looking for contemporary furniture, this is a source you should check out. Their quality is excellent, and their prices are quite good for what you get.

If you're considering ordering stone, metal, and glass furniture from another brand, go to Ironstone Galleries' Web site first and check their catalog. You may well find a similar style at a much better price.

Phone orders accepted:	**Yes**
Discount:	**40%-50% off mfrs. suggested retail**
Payment methods:	**VISA, MC, personal checks**
In-house financing available:	**No**
Deposits required:	**50% deposit when order is placed, balance due when furniture is ready to be shipped**
Catalog available:	**Yes, at their Web site**
Clearance center:	**Not applicable**
Delivery:	**Full service in-home delivery and set-up. Customer pays freight company directly for shipping costs.**

Directions: Please see *Hickory Furniture Mart* for complete directions.

Ironstone Galleries Factory Outlet (cont.)

Leather-topped table and chairs from Ironstone Galleries

Retail: $4,956.00   Discounted price: $2,500.00
Savings at the Ironstone Galleries Factory Outlet: $2,456.00 = 50% off retail

Jones Brothers Furniture

1324 N. Bright Leaf Blvd.
Smithfield, NC 27577

Phone:	**(919) 934-4162**	**Hours:**	**Mon & Fri 9:00-9:00**
Toll Free:	**None**		**Tues, Wed, Thurs, Sat 9:00-5:00**
Fax:	**(919) 989-7500**	**E-mail:**	**sales@jonesbrothersfurniture.com**
		Web site:	**www.jonesbrothersfurniture.com**

Jones Brothers Furniture is located in Smithfield, NC, just west of Raleigh, NC. They have a good selection of medium to high-end lines, including Lexington, Wellington Hall, Hekman, and Hooker.

They don't have a clearance center or any floor samples or discontinued pieces on display. For this reason, there is no monetary advantage to visiting in person. They do have great deals on many lines sold over the phone, though. They also have a good reputation for customer service.

Lines carried:

Action By Lane	Craftique	Lane	Sealy
American Drew	Emerson Et Cie	Lane/Venture	Sligh
Ardley Hall	Fairfield Chair	Leisters	Southhampton
Artistica	Fauld	Lexington	Stanley
Athol	Frederick Cooper Lamps	Lloyd Buxton	Stiffel Lamps
Bernhardt	French Heritage	Madison Square	Sumter Cabinet
Bob Timberlake	Hammary	Maitland-Smith	Superior
Bradington Young	Hancock & Moore	McKinley Leather	Taylor King
Bristol House	Hekman	Michael Thomas	Tradition House
Broyhill	Henkel-Harris	Miles Talbot	Universal
C. R. Laine	Henkel-Moore	Nichols and Stone	Vaughan Bassett
Carlton McLendon	Henry Link	Parker Southern	Venture By Lane
Carolina's Choice	Hickory Chair	Pulaski	Virginia House
Charleston Forge	Hooker	Richardson Brothers	Waterford
Classic Rattan	Jasper	Riverside	Wellington Hall
Cochrane	Jessica Charles	Salem Square	Woodmark
Colonial	John Richard	Saloom	Wright Table
Cox	La Barge	Sarried	

Phone orders accepted:	**Yes**
Discount:	**35%-50% off mfrs. suggested retail**
Payment methods:	**Personal checks. No credit cards.**
In-house financing available:	**No**
Deposits required:	**35% deposit when order is placed, balance due when furniture is ready to be shipped**
Catalog available:	**No**
Clearance center:	**No**
Delivery:	**Full service in-home delivery and set-up. Customer pays freight company directly for shipping costs.**

Directions: From I-95, take exit #97, and go west on Hwy. 70. Turn left on Hwy. 301. Jones Brothers is one-half mile down on the left side of the road.

K-Town Furniture Outlet

Cannon Village
136 Oak Avenue
Kannapolis, NC 28081

Phone:	**(704) 932-3111**	**Hours:**	**M-F 9:00-7:00, Sat 9:00-6:00,**
Toll Free:	**None**		**Sun 1:30-5:30**
Fax:	**(704) 932-3540**	**E-mail:**	**info@cannonvillage.com**
		Web site: www.cannonvillage.com	

K-Town Furniture Outlet is a reputable deep discounter at Cannon Village in Kannapolis. It's owned and operated by the same people who own and operate Village Furniture House and Carolina Interiors in Cannon Village. Please see Carolina Interiors for a full listing of lines available through this company. Their discounts run about 25%-60% off retail.

They've got a good variety of lines, including a few lines of appliances and televisions. Shoppers who visit in person will also find some very good deals on market samples from time to time, particularly during May and November after the High Point wholesale furniture market ends.

For example, on a recent visit, I found a great deal on a market sample leather chair (pictured on the following page). This chair retails for $1,250.00, but you could get this sample in first-quality condition for $699.00, a discount of 45% off retail. You can special order the identical chair through K-Town for $949.00, a discount of 25% off retail.

They do have good deals on many lines here, and I've found the staff very accommodating. If you plan to order furniture by phone, do give them a call to compare prices.

Lines carried:	**Please see *Carolina Interiors* for a full listing of the lines available through this company.**
Phone orders accepted:	Yes
Discount:	**25%-60% off mfrs. suggested retail**
Payment methods:	**Personal checks. No credit cards.**
In-house financing available:	No
Deposits required:	**1/3 deposit when order is placed, balance due when furniture is ready to be shipped**
Catalog available:	No
Clearance center:	No
Delivery:	**Full service in-home delivery and set-up. Customer pays freight company directly for shipping costs.**

Directions: From I-85, take exit #63, and follow the signs to Cannon Village.

K-Town Furniture Outlet (cont.)

Leather chair at K-Town Furniture Outlet

Retail: $1,250.00   Discounted price: $699.00
Savings at the K-Town Furniture Outlet: $551.00 = 45% off retail

Kagan's American Drew

The Atrium
430 S. Main St.
High Point, NC 27260

Phone:	**(336) 885-8568**	**Hours:**	**M-F 9:00-6:00, Sat 9:00-5:00**
Toll Free:	**None**	**E-mail:**	**info@kaganfurniture.com**
Fax:	**(336) 885-8566**	**Web site:**	**www.kaganfurniture.com**

Prices at Kagan's American Drew gallery at the Atrium Furniture Mall in High Point run 40%-50% off retail. All of the furniture here is new and first-quality.

Kagan's has a clearance center in their National Home Furnishings Center showroom on the south side of High Point where they liquidate their floor samples and discontinued styles.

If you're thinking of ordering any of the lines below by phone, call this source to compare prices.

Lines carried:

American Drew
Canal Dover
Cherry Grove

Phone orders accepted:	**Yes**
Discount:	**30%-50% off mfrs. suggested retail**
Payment methods:	**Personal checks. No credit cards.**
In-house financing available:	**No**
Deposits required:	**50% deposit when order is placed, balance due when furniture is ready to be shipped**
Catalog available:	**No**
Clearance center:	**Yes - See *Kagan's Furniture Galleries***
Delivery:	**Full service in-home delivery and set-up. Customer pays freight company directly for shipping costs.**

Directions: Kagan's American Drew is located inside the Atrium complex in downtown High Point. Please see *The Atrium* for complete directions.

Kagan's Furniture Galleries

1628 S. Main St.
High Point, NC 27261

Phone:	(336) 883-7113	**Hours:**	M-Sat 9:00-6:00
Toll Free:	None	**E-mail:**	info@kaganfurniture.com
Fax:	None	**Web site:**	www.kaganfurniture.com

Kagan's Furniture Galleries is the main occupant of the National Home Furnishings Center on the south side of High Point. Their discounts on new furniture run 40%-50% off retail.

They have a small clearance center in the front corner of the store, but it doesn't have much stock. If your shopping time is limited, you may want to spend your time visiting the many factory outlets and clearance centers in the area that have much more to choose from.

If you plan to order by phone, do call them to compare prices.

Lines carried:

A-America	Carsons of High Point	Laurier	Robin Bruce
Aico	Catnapper	Lea	Rowe
American Drew	Crawford	Magnussen	Samuel Lawrence
Artmax	D & W Silks	Master Design	Schnadig
Ashley	Dall Agnese	McKay Table Pads	Sealy Mattress
Barn Door	Distinctive Designs	Millennium	Signature Rugs
Bassett Mirror Co.	Excelsior	Muniz Acrylic Furniture	Sitza Leather
Bassett	Fairmont Designs	Ohio Table Pads	Spring Air Mattress
Bauhaus USA	Heather Brooke	Orleans	Steinworld
Benchcraft	High Point Furniture	Overnight Sofas	Sunrise Furniture
Broyhill	Howard Miller	RiversEdge	Union City Imports
Cambridge Chair	Jami L. Designs	Riverside	Vaughn Furniture
Canal Dover	Johnston Casuals	Peoplelounger	Vineyard Furniture
Carlisle Lighting	Kingsley	Primo Designs	Webb
Carlton-McLendon	Lane	Relax-R-Motion	Winner's Only

Phone orders accepted:	No
Discount:	30%-50% off mfrs. suggested retail
Payment methods:	Personal checks. No credit cards.
In-house financing available:	No
Deposits required:	Not applicable
Catalog available:	Not applicable
Clearance center:	Not applicable
Delivery:	Full service in-home delivery and set-up. Customer pays freight company directly for shipping costs.

Directions: From I-85, take exit #111 (Hwy. 311), and head northwest into High Point. After several miles, when you reach downtown High Point, Hwy. 311 will become S. Main St. Kagan's is on the left side of Main St.

Kagan's Gallery

Jennie

The Atrium
430 S. Main St.
High Point, NC 27260

914.
110.00

Phone:	**(336) 885-8300**	**Hours:**	**M-F 9:00-6:00, Sat 9:00-5:00**
Toll Free:	**None**	**E-mail:**	**info@kaganfurniture.com**
Fax:	**(336) 885-8307**	**Web site:**	**www.kaganfurniture.com**

Prices at Kagan's American Drew gallery at the Atrium Furniture Mall in High Point run 40%-50% off retail. All of the furniture here is new and first-quality.

Kagan's has a clearance center in their National Home Furnishings Center showroom on the south side of High Point where they liquidate their floor samples and discontinued styles.

If you're thinking of ordering any of the lines below by phone, call this source to compare prices.

Lines carried:

A-America	Carsons of High Point	Laurier	Robin Bruce
Aico	Catnapper	Lea	Rowe
American Drew	Crawford	Magnussen	Samuel Lawrence
Artmax	D & W Silks	Master Design	Schnadig
Ashley	Dall Agnese	McKay Table Pads	Sealy Mattress
Barn Door	Distinctive Designs	Millennium	Signature Rugs
Bassett Mirror Co.	Excelsior	Muniz Acrylic Furniture	Sitza Leather
Bassett	Fairmont Designs	Ohio Table Pads	Spring Air Mattress
Bauhaus USA	Heather Brooke	Orleans	Steinworld
Benchcraft	High Point Furniture	Overnight Sofas	Sunrise Furniture
Broyhill	Howard Miller	RiversEdge	Union City Imports
Cambridge Chair	Jami L. Designs	Riverside	Vaughn Furniture
Canal Dover	Johnston Casuals	Peoplelounger	Vineyard Furniture
Carlisle Lighting	Kingsley	Primo Designs	Webb
Carlton-McLendon	Lane	Relax-R-Motion	Winner's Only

Phone orders accepted:	**Yes**
Discount:	**30%-50% off mfrs. suggested retail**
Payment methods:	**Personal checks. No credit cards.**
In-house financing available:	**No**
Deposits required:	**50% deposit when order is placed, balance due when furniture is ready to be shipped**
Catalog available:	**No**
Clearance center:	**Yes - See *Kagan's Furniture Galleries***
Delivery:	**Full service in-home delivery and set-up. Customer pays freight company directly for shipping costs.**

Directions: Kagan's Gallery is located inside the Atrium complex in downtown High Point. Please see *The Atrium* for complete directions.

Kathy Ireland Home Collection

Catawba Furniture Mall
377 Hwy. 70 SW
Hickory, NC 28602

Phone:	**(828) 327-2363**	**Hours:**	**M-Sat 9:00-7:00**
Toll Free:	**None**	**E-mail:**	**info@catawbafurniture.com**
Fax:	**(828) 327-4036**	**Web site:**	**www.catawbafurniture.com**

The Kathy Ireland Home Collection showroom in the Catawba Furniture Mall just opened in January 2004. Discounts run 40-50% off retail. It's owned and operated by Designer's Choice, which operates most of the showrooms in the mall. They have a good reputation for customer service.

All of the furniture at Designer's Choice is special order. If you see something you like, be sure to check upstairs at Designer's Outlet before buying. Designer's Outlet liquidates samples, overstock items, discontinued pieces, and customer returns for Designer's Choice. They have a nice variety of outlet pieces from the lines below at substantially greater savings: 50%-70% off retail. You may well find what you're looking for in stock at the outlet.

Please see the listing in this book for the Catawba Furniture Mall if you are planning a visit here. The Mall offers discounts on hotel rooms and coupons toward your furniture purchase during their big sale weekends four times each year.

Phone orders accepted:	**Yes**
Discount:	**40%-50% off mfrs. suggested retail**
Payment methods:	**VISA, MC, personal checks**
In-house financing available:	**Yes, 90 days same as cash with 25% down pmt.**
Deposits required:	**50% deposit when order is placed; balance due when furniture is ready to be shipped**
Catalog available:	**No**
Clearance center:	**No**
Delivery:	**Full service in-home delivery and set-up. Customer pays freight company directly for shipping costs.**

Directions: **The Catawba Furniture Mall is in Hickory, NC. From I-40, take exit #123-B and turn right. The mall will be about half a mile down on your right.**

Kincaid Factory Outlet

Manufacturer-Owned Factory Outlets
4916 Hickory Blvd
Hickory, NC 28601

Phone:	**(828) 496-2262**	**Hours:**	**M-Sat 9:00-6:00**
Toll Free:	**None**	**E-mail:**	**None**
Fax:	**(828) 496-2386**	**Web site:**	**None**

This is Kincaid's only true factory outlet, in the Manufacturer-Owned Factory Outlets at Lenoir Mall, just north of Hickory, NC. This outlet is considerably larger than Kincaid's former factory outlet in Lenoir. It has a very nice selection of case goods and upholstery.

This outlet also serves as a factory outlet for La-Z-Boy, which owns Kincaid Furniture, so there an area toward the back with La-Z-Boy recliners.

There are virtually no seconds here. Most of the items in stock are floor samples from the bi-annual wholesale furniture markets in High Point and discontinued styles.

On a recent visit here, I found a great deal on a cherry china cabinet from Kincaid (pictured on the following page). This piece normally retails for $3,068.00, but the outlet had this overstock piece for only $1,250.00. There were no flaws of any kind.

If you're in the Hickory area, and you're looking for medium-quality furniture, you may wish to visit this outlet.

Phone orders accepted:	**No**
Discount:	**50%-75% off mfrs. suggested retail**
Payment methods:	**VISA, MC, personal checks**
In-house financing available:	**No**
Deposits required:	**Not applicable**
Catalog available:	**Not applicable**
Clearance center:	**Not applicable**
Delivery:	**Full service in-home delivery and set-up. Customer pays freight company directly for shipping costs.**

Directions: From I-40, take exit #123 (Hwy. 321) and head north through Hickory. The outlet will be on the right, approximately 6 miles north of I-40.

Kincaid Factory Outlet (cont.)

Solid cherry china cabinet from Kincaid

Retail: $3,068.00   Discounted price: $1,250.00
Savings at the Kincaid Factory Outlet: $1,818.00 = 59% off retail

Klaussner Home

Catawba Furniture Mall
377 Hwy. 70 SW
Hickory, NC 28602

Phone:	**(828) 327-0501**		**Hours:**	**M-Sat 9:00-7:00**
Toll Free:	**None**		**E-mail:**	**info@catawbafurniture.com**
Fax:	**(828) 327-4036**		**Web site:**	**www.catawbafurniture.com**

The Klaussner Home showroom in the Catawba Furniture Mall is owned and operated by Designer's Choice, which operates most of the showrooms in the mall. They have a good reputation for customer service. Discounts run 40-50% off retail.

All of the furniture at Designer's Choice is special order. If you see something you like, be sure to check upstairs at Designer's Outlet before buying. Designer's Outlet liquidates samples, overstock items, discontinued pieces, and customer returns for Designer's Choice. They have a nice variety of outlet pieces from the lines below at substantially greater savings: 50%-70% off retail. You may well find what you're looking for in stock at the outlet.

Please see the listing in this book for the Catawba Furniture Mall if you are planning a visit here. The Mall offers discounts on hotel rooms and coupons toward your furniture purchase during their big sale weekends four times each year.

Phone orders accepted:	**Yes**
Discount:	**40%-50% off mfrs. suggested retail**
Payment methods:	**VISA, MC, personal checks**
In-house financing available:	**Yes, 90 days same as cash with 25% down pmt.**
Deposits required:	**50% deposit when order is placed, balance due when furniture is ready to be shipped**
Catalog available:	**No**
Clearance center:	**No**
Delivery:	**Full service in-home delivery and set-up. Customer pays freight company directly for shipping costs.**

Directions:	**The Catawba Furniture Mall is in Hickory, NC. From I-40, take exit #123-B and turn right. The mall will be about half a mile down on your right.**

Knight Galleries Inc.

835 Creekway Dr. NW
Lenoir, NC 28645

Phone:	(828) 758-8422		**Hours:**	M-F 9:00-5:00
Toll Free:	(800) 334-4721		**E-mail:**	knightgalleries@charter.net
Fax:	(828) 754-1592		**Web site:**	www.knightgalleriesinc.com

Knight Galleries is located in Lenoir, just a few miles north of Hickory, NC. They have a fairly small store with a few pieces of furniture from Lexington and Stanley. Most of their business is done by phone.

They don't have a clearance center or any floor samples or discontinued pieces on display. For this reason, there is no monetary advantage to visiting in person. They do have good deals on many lines sold over the phone, though. So, if you're planning to order your furniture by phone, definitely give this source a call to compare their prices.

Lines carried:

Action By Lane	Dixie	Lea	Serta Mattress
American Drew	Fairfield Chair	Lexington	Southern Reproductions
American Of Martinsville	Flexsteel	Link Taylor	Stanley
Barcalounger	Hammary	Lyon Shaw	Stanton Cooper
Bassett	Hekman	Mobel	Stratford
Blacksmith Shop	Henry Link	Nathan Hale	Stratolounger
Broyhill	Hickory Tavern	National Mt. Airy	Swan Brass Beds
C & M Furniture	Hickory White	Nichols & Stone	Tell City Chair
C. R. Laine	Highland House	Null Industries	Temple
Clark Casual	Hooker	Ohio Table Pad Co.	Universal
Clayton Marcus	Jasper	Pearson	Venture By Lane
Cochrane	Keller	Peoplelounger	Virginia House
Corsican Beds	King Hickory	Pulaski	Young Hinkle
Craftique	Lane	Richardson Brothers	
Crawford	Lane/Venture	Riverside	

Phone orders accepted:	Yes
Discount:	40%-50% off mfrs. suggested retail
Payment methods:	VISA, MC, personal checks
In-house financing available:	No
Deposits required:	1/3 deposit when order is placed, balance due when furniture is ready to be shipped
Catalog available:	No
Clearance center:	No
Delivery:	Full service in-home delivery and set-up. Customer pays freight company directly for shipping costs.

Directions: From I-40, take exit #123 and drive north on Hwy. 321 to Lenoir. Turn left on 321A South, and go 1 mile to the first traffic light. Then, turn right on Creekway Dr. Knight Galleries is immediately on the right.

Lake Hickory Furniture

4360 Hickory Blvd.
Granite Falls, NC 28630

Phone:	**(828) 396-2194**	**Hours:**	**M-Sat 9:00-5:00**
Toll Free:	**None**	**E-mail:**	**None**
Fax:	**(828) 396-1226**	**Web site:**	**None**

Lake Hickory Furniture is located just a few miles north of Hickory, NC. They have a good selection of medium to high-end lines, including Lexington, Lane, Universal, and Stanley.

They don't have a clearance center, and they have very few floor samples or discontinued pieces on display. There really isn't much reason to go by this store in person. They do have good deals on many lines sold over the phone, though. So, if you're planning to order your furniture by phone, give this source a call to compare their prices.

Lines carried:

American Drew	Crawford	Lexington	Southern Reproductions
American Of Martinsville	Distinction Leather	Marlow	Stanley
Benicia Brass Beds	Habersham Plantation	Mobel	Superior
Bob Timberlake	Hammary	Null Industries	Tell City Chair
Borkholder	Hitchcock Chair	Old Salem	Timeless Bedding
Brady Furniture	Hooker	Peters Revington	Two Day Designs
Brown Street	Huntington House	Phillips Leather	Universal
Cambridge Glider Rockers	Jasper	Pulaski	Virginia House
Chatham County	Johnston Casuals	Richardson Brothers	Wisconsin Furniture
Conover Chair	Key City.	Simply Southern	
County Seat	Lane	Sleepworks	

Phone orders accepted:	**Yes**
Discount:	**35%-50% off mfrs. suggested retail**
Payment methods:	**VISA, MC, personal checks**
In-house financing available:	**No**
Deposits required:	**50% deposit when order is placed, balance due when furniture is ready to be shipped**
Catalog available:	**No**
Clearance center:	**No**
Delivery:	**Full service in-home delivery and set-up. Customer pays freight company directly for shipping costs.**

Directions: **From I-40, take exit #123 and drive north on Hwy. 321 to Granite Falls. Lake Hickory Furniture is on the right side of the road.**

Lane Factory Outlet

107 East Church Street
Martinsville, VA 24112

Phone:	**(276) 632-2575**	**Hours:**	**M-Sat 10:00-6:00**
Toll Free:	**None**	**E-mail:**	**lane.furniture.outlet@fm-a.com**
Fax:	**(276) 632-2575**	**Web site:**	**www.fm-a.com**

The Lane Factory Outlet in Martinsville, VA adjoins the Hooker Furniture Factory Outlet and is operated by the same staff. It's about an hour's drive north of High Point. This is now the only Lane Factory Outlet since the one in Raleigh closed.

The majority of the stock at this outlet is new and in first-quality condition. Most pieces are 65% off retail. The staff is great to work with, and all the outlets in downtown Martinsville have a great reputation for service.

Unlike most factory outlets, this one will take phone orders. If there is a certain item you want from Lane, just call the outlet to see if they have one in stock. If they do, they'll be happy to take your order over the phone and ship it.

Unfortunately, there aren't many Lane pieces here to choose from. On my last visit, they had about 3 dozen pieces total. The Lane factory nearby has recently closed, so they are receiving much less outlet stock from the factory. However, the company which owns this outlet also sells a lot of Lane products by special order, so they do expect to be able to keep a small supply of Lane product in this outlet from their floor samples and discontinued items.

If you plan to visit High Point, you may wish to take a day to drive to the Martinsville, VA area, which has outlets for Hooker, Lane, Stanley, and Bassett, as well as a great clearance center (Martin Plaza). The bargains here are well worth the extra travel time.

Phone orders accepted:	Yes
Discount:	**65% off mfrs. suggested retail**
Payment methods:	**VISA, MC, AMEX, Discover, personal checks**
In-house financing available:	**No**
Deposits required:	**Not applicable**
Catalog available:	**Not applicable**
Clearance center:	**Not applicable**
Delivery:	**Full service in-home delivery and set-up. Customer pays freight company directly for shipping costs.**

Directions: From I-40 in Greensboro, NC, take the Hwy. 68/Airport exit (#210), and head north on Hwy. 68. After about 30 minutes, turn onto Hwy. 220 toward Martinsville/Roanoke. After about another 20 minutes, you'll enter Martinsville. Be sure to stay on Business 220 through town, not on the 220 bypass which goes around Martinsville. About 10 miles after you get on Business 220, you'll come to Broad St. There's a green "John Deere" dealership sign on the corner. Broad St. will dead end into Church St. The Lane Factory Outlet will be directly in front of you.

La-Z-Boy Factory Outlet

Manufacturer-Owned Factory Outlets
4916 Hickory Blvd
Hickory, NC 28601

Phone:	**(828) 496-2262**	**Hours:**	**M-Sat 9:00-6:00**
Toll Free:	**None**	**E-mail:**	**None**
Fax:	**(828) 496-2386**	**Web site:**	**None**

This is La-Z-boy's only true factory outlet. It's located in the Manufacturer-Owned Factory Outlets in Lenoir Mall, just north of Hickory, NC. It occupies a back corner of the Kincaid Factory Outlet, which is also owned by La-Z-Boy.

Unfortunately, there isn't much of a selection here. On my last visit, there were only a few dozen chairs to choose from, and no sofas in stock. If you do find the chair you're looking for here, you'll definitely get a great bargain.

Phone orders accepted:	**No**
Discount:	**50%-75% off mfrs. suggested retail**
Payment methods:	**VISA, MC, personal checks**
In-house financing available:	**No**
Deposits required:	**Not applicable**
Catalog available:	**Not applicable**
Clearance center:	**Not applicable**
Delivery:	**Full service in-home delivery and set-up. Customer pays freight company directly for shipping costs.**

Directions: From I-40, take exit #123 (Hwy. 321) and head north through Hickory. The outlet will be on the right, approximately 6 miles north of I-40.

Leather & More

Atrium Furniture Mall
430 S. Main St.
High Point, NC 27260

Phone:	(336) 882-3042	**Hours:**	M-F 9:00-6:00, Sat 9:00-5:00
Toll Free:	None	**E-mail:**	None
Fax:	(336) 882-3043	**Web site:**	www.leatherandmoreinhighpoint.com

   Leather & More just opened in 2003 at the Atrium Furniture Mall in High Point. Their staff is very helpful, and their prices are good. They specialize in high quality leather. There's an extensive product catalog at their Web site.

   Pricing here runs about 25% off retail. Occasionally, they have market samples in stock at bigger discounts, especially during May and November.

   You may find more competitive pricing on special orders elsewhere. As always, call around to compare prices.

Lines carried:

Collezione Divani
Legacy International
Omnia Leather

Phone orders accepted:	Yes
Discount:	25% off mfrs. suggested retail
Payment methods:	VISA, MC, personal checks
In-house financing available:	No
Deposits required:	50% deposit when order is placed, balance due when furniture is ready to be shipped
Catalog available:	Yes, at their Web site
Clearance center:	No
Delivery:	Full service in-home delivery and set-up. Customer pays freight company directly for shipping costs.

Directions: Please see *The Atrium* for complete directions.

LeatherLand USA

Atrium Furniture Mall
430 S. Main St.
High Point, NC 27260

Phone:	**(336) 454-2215**	**Hours:**	**M-F 9:00-6:00, Sat 9:00-5:00**
Toll Free:	**None**	**E-mail:**	**Leatherland@northstate.net**
Fax:	**(336) 454-6983**	**Web site:**	**www.leatherlandusa.com**

LeatherLand Furniture opened at the Atrium Furniture Mall in 2003. They have a good selection of medium quality traditional and transitional furniture. Their discounts run 40%-50% off retail.

Their Web site shows a wide range of their styles. Definitely compare prices with them before ordering leather.

Lines carried:

Ashley Leather
Elite
El Ran Motion
Lafer
Leather Land
Leather Mart
Legacy Leather
Millenium Leather

Phone orders accepted:	**Yes**
Discount:	**40%-50% off mfrs. suggested retail**
Payment methods:	**VISA, MC, AMEX, Discover, personal checks**
In-house financing available:	**Yes**
Deposits required:	**50% deposit when order is placed, balance due when furniture is ready to be shipped**
Catalog available:	**Yes, online**
Clearance center:	**No**
Delivery:	**Full service in-home delivery and set-up. Customer pays freight company directly for shipping costs.**

Directions: Please see *The Atrium* for complete directions.

LeatherTrend Factory Outlet

Level 4
Hickory Furniture Mart
U. S. Hwy. 70 SE
Hickory, NC 28602

Phone:	**(828) 327-0244**	**Hours:**	**M-Sat 9:00-6:00**
Toll Free:	**None**	**E-mail:**	**moutlet@charterinternet.com**
Fax:	**(828) 327-4544**	**Web site:**	**www.hickoryfurniture.com**

The LeatherTrend factory outlet is part of Manufacturer's Outlet, a very reputable company with a long-standing reputation for service. Manufacturer's Outlet also operates the factory outlets for Hickory White and Theodore Alexander at the Hickory Furniture Mart.

The stock is made up of floor samples, discontinued styles, and customer returns. All of the furniture here is upholstery: sofas and occasional chairs. The discounts run from 50%-70% off retail. Virtually all of the furniture here is in new first-quality condition.

This factory outlet also features Simex, Clayton-Marcus, SofaTrend, and Mirador. In addition to furniture, they also have a line of European oil paintings at good prices and some Asian antique pieces.

They also participate in the regular mall-wide sales run by the Hickory Furniture Mart in February, May, July, and November. Please check out Web site at www.smartdecorating.com for upcoming sale dates.

Phone orders accepted:	**No**
Discount:	**50%-70% off mfrs. suggested retail**
Payment methods:	**VISA, MC, personal checks**
In-house financing available:	**Yes**
Deposits required:	**Not applicable**
Catalog available:	**Not applicable**
Clearance center:	**Not applicable**
Delivery:	**Full service in-home delivery and set-up. Customer pays freight company directly for shipping costs.**

Directions: Please see *Hickory Furniture Mart* for complete directions.

Lindy's Furniture Co.

Hwy. 70
Connelly Springs, NC 28612

Phone:	**(828) 879-3000**	**Hours:**	**Mon, Tues, Thurs, & Fri 9:00-5:00**
Toll Free:	**None**		**Sat 9:00-3:00**
Fax:	**(828) 874-1600**	**E-mail:**	**lindys@charter.net**
		Web site:	**www.lindysfurniture.com**

Lindy's Furniture Co. takes Southern style <u>very</u> seriously. The store, perched high on a hill in the tiny town of Connelly Springs, looks a lot like "Tara" from *Gone With the Wind*. Thankfully, this makes it very easy to spot going down the road.

They've been discounting furniture for over 83 years. This store has an excellent reputation for customer service. It's owned by the same family that owns and operates Hudson Discount Furniture and Better Homes Discount Furniture. They are very reputable and pleasant to work with.

The store is huge. In addition to the four-story main building, there are 6 interconnected warehouses behind it filled with wall-to-wall furniture. The staff estimates that it takes one and a half hours to tour the entire facility straight through.

They do occasionally have floor samples, seconds, and market samples available for sale below wholesale prices. They will also sell any item off the floor, which can help you avoid shipping delays. Their special order prices are among the best.

They carry hundreds of lines, far more than their published list on the following page. They also promise to meet or beat any competitor's written price quote, so hold them to it! Any customer who plans to order their furniture over the phone would do well to call this source and compare their prices.

Phone orders accepted:	**Yes**
Discount:	**Up to 70% off mfrs. suggested retail**
Payment methods:	**VISA, MC, personal checks**
In-house financing available:	**Yes, 90 days no interest**
Deposits required:	**25% deposit when order is placed, balance due when furniture is ready to be shipped**
Catalog available:	**No**
Clearance center:	**No**
Delivery:	**Full service in-home delivery and set-up. Customer pays freight company directly for shipping costs.**

Directions: From I-40, take exit #113, and go south on Connelly Springs Rd. At the first stop sign, turn left. Go about 3 miles until you reach Hwy. 70. Turn right on Hwy. 70. Lindy's is about one mile down on the right side of the road. It's the large building at the top of the hill that looks like "Tara" from *Gone With the Wind*.

Lindy's Furniture Co. (cont.)

Lindy's Furniture Co.

Lines carried:

Aico	Hickory Hill	Sam Moore
American Drew	Hooker	Schnadig
Barn Door	Howard Miller	Shamrock
Bassett Mirror Company	Jackson Furniture	South Sea Rattan
Benchcraft	Jami L. Designs	Standard
Berkline	Keller	Stoneville
Bermex	Kimball	Stylecraft Lamps
Best Chair	King Hickory	Sumter Cabinet
Broyhill	Kingsdown	Universal
Bruards	Kroehler	Vaughan
Casapelle Leather	La-Z-Boy	Vaughan Bassett
Chromcraft	Lea	Webb
Clayton Marcus	Legacy Classics	Winners Only
Cochrane	Liberty	
Craftique	Ligo	
Davis Int'l	Magnussen Presidential	
DMI	Morgan Stewart	
England Corsair	Ohio Table Pad	
Fairfield	Platinum	
Fashion Bed	Pulaski	
Flexsteel	Relax-R	
Hammary	Richardson Bros.	
Harbor Home	Riverside	
Hekman	Rowe	

Loftin Black Furniture Co.

111 Sedgehill Dr.
Thomasville, NC 27360

Phone:	**(336) 472-6117**	**Hours:**	**M-Sat 8:00-5:30**
Toll Free:	**(800) 334-7398**	**E-mail:**	**None**
Fax:	**(336) 472-2052**	**Web site:**	**www.ncnet.com/ncnw/tho-loft.html**

Loftin-Black Furniture Co. has a good selection of medium to high-end lines: Hooker, Lexington, Universal, Stanley, etc. Their discounts run about 35%-50% off retail on new first-quality furniture.

They have very few discontinued pieces and floor samples available, and these are only discounted about 30%, which is far less than the discounts offered on comparable furniture by other discounters and factory outlets.

Unfortunately, Loftin-Black has also been accumulating complaints at the BBB, including at least one that is unresolved. Until these unresolved complaints have been taken care of, I recommend my readers shop elsewhere.

Phone orders accepted:	**Yes**
Discount:	**35%-50% off mfrs. suggested retail**
Payment methods:	**VISA, MC, Discover, personal checks**
In-house financing available:	**No**
Deposits required:	**50% deposit when order is placed, balance due when furniture is ready to be shipped**
Catalog available:	**No**
Clearance center:	**No**
Delivery:	**Full service in-home delivery and set-up. Customer pays freight company directly for shipping costs.**

Directions: From I-85, take exit #103 (Hwy. 109). Turn left on Sedgehill Dr. You'll see a Shoney's on the corner. Loftin-Black is right behind Shoney's.

The Lounge Shop

2222 E. Patterson St.
Greensboro, NC 27410

Phone:	(336) 852-3088	**Hours:**	M-F 10:00-6:00, Sat 10:00-4:00
Toll Free:	None	**E-mail:**	None
Fax:	None	**Web site:**	None

The Lounge Shop doesn't publish a list of the lines they can special order, but they have access to about 250 brands, including most popular medium to high-end lines. The discounts on phone orders or in person sales run about 60%-75% off retail. They have particularly good deals on Lexington.

This is a very impressive store. On a recent visit here, I found a great deal on a Henry Link wicker set (pictured on the following page). Normally, the sofa, chair, and two end tables retail for $3,928.00, but the Lounge Shop had this set in stock for $1,848.00, including the cushions.

There's no real monetary advantage to going in person because they will match their store prices on orders placed by phone. However, anyone ordering furniture by phone should definitely compare prices here. I was very impressed with the staff at this store, as well as the service and the discounts.

Phone orders accepted:	Yes
Discount:	60%-75% off mfrs. suggested retail
Payment methods:	Personal checks. No credit cards.
In-house financing available:	No
Deposits required:	50% deposit when order is placed, balance due when furniture is ready to be shipped
Catalog available:	No
Clearance center:	No
Delivery:	Full service in-home delivery and set-up. Customer pays freight company directly for shipping costs.

Directions: From I-85, take the Holden Rd. exit and head north into Greensboro. Then, after a few miles, turn right on Patterson St. The Lounge Shop is a few miles down on the left.

The Lounge Shop (cont.)

The Lounge Shop

Wicker living room set from Henry Link

Retail: $3,928.00   Discounted price: $1,848.00
Savings at The Lounge Shop: $2,080.00 = 53% off retail

Mackie Furniture Co.

13 N. Main St.
Granite Falls, NC 28630

Phone:	**(828) 396-3313**	**Hours:**	**M-Sat 8:30-5:00**
Toll Free:	**None**	**E-mail:**	**info@mackiefurniture.com**
Fax:	**(828) 396-3314**	**Web site:**	**www.mackiefurniture.com**

Mackie Furniture Co. is a very quaint small-town furniture store in tiny Granite Falls, NC. It's been in business since 1916. The store isn't very big, but they do have some nice pieces in stock from medium to high-end lines such as Lexington, Lane, Stanley, and Hooker.

They don't have a clearance center or any floor samples or discontinued pieces on display. For this reason, there is no monetary advantage to visiting in person. They do have good deals on many lines sold over the phone, though. So, if you're planning to order your furniture by phone, give this source a call to compare their prices.

Lines carried:

Action By Lane	Clayton Marcus	Keller	Powell
American Drew	Cochrane	Kincaid	Pulaski
Ashley Furniture	Eddie Bauer	Kingsdown Mattress	Riverside
Bassett	Fairfield Chair	Lane	Telescope
Bob Mackie	Fashion Bed Group	Lea	Timmerman
Broyhill	Heather Brooke	Lloyd/Flanders	Universal
Carolina Mattress	Hooker	McKay Table Pads	Vaughan
Carolina Mirror	Jessica McClintock	Phillip Reinisch	

Phone orders accepted:	**Yes**
Discount:	**35%-50% off mfrs. suggested retail**
Payment methods:	**VISA, MC, personal checks**
In-house financing available:	**No**
Deposits required:	**50% deposit when order is placed, balance due when furniture is ready to be shipped**
Catalog available:	**Yes, limited catalog at Web site**
Clearance center:	**No**
Delivery:	**Full service in-home delivery and set-up. Customer pays freight company directly for shipping costs.**

Directions: **From I-40, take exit #123 and drive north on Hwy. 321 to Granite Falls. Turn left on 321-A North, and go into downtown Granite Falls. 321-A will become Main St. Mackie Furniture is on the left.**

Maitland Smith Factory Outlet

411 Tomlinson St.
High Point, NC 27260

Phone:	**(336) 812-2441**	**Hours:**	**M-F 9:00-5:00**
Toll Free:	**None**	**E-mail:**	**None**
Fax:	**(336) 887-2625**	**Web site:**	**None**

This outlet is amazing. It's huge, adjoining Maitland-Smith's main wholesale showroom in High Point. There are two huge connected warehouses filled with traditional and oriental style furniture and accessories. Maitland Smith is a very, very high-end line, and the furniture here is exceptional. There are also some La Barge occasional tables here.

Most of the furniture in stock is in new first-quality condition. The discounts range from 50%-75% off retail, with most pieces priced about 65% off. There are a few seconds and damaged returns mixed in.

On a recent visit here, I found an amazing deal on a leather-topped game table. This table has an insert that lifts out of the top to display a checkerboard and a backgammon board. The retail on this piece is normally $4,326.00, but this table was only $595.00. It was a slightly damaged piece with two superficial scratches about a centimeter long each.

A local refinisher told me that the scratches would cost no more than $150.00 to invisibly repair. So, you save $3,731.00 off retail and pay back $150.00 to restore it to perfect condition. This the kind of fixer-upper that you should be on the lookout for.

This is an amazing outlet. Anyone visiting the High Point area should make a point of stopping in here.

Phone orders accepted:	**No**
Discount:	**50%-75% off mfrs. suggested retail**
Payment methods:	**Personal checks. No credit cards.**
In-house financing available:	**No**
Deposits required:	**Not applicable**
Catalog available:	**Not applicable**
Clearance center:	**Not applicable**
Delivery:	**Customer must make own arrangements to take furniture home.**

Directions: From I-85, take exit #111 (Hwy. 311), and head northwest into High Point. After several miles, when you reach downtown High Point, Hwy. 311 will become S. Main St. When you reach downtown High Point, turn left on Grimes Ave. After a block, turn left on Tomlinson St. The Maitland Smith Factory Outlet is immediately on the right.

Maitland Smith Factory Outlet (cont.)

Maitland Smith Factory Outlet in High Point, NC

Leather-topped game table from Maitland Smith

Retail: $4,326.00   Discounted price: $595.00
Savings at the Maitland Smith Factory Outlet: $3,731.00 = 86% off retail

Manufacturer's Outlet

Level 4
Hickory Furniture Mart
U. S. Hwy. 70 SE
Hickory, NC 28602

Phone:	**(828) 327-0244**	**Hours:**	**M-Sat 9:00-6:00**
Toll Free:	**None**	**E-mail:**	**moutlet@charterinternet.com**
Fax:	**(828) 327-4544**	**Web site:**	**www.hickoryfurniture.com**

Manufacturer's Outlet at the Hickory Furniture Mart is a very reputable company with a long-standing reputation for service. This showroom houses the factory outlets for Clayton-Marcus, LeatherTrend, SofaTrend, Mirador, and Simex. Manufacturer's Outlet also operates the factory outlets for Hickory White and Theodore Alexander in separate showrooms at the Hickory Furniture Mart.

The stock is made up of floor samples, discontinued styles, and customer returns. All of the furniture here is upholstery: sofas and occasional chairs. The discounts run from 50%-70% off retail. Virtually all of the furniture here is in new first-quality condition.

In addition to furniture, they also have a line of European oil paintings at good prices and some Asian antique pieces.

They also participate in the regular mall-wide sales run by the Hickory Furniture Mart in February, May, July, and November. Please check out Web site at www.smartdecorating.com for upcoming sale dates.

Phone orders accepted:	**No**
Discount:	**50%-70% off mfrs. suggested retail**
Payment methods:	**VISA, MC, personal checks**
In-house financing available:	**Yes**
Deposits required:	**Not applicable**
Catalog available:	**Not applicable**
Clearance center:	**Not applicable**
Delivery:	**Full service in-home delivery and set-up. Customer pays freight company directly for shipping costs.**

Directions: Please see *Hickory Furniture Mart* for complete directions.

Martin Plaza

115 East Church Street
Martinsville, VA 24112

Phone:	**(276) 638-2040**	**Hours:**	**M-Sat 10:00-6:00**
Toll Free:	**None**	**E-mail:**	**showroom@fm-a.com**
Fax:	**(276) 632-2575**	**Web site:**	**http://www.fm-a.com**

Martin Plaza in Martinsville, VA is the clearance center for The Showroom, owned by Fred Martin Associate. FMA also owns and operates the Lane Factory Outlet and the Hooker Furniture Factory Outlet on the same street. They have a great reputation for service, and the staff is very helpful. Martinsville is about an hour's drive north of High Point.

The most of the stock at this outlet are floor samples and discontinued items in very good condition. A few pieces may have slight flaws, but I didn't see any flawed pieces on my last visit. Most pieces are 50%-60% off retail.

They may have pieces from any line sold by The Showroom, but the majority of the stock here is from Klaussner and Century. Please see the listing in this book for *The Showroom* for a complete list of lines which may be carried here.

Unlike most factory outlets and clearance centers, this one will take phone orders. If there is a certain item you want, just call the clearance center to see if they have one in stock.

If you plan to visit High Point, you may wish to take a day to drive to the Martinsville, VA area, which also has outlets for Hooker, Lane, Stanley, and Bassett. The bargains here are well worth the extra travel time.

Phone orders accepted:	**Yes**
Discount:	**50%-60% off mfrs. suggested retail**
Payment methods:	**VISA, MC, AMEX, Discover, personal checks**
In-house financing available:	**No**
Deposits required:	**100% due with order. All items are in stock and ship immediately.**
Catalog available:	**No**
Clearance center:	**No**
Delivery:	**Full service in-home delivery and set-up. Customer pays freight company directly for shipping costs.**

Directions: From I-40 in Greensboro, NC, take the Hwy. 68/Airport exit (#210), and head north on Hwy. 68. After about 30 minutes, turn onto Hwy. 220 toward Martinsville/Roanoke. After about another 20 minutes, you'll enter Martinsville. Be sure to stay on Business 220 through town, not on the 220 bypass which goes around Martinsville. About 10 miles after you get on Business 220, you'll come to Broad St. There's a green "John Deere" dealership sign on the corner. Broad St. will dead end into Church St. You'll see Martin Plaza right across the street to the right.

Mecklenburg Furniture

520 Providence Rd.
Charlotte, NC 28207

Phone:	**(704) 376-8401**	**Hours:**	**M-Sat 9:00-5:30, Thurs 9-8**
Toll Free:	**None**	**E-mail:**	**None**
Fax:	**(704) 347-0499**	**Web site:**	**None**

Mecklenburg Furniture is located in Charlotte, NC, about an hour south of Charlotte. They have a very nice selection of high-end lines, including Lexington, Broyhill, Stanley, and Hooker.

They don't have a clearance center or any floor samples or discontinued pieces on display. For this reason, there is no monetary advantage to visiting in person. They do have great deals on many lines sold over the phone, though. So, if you're planning to order your furniture by phone, definitely give this source a call to compare their prices.

Lines carried:

Accentrics By Pulaski	Bassett Mirror	Carolina Mirror	Clayton Marcus
Action By Lane	Bevan Funnell	Carsons	Colonial
Alexvale	Bigelow Carpet	Carvers Guild	Corsican
American Drew	Blacksmith Shop	Casa Bique	Council-Craftsmen
American Of Martinsville	Boos Co.	Casa Stradivari	Couristan Rugs
Armstrong Vinyl	Borkholder	Century	Courtleigh
Artisan House	Bradington Young	Chapman Lamps	Cowtan & Tout
As You Like It Lamps	Braxton Culler	Charleston Forge	Cox
Austin Sculpture	Brown Street	Chelsea House/Port Royal	Craftique
Baker	Broyhill	Christelle Collection	Craftwork Guild
Baldwin Brass	Brunschwig & Fils	Chromcraft	Crestline
Barcalounger	Buccola	CJC Decorative Pillows	Crystal Clear Lighting
Barlow Tyne	Butler Specialty	Clarence House	CTH Sherrill
Bashian Oriental Rugs	C. R. Laine	Clark Casual	D & F Wicker and Rattan
Bassett	Cal-Style	Classic Rattan	Dansen Contemporary

Phone orders accepted:	**Yes**
Discount:	**30%-70% off mfrs. suggested retail**
Payment methods:	**Personal checks. No credit cards.**
In-house financing available:	**No**
Deposits required:	**1/3 deposit when order is placed, balance due when furniture is ready to be shipped**
Catalog available:	**No**
Clearance center:	**No**
Delivery:	**Full service in-home delivery and set-up. Customer pays freight company directly for shipping costs.**

Directions: From I-77 in Charlotte, take the Providence Rd. exit, and head south-east. Mecklenburg Furniture is a few miles down on the right.

Mecklenburg Furniture (cont.)

Lines carried (cont.):

Dapha
Davis & Davis Rugs
Daystrom
Decorative Crafts
Dillon
Dinaire
Distinction Leather
DMI
Duralee Fabrics
Elan International
Elements By Grapevine
Ello
Emerson Leather
Englander Bedding
Fairfield Chair
Fashion Bed Group
Ficks Reed
Fine Art Lamps
Fitz & Floyd
Flexsteel
Frederick Cooper Lamps
Frederick Edward
Friedman Brothers
Fritz & LaRue Rugs
George Kovacs Lamps
Garcia Imports
Georgian Reproductions
Glass Arts
Great City Traders
Guildmaster
Habersham Plantation
Hammary
Hancock & Moore
Hekman
Helios Carpet
Hen Feathers
Hickory Chair
Hickory Fry
Hickory Hill
Hickory Leather
Highland House
High Point Desk
Hitchcock Chair
Hobe Sound Lamps
Hood
Hooker
House Of France
House Parts
Hyundai Furniture

JSF Industries
Jasper
Johnston Casuals
John Richard Lamps
John Widdicomb
Karges
Kay Lyn
Keller
Kessler
Key City
Kimball
Kinder-Harris
Kincaid
Kingsdown Mattress
Kirk Steiff
Kittinger
La Barge
L & S Imports
Lane
Lane/Venture
Lea
Lees Carpet
Lenox Lamps
Lexington
Lloyd/Flanders
Lyon Shaw
Mannington Vinyl
Madison Square
Maitland Smith
Marbro Lamps
Masland Carpet
Masterlooms Carpet
McGuire
McKay Table Pad Co.
McKinley Leather
Michael Thomas
Michaels Co.
Millender
Millennium
Milliken Carpets
Mirror Fair
Moosehead
Motion Craft
Mottahedeh
Nathan Hale
Nichols & Stone
Norman Perry Lamps
O'Asian
Ohio Table Pad Co.

Old Hickory Tannery
Palazzetti
PAMA
Paoli
Pande Cameron Rugs
Paul Roberts
Payne Fabrics
Pearson
Pennsylvania Classics
Pennsylvania House
Port Royal
Pulaski
Rex
Ridgeway Clocks
Riverside
Robert Allen Fabrics
Rowe
Rustic Crafts
      Fireplaces
Salem Square
Saloom
Sarreid
Scalamandre Fabrics
Schumacher Fabrics
Sedgefield Lamps
SEE Imports
Selig
Shoal Creek Lighting
Shuford
Silvestri
Simply Southern
Sligh Furniture
Southampton
Southern
      Reproductions
Southwood
      Reproductions
Speer Lamps
Stanford
Stanley
Stanton Cooper
Stark Carpet
Statesville Chair
Statton
Stein World
Stiffel Lamps
Stoneleigh
Stroheim and Romann
Swaim Originals

Swan Brass Beds
Taylorsville
Taylor Woodcraft
Thayer Coggin
Thonet
Tianjin Philadelphia
      Carpets
Touch Of Brass
Tropitone
Trosby
Union National
Universal
Vanguard
Venture By Lane
Virginia House
Virginia Metalcrafters
Waterford Furniture
Waterford
      Crystal Lamps
Waverly Fabrics
Weathercraft By Lane
Weiman
Wellington Hall
Wesley Allen
      Brass Beds
Wesley Hall
Westgate Fabrics
Whitecraft Rattan
Wildwood Lamps
Winston
Woodard
Woodmark
Wright Table

Medallion Furniture

Atrium Furniture Mall
430 S. Main St.
High Point, NC 27260

Phone:	**(336) 889-3432**	**Hours:**	**M-F 9:00-6:00, Sat 9:00-5:00**
Toll Free:	**(866) 584-4140**	**E-mail:**	**sales@medallionfurniturestore.com**
Fax:	**(336) 889-3432**	**Web site:**	**www.medallionfurniturestore.com**

Medallion Furniture has been in business for over 10 years with no customer complaints on record. They have a good selection of imported contemporary furniture, mostly from Italy, Canada, and China.

Their discounts run 15%-25% off retail, which isn't as competitive as you'll find from most High Point area discounters. They also sell floor samples at 30%-35% off retail. The quality of the lines they carry is quite good.

If you're at the Atrium, it would certainly be worth checking to see if they have a floor sample you're interested in at a good price. For special orders, you'll be able to do significantly better than a 15%-25% discount on some of the lines at other discounters.

Lines carried:

Cassetti	Fruil	Jesper	Schillig
Catskill Craftsmen	Fruil Cassetti	Kent Upholstery	Sitcom
De Moma	Galerkin	Naos	Sofa Art
Directions	Global Furniture Ind.	Nicholetti	
Ermes Salotti	Hjellagarde	Nord Furniture	
Fine Art Pictures	Jaymar	Northern Comfort	

Phone orders accepted:	**Yes**
Discount:	**15%-25% off mfrs. suggested retail**
Payment methods:	**VISA, MC, AMEX, Discover, personal checks**
In-house financing available:	**Yes**
Deposits required:	**50% deposit when order is placed, balance due when furniture is ready to be shipped**
Catalog available:	**Yes, online**
Clearance center:	**No**
Delivery:	**Full service in-home delivery and set-up. Customer pays freight company directly for shipping costs.**

Directions: Please see *The Atrium* for complete directions.

Mirador Factory Outlet

Level 4
Hickory Furniture Mart
U. S. Hwy. 70 SE
Hickory, NC 28602

Phone:	**(828) 327-0244**	**Hours:**	**M-Sat 9:00-6:00**
Toll Free:	**None**	**E-mail:**	**moutlet@charterinternet.com**
Fax:	**(828) 327-4544**	**Web site:**	**www.hickoryfurniture.com**

The Mirador factory outlet is part of Manufacturer's Outlet, a very reputable company with a long-standing reputation for service. Manufacturer's Outlet also operates the factory outlets for Hickory White and Theodore Alexander at the Hickory Furniture Mart.

The stock is made up of floor samples, discontinued styles, and customer returns. All of the furniture here is upholstery: sofas and occasional chairs. The discounts run from 50%-70% off retail. Virtually all of the furniture here is in new first-quality condition.

This factory outlet also features Simex, Clayton-Marcus, LeatherTrend, and SofaTrend. In addition to furniture, they also have a line of European oil paintings at good prices and some Asian antique pieces.

They also participate in the regular mall-wide sales run by the Hickory Furniture Mart in February, May, July, and November. Please check out Web site at www.smartdecorating.com for upcoming sale dates.

Phone orders accepted:	**No**
Discount:	**50%-70% off mfrs. suggested retail**
Payment methods:	**VISA, MC, personal checks**
In-house financing available:	**Yes**
Deposits required:	**Not applicable**
Catalog available:	**Not applicable**
Clearance center:	**Not applicable**
Delivery:	**Full service in-home delivery and set-up. Customer pays freight company directly for shipping costs.**

Directions: Please see *Hickory Furniture Mart* for complete directions.

Mitchell Gold Factory Outlet

930 Hwy. 70 SW
Hickory, NC 28602

Phone:	**(828) 261-0051**	**Hours:**	**M-Sat 9:00-5:00**
Toll Free:	**None**	**E-mail:**	**None**
Fax:	**(828) 261-0344**	**Web site:**	**None**

This is a true factory outlet for Mitchell Gold upholstery. If you must have furniture with the "Mitchell Gold" name on it, you'll get it for the least outrageous price available here.

However, if you want better quality furniture at lower prices, check just about any other factory outlet within a 10 minute radius of this store. In my experience, this outlet does not offer good value for money.

Phone orders accepted:	**No**
Discount:	**50%-60% off mfrs. suggested retail**
Payment methods:	**VISA, MC, personal checks**
In-house financing available:	**No**
Deposits required:	**Not applicable**
Catalog available:	**Not applicable**
Clearance center:	**Not applicable**
Delivery:	**Full service in-home delivery and set-up. Customer pays freight company directly for shipping costs.**

Directions:	**From I-40, take exit #123 (Hwy. 321), and go north toward Hickory. After a few miles, take the Hwy. 70 exit, and go east. The Furniture Factory Outlet Shoppes is immediately on your left as you exit onto Hwy. 70.**

Murrow Furniture Galleries

3514 S. College Rd.
Wilmington, NC 28406

Phone:	**(910) 799-4010**	**Hours:**	**M-F 8:30-5:30, Sat 9:00-5:30**
Toll Free:	**None**	**E-mail:**	**None**
Fax:	**(910) 791-2791**	**Web site:**	**www.murrowfurniture.com**

Murrow Furniture Galleries has a huge 45,000 square-foot store in Wilmington, NC, near the Atlantic coast. They have a very impressive stock of high-end lines such as Bernhardt, Lexington, Baker, Century, Thomasville, and others. Their discounts generally run from 40%-50% off retail.

They do sell floor samples for immediate shipment. However, they are also about a 3 hour drive from the major furniture factory outlet centers in Hickory and High Point. If your travel time is limited, you may not wish to visit this store in person. You'll find a much larger selection of in-stock furniture at better prices in Hickory and High Point.

However, their prices on furniture sold by phone are quite good, and they have an excellent reputation for customer service. If you plan to order furniture by phone, definitely give this source a call and compare their prices.

Discount:	**40%-50% off mfrs. suggested retail**
Payment methods:	**VISA, MC, personal checks**
In-house financing available:	**No**
Deposits required:	**50% deposit when order is placed, balance due when furniture is ready to be shipped**
Catalog available:	**No**
Clearance center:	**No**
Delivery:	**Full service in-home delivery and set-up. Customer pays freight company directly for shipping costs.**

Directions: **From I-40, take exit #420, and head south on Hwy. 132. After a few miles, Hwy. 132 will change name to S. College Rd. Murrow Furniture Galleries is about 10 miles south of the interstate on the right side of the road.**

Murrow Furniture Galleries (cont.)

Lines carried:

Action By Lane	DSF	Lea	Southwood
Ambiance	Duralee Fabrics	Leathermans Guild	Speer
American Drew	Dutalier	Lexington	Stanley
American Heritage	Ekornes	Lillian August	Statesville Chair
Art de Mexico	Ello	Lloyd Flanders	Statton
Artistica	Elements by Grapevine	Lyon Shaw	Stiffel
Artmark	Emerson Et Cie	McGuire	Stroheim & Romann
Asmara Rugs	Fairfield Chair	McKay Table Pads	Superior
Baker	Fashion Bed Group	Madison Square	Swaim
Baldwin Brass	Ficks Reed	Maitland-Smith	Taylor King
Barcalounger	Fine Arts Lamps	Marbro Lamps	Taylorsville
Bassett Mirror	Frederick Cooper	Maryland Classics	Taylor Woodcraft
Bernhardt	Friedman Bros. Mirrors	Masland Carpet & Rugs	Thayer Coggin
Bevan Funnell	Garcia Imports	Mastercraft	Thomasville
Blacksmith Shop	Georgian Furnishings	Michael Thomas	Tradition House
Bob Timberlake	Glober	Motioncraft	Tropitone
Bradington Young	Glass Arts	Murray Feiss Lamps	Trosby
Brass Beds of Va.	Grace	Natural Light	Universal
Braxton Culler	Greeff Fabrics	Nathan Hale	Vanguard
Broyhill Premier	Guildmaster	Nichols & Stone	Vaughan
Cambridge	Habersham Plantation	Norbar Fabrics	Venture By Lane
Canadel	Hammary	Norman Perry Lamps	Vermont Tubbs
Carolina Mirror	Hancock & Moore	Ohio Table Pad Company	Virginia House
Carson's	Hart Country Shop	Pande Cameron Rugs	Virginia Metalcrafters
Carvers Guild	Hekman	Parker Southern	Waterford Furniture
Casa Bique	Hen Feathers	Paul Hansen Lamps	Waverly
Casa Stradivari	Henry Link	Pennsylvania House	Wedgewood
Century	Hickory Chair	Platt	Wellesley Guild
Charleston Forge	Hickory White	Pulaski	Wellington Hall
Chapman Lamps	Hooker	Reliance Lamp	Wesley Allen Brass
Chelsea House	Howard Miller	Rex	Wesley Hall
Chromcraft	Hyundai	Ridgewood Furniture	Westgate Fabrics
Clark Casual	Jasper Cabinet	Riverside	Whittemore-Sherrill
Classic Leather	Jeffco	Robert Allen Fabrics	Wildwood
Classic Rattan	John Richard Lamps	Royal Patina	William Alan
Colonial Furniture	John Widdicomb	Salem Square	Winston Furniture
Councill Craftsman	Johnston Casuals	Saloom	Woodard
Cooper Classics	J. Royale	Sam Moore	Woodmark
Country Affair/Elden	J.T.B.	Sarreid	Wright Table Co.
Cox	Karges	S. Bent	
Craftique	Keller	Schumacher	
Craftwork Guild	Kimball	Seabrook Wallcovering	
Crawford	Kincaid	Sedgefield Lamps	
Crystal Clear	King Hickory	Serta Mattress	
Clyde Pearson	Koch Originals	Sherrill	
Design South	Koch & Lowy	Shuford	
Decorative Crafts	Kravet Fabrics	Sligh	
Dillon	LaBarge	Southern Furniture	
Distinction Leather	Lane	Southhampton	

National Home Furnishing Center

Level 1
Hickory Furniture Mart
U. S. Hwy. 70 SE
Hickory, NC 28602

Phone:	(828) 324-7110	**Hours:**	**M-Sat 9:00-6:00**
Toll Free:	None	**E-mail:**	**ike@kaganfurniture.com**
Fax:	(828) 324-7116	**Web site:**	**www.kaganfurniture.com**

NHFC is owed by Ike Kagan, of Kagan's Furniture in High Point. Even though this showroom only opened in September 2002, the parent company has been in business for many years and has a good reputation. They have a great selection of contemporary and transitional furniture.

As an example, on a recent visit to the new store, I found a very nice "Cortina" dining room set by Excelsior. NHFC's price on this 8 piece set, including the hutch, was $5,930.00. According to owner Ike Kagan, the identical set retails for $7,500.00 to $8,500.00 nationwide, depending on the city. That's a discount of 20%-30% off the prevailing retail, which is pretty standard for all of Kagan's stores.

There are a few floor samples on display for immediate sale, but the vast majority of sales are special order. Some products are in stock at Kagan's warehouses for immediate shipment, but others must be ordered directly from the manufacturer. They do have a very small clearance center at one of their High Point stores.

If you visit the Hickory Furniture Mart and you're looking for good deals on contemporary furniture, definitely stop in this showroom to check out their selection. Before you buy, though, be sure to check the brand index in the back of this book to compare NHFC/Kagan's discounts to their competitors. Sometimes, this showroom does have the best deal on a given brand, but I have frequently found that some of their competitors offer better deals.

Lines carried:

A-America	Cambridge Chair	Monarch	Robin Bruce
Aico	Carsons of High Point	Montage	Schnadig
Art As Antiques	Dall Agnese	Millennium	Sealy Mattress
Artmax	Excelsior	Orleans	Serta Mattress
Ashley	Fairmont Designs	Palliser	Sigla
BMC	J. Royale	Powell	Signature Rugs
Butler Specialty	Jami L. Designs	Reinisch Curios	Sumer
CMI	McKay Table Pads	Rentwil	Wynwood

Phone orders accepted:	**Yes**
Discount:	**20%-40% off mfrs. suggested retail**
Payment methods:	**Personal checks. No credit cards.**
In-house financing available:	**No**
Deposits required:	**50% deposit when order is placed, balance due when furniture is ready to be shipped**
Catalog available:	**No**
Clearance center:	**Yes - See *Kagan's Furniture Galleries***
Delivery:	**Full service in-home delivery and set-up. Customer pays freight company directly for shipping costs.**

Directions: Please see *Hickory Furniture Mart* for complete directions.

Nostalgia Furniture

5114 Hwy. 182
Columbus, MS 39702

Phone:	**(662) 328-7310**	**Hours:**	**M-Sat 9:00-6:00**
Toll Free:	**None**	**E-mail:**	**info@nostalgiafurniture.com**
Fax:	**None**	**Web site:**	**www.nostalgiafurniture.com**

Nostalgia Furniture has two factory-direct showrooms: this one at their factory in Columbus, MS, and another in the Hickory Furniture Mart. This small family manufacturing business was started by former employees of Kincaid Furniture and several other manufacturers in the Hickory and Tupelo areas.

Nostalgia has chosen to sell directly to consumers through their Web site and showrooms, skipping the retailer altogether. Their prices run about 55%-65% off retail prices charged by other companies for comparable pieces.

Their quality is excellent. They have a wide variety of traditional styles in cherry and mahogany. They manufacture case goods only (all wood furniture). The only upholstery you will find here are simple dining room and occasional chairs.

Their prices are very good for what they offer. If you are in the market for a traditional bedroom set, dining room set, entertainment center, or occasional table, you should definitely compare Nostalgia's prices before you buy. Nostalgia also sells directly to the public through their internet catalog at www.nostalgiafurniture.com.

I have found the owners to be very cooperative and helpful, and I've heard absolutely no complaints about them.

Phone orders accepted:	**Yes**
Discount:	**55%-65% off retail prices on comparable pieces**
Payment methods:	**VISA, MC, personal checks.**
In-house financing available:	**No**
Deposits required:	**50% deposit when order is placed, balance due when furniture is ready to be shipped**
Catalog available:	**Yes-internet only**
Clearance center:	**No**
Delivery:	**Full service in-home delivery and set-up. Customer pays freight company directly for shipping costs.**

Directions: From I-20 in east Mississippi, take exit 71B (I-359 N/AL-69 N) exit and take AL-69 north to U. S. Hwy. 43 north. After about three miles, get onto U. S. Hwy. 82 west. Go about 50 miles west and take the MS-50 exit. Go west on MS Hwy. 50 for about a mile. Then, turn left onto Gardner Blvd. After about a mile, turn left onto MS Hwy. 182.

Nostalgia Furniture

Level 4
Hickory Furniture Mart
U. S. Hwy 70 SE
Hickory, NC 28602

Phone:	**(828) 325-4800**	**Hours:**	**M-Sat 9:00-6:00**
Toll Free:	**None**	**E-mail:**	**info@nostalgiafurniture.com**
Fax:	**(828) 325-4805**	**Web site:**	**www.nostalgiafurniture.com**

Nostalgia Furniture has two factory-direct showrooms: one in the Hickory Furniture Mart, and one at their factory in Columbus, MS. This small family manufacturing business was started by former employees of Kincaid Furniture and several other manufacturers in the Hickory and Tupelo areas.

Nostalgia has chosen to sell directly to consumers through their Web site and showrooms, skipping the retailer altogether. Their prices run about 55%-65% off retail prices charged by other companies for comparable pieces.

Their quality is excellent. They have a wide variety of traditional styles in cherry and mahogany. They manufacture case goods only (all wood furniture). The only upholstery you will find here are simple dining room and occasional chairs.

Their prices are very good for what they offer. For example, on a recent visit I found a terrific deal on a solid mahogany dining room set (pictured on the following page). This set would normally retail for about $7,000.00 including the eight foot trestle table and six chairs, but you could special order this set new from Nostalgia for only $2,495.00, as savings of 64% off retail. The design is copied from an antique set the owners found in England, as are many of Nostalgia's designs.

If you are in the market for a traditional bedroom set, dining room set, entertainment center, or occasional table, you should definitely compare Nostalgia's prices before you buy. Nostalgia also sells directly to the public through their internet catalog at www.nostalgiafurniture.com.

This is a relatively new business, and as such, has not had the opportunity to establish a long track record for service. However, I have found the owners to be very cooperative and helpful, and I've heard absolutely no complaints about them. They do participate in the Hickory Furniture Mart consolidated shipping program, which is well-established and very reliable.

Phone orders accepted:	**Yes**
Discount:	**55%-65% off retail prices on comparable pieces**
Payment methods:	**VISA, MC, AMEX, Discover, personal checks.**
In-house financing available:	**No**
Deposits required:	**50% deposit when order is placed, balance due when furniture is ready to be shipped**
Catalog available:	**Yes-internet only**
Clearance center:	**No**
Delivery:	**Full service in-home delivery and set-up. Customer pays freight company directly for shipping costs.**

Directions: Please see *Hickory Furniture Mart* for complete directions.

Nostalgia Furniture (cont.)

Solid mahogany dining room set from Nostalgia Furniture

Retail: $7,000.00   Discounted price: $2,495.00
Savings at Nostalgia Furniture: $4,505.00 = 64% off retail

Parkway Furniture

2815 Hwy. 105 S.
Boone, NC 28607

Phone:	**(828) 264-3993**	**Hours:**	**M-Sat 9:00-5:00**
Toll Free:	**None**	**E-mail:**	**sales@stevensfurniture.com**
Fax:	**(828) 262-3530**	**Web site:**	**www.stevensfurniture.com**

Parkway Furniture in Boone, NC, has a very impressive showroom with large galleries for Stanley, Broyhill, and Lexington, among other lines.

You can buy furniture off the floor if you wish, but the discount you receive in person is no better than the discount you receive over the phone. Their discounts run about 40%-50% off retail.

Unfortunately, this source has also been accumulating complaints at the BBB, some of which have not even been answered by the company, much less resolved. Under these circumstances, I must recommend that my readers not shop here.

Phone orders accepted:	**Yes**
Discount:	**40%-50% off mfrs. suggested retail**
Payment methods:	**VISA, MC, personal checks.**
In-house financing available:	**Yes**
Deposits required:	**50% deposit when order is placed, balance due when furniture is ready to be shipped**
Catalog available:	**No**
Clearance center:	**Yes**
Delivery:	**Full service in-home delivery and set-up. Customer pays freight company directly for shipping costs.**

Directions: From I-40, take exit #123 and head north into Hickory, NC, on Hwy. 321. Go 25 miles north on Hwy. 321 to Boone, and turn left on Hwy. 105. Parkway Furniture is about two miles down on the left side of the road.

Pennsylvania House at the Mart

Level 4
Hickory Furniture Mart
U. S. Hwy. 70 SE
Hickory, NC 28602

Phone:	**(828) 261-2026**	**Hours:**	**M-Sat 9:00-6:00**
Toll Free:	**None**	**E-mail:**	**None**
Fax:	**(828) 261-2049**	**Web site:**	**None**

Pennsylvania House at the Mart is a discounter for Pennsylvania House, not a factory outlet. Their prices run about 40% off retail, which is the maximum discount allowed by the manufacturer.

This is the largest Pennsylvania House showroom in the U. S., so it's a great place to see their entire line. They have a sister store in High Point, Pennsylvania House Collectors Gallery, which has the same ownership, prices, policies, etc.

They don't carry general outlet stock such as showroom samples or discontinued items, but they occasionally sell a floor sample from their own showroom if it has a slight flaw or is scheduled to be replaced by a new display. These prices are set individually. It's unfortunate that Pennsylvania House no longer sells off their outlet stock to the public.

According to the manager, the prices here are approximately 20% below most of his competitors who carry Pennsylvania House. However, as Pennsylvania House restricts their dealers from going below a certain discount, I would expect you to find that many other North Carolina discounters carry Pennsylvania House at the minimum price allowed just as this showroom does.

If you're at the Hickory Furniture Mart, you may wish to see if they have a floor sample at a good price that interests you. Otherwise, I find that you can generally do much better on pricing and value by not special ordering from brands that restrict their discounts. Pennsylvania House has many competitors with similar styles and equivalent quality who allow deep discounters to offer better discounts.

Phone orders accepted:	**Yes**
Discount:	**40% off mfrs. suggested retail**
Payment methods:	**VISA, MC, AMEX, Discover, personal checks**
In-house financing available:	**No**
Deposits required:	**50% deposit when order is placed, balance due when furniture is ready to be shipped**
Catalog available:	**Yes**
Clearance center:	**No**
Delivery:	**Full service in-home delivery and set-up. Customer pays freight company directly for shipping costs.**

Directions: Please see *Hickory Furniture Mart* for complete directions.

Pennsylvania House Collectors Gallery

2001 Brentwood Street
High Point, NC 27260

Phone:	**(336) 887-3000**	**Hours:**	**M-F 9:00-5:30, Sat 9:00-5:00**
Toll Free:	**None**	**E-mail:**	**None**
Fax:	**None**	**Web site:**	**None**

Pennsylvania House Collectors Gallery is a discounter for Pennsylvania House, not a factory outlet. Their prices run 40% off retail, which is the maximum allowed by the manufacturer. They have a sister store in Hickory, Pennsylvania House at the Mart, which has the same ownership, prices, policies, etc.

They don't carry general outlet stock such as showroom samples or discontinued items, but they occasionally sell a floor sample from their own showroom if it has a slight flaw or is scheduled to be replaced by a new display. These prices are set individually. It's unfortunate that Pennsylvania House no longer sells off their outlet stock to the public.

If you're in the area, you may wish to see if they have a floor sample at a good price that interests you. Otherwise, I find that you can generally do much better on pricing and value by not special ordering from brands that restrict their discounts. Pennsylvania House has many competitors with similar styles and equivalent quality who allow deep discounters to offer better discounts.

Phone orders accepted:	**Yes**
Discount:	**40% off mfrs. suggested retail**
Payment methods:	**VISA, MC, AMEX, Discover, personal checks**
In-house financing available:	**No**
Deposits required:	**50% deposit when order is placed, balance due when furniture is ready to be shipped**
Catalog available:	**Yes**
Clearance center:	**No**
Delivery:	**Full service in-home delivery and set-up. Customer pays freight company directly for shipping costs.**

Directions: Take Business I-85 to the Brentwood Exit. You'll see the Pennsylvania House Collector's Gallery right off the northbound exit.

Piedmont Furniture

1928 S. College Dr.
High Point, NC 27260

Phone:	**(336) 889-0819**	**Hours:**	**M-Sat 9:00-5:30**
Toll Free:	**None**	**E-mail:**	**None**
Fax:	**(336) 889-8997**	**Web site:**	**www.piedmontfurniture.com**

Piedmont Furniture in High Point is a fantastic source for Thomasville and Lexington. Thomasville does have three factory outlets which also have great deals, but there is no other source for outlet merchandise from Lexington.

They're also able to order many other lines at good prices. If there's a particular line you're interested in, they invite you to call and ask for a price comparison from them.

Piedmont Furniture works with a wholesale company that refurbishes seconds and damaged pieces from Thomasville and Lexington. I've been to their facility, and the results are stunning. When they get through with a piece, it looks absolutely fresh from the factory. Please note that the refurbished items are casegoods only, no upholstery.

If you visit High Point to shop and you're interested in fine quality traditional casegoods, this store is a must visit!

Phone orders accepted:	**Yes**
Discount:	**40%-70% off mfrs. suggested retail**
Payment methods:	**VISA, MC, Discover, personal checks**
In-house financing available:	**No**
Deposits required:	**33% deposit when order is placed, balance due when furniture is ready to be shipped**
Catalog available:	**Yes**
Clearance center:	**No**
Delivery:	**Full service in-home delivery and set-up. Customer pays freight company directly for shipping costs.**

Directions: From I-85, take exit #111 (Hwy. 311), and head northwest into High Point. After several miles, when you reach downtown High Point, Hwy. 311 will become S. Main St. Turn right on S. College Dr., right past Rose On Main. Piedmont Furniture will be immediately on your left.

Pottery Barn Furniture Outlet

Multiple locations nationwide

Phone:	**Varies by location**	**Hours:**	**Varies by location**
Toll Free:	**(888) 779-5176**	**E-mail:**	**Please visit Web site**
Fax:	**None**	**Web site:**	**www.potterybarn.com**

There are approximately a dozen "Pottery Barn Furniture Outlets" all over the US, with more opening all the time. Please check their Web site or call their 800 number for the most up to date information on new locations.

I was very disappointed to find that these "furniture outlets" hardly carry any furniture at all. Easily 80%-90% of the items in stock are accessories.

At the Pottery Barn Furniture Outlet in Dawsonville, GA, I was able to fit their entire furniture selection into one photo (on the following page). Their entire selection consisted of 3 sofas and about a dozen bedframes, all in very poor condition.

The three sofas in the picture are all Pottery Barn's "Hamilton" style. Two were upholstered in a green fabric and marked at $1,499.00 retail discounted to $899.00 outlet price. Both showed significant use and wear. For $899.00 (or considerably less), I can find you much better quality sofas in new first-quality condition at pretty much any furniture factory outlet in North Carolina.

The third sofa in the picture was just a frame covered in muslin, priced at a whopping $674.00! That's beyond a bad deal; it's a bad joke. You can buy plain frames like that from any upholsterer for less than $100.00. I can't imagine why they believe anyone would want to spend so much on a plain furniture frame.

This is the kind of "outlet" that gives real furniture factory outlets a bad name. Visiting a Pottery Barn "Furniture Outlet" is a total waste of time.

You can find better quality furniture at much lower prices at many of the factory outlets and clearance centers in North Carolina. One good places to find similar styles is Boyles Country Shop and Clearance Center in Hickory, NC. You could also check out the Broyhill Factory Outlet in Lenoir, NC, and the Furnitureland South Clearance Center in High Point, NC.

Phone orders accepted:	**Yes**
Discount:	**None-40% off mfrs. suggested retail**
Payment methods:	**VISA, MC, AMEX, Discover, personal checks.**
In-house financing available:	**Yes, through their Pottery Barn credit card.**
Deposits required:	**Not applicable**
Catalog available:	**Yes**
Clearance center:	**Not applicable**
Delivery:	**Common carrier only.**

Directions: Varies by location. Please visit www.potterybarn.com or call (888) 779-5176 or for complete directions to the Pottery Barn Furniture Outlet in your area.

Pottery Barn Furniture Outlet (cont.)

Pottery Barn Furniture Outlet in Dawsonville, GA

Furniture selection at the Pottery Barn Furniture Outlet in Dawsonville, GA

Priba Furniture Sales and Interiors

210 Stage Coach Trail
Greensboro, NC 27415

Phone:	(336) 855-9034	**Hours:**	M-F 9:00-5:30, Sat 9:00-5:00
Toll Free:	(800) 296-7977	**E-mail:**	info@pribafurniture.com
Fax:	(336) 855-1370	**Web site:**	www.pribafurniture.com

Priba Furniture Sales and Interiors is located in Greensboro, NC, just north of High Point. They have a good selection of medium to high-end lines, including Wellington Hall, Century, and Bernhardt.

Also, this store offers a 1% rebate toward the cost of one night's hotel bill if you visit their store and make a purchase.

They don't have a clearance center or any floor samples or discontinued pieces on display. They do have great deals on many lines sold over the phone, though. So, if you're planning to order your furniture by phone, definitely give this source a call to compare their prices.

Phone orders accepted:	Yes
Discount:	35%-48% off mfrs. suggested retail
Payment methods:	VISA, MC, personal checks
In-house financing available:	Yes
Deposits required:	30% deposit when order is placed, balance due when furniture is ready to be shipped
Catalog available:	No
Clearance center:	No
Delivery:	Full service in-home delivery and set-up. Customer pays freight company directly for shipping costs.

Directions: From I-40, take exit #212, and go north 1/2 mile on Chimney Rock Rd. Turn right on Market St. Go 3/10 of a mile, and turn left on Stage Coach Trail. Priba Furniture Sales and Interiors is on the right.

Priba Furniture Sales and Interiors (cont.)

Lines carried:

Action By Lane
American Drew
Ardley Hall
Artistica Metal Designs
Baker
Barcalounger
Bernhardt
Bevan Funnell
Bradington Young
Braxton Culler
Brown Jordan
CBS
CEBU
Century
Canal Dover
Carolina Tables
Casa Bique
Casa Stradivari
Charleston Forge
Chromcraft
Clark Casual
Classic Leather
Colonial Furniture
Conover
Councill-Craftsmen
Cox
Craftique
Crawford
Creative Metal
Customcraft
Designs South
Dillon
Dinaire
Dinec
Directional
Distinction Leather
Ello
Emerson et Cie
Fairfield Chair
Fashion Bed Group
Fauld
Ficks Reed
Flat Rock
Fremarc
Froelich Company
Garcia
Glass Arts
Guy Chaddock
Habersham Plantation

Hammary
Hekman
Henry Link
Hickory Chair
Hickory White
Highborn Manor
Hitchcock Chair
Hooker
Howard Miller
Hunt Country Furniture
HTB
Hyundai Furniture
Jasper
Johnston Casuals
John Widdicomb
Karges
Kincaid
Kingsdown
La Barge
Lane
Lane/Venture
Leathercraft
Leathermen's Guild
Leather Shop
Lee Industries
Lexington
Lillian August
Lloyd/Flanders
Lowenstein
Lyon Shaw
Madison Square
Maitland Smith
Marboro Lamps
Mar-Kel Lighting
Maryland Classics
Masland Carpets
McGuire
McKay Table Pad
McKinley Leather
Meadowcraft
Motioncraft
Murray Feiss
Nathan Hale
National Mt. Airy
Natuzzi Leather
Nichols & Stone
Nora Fenton
Norman Perry
North Hickory

Ohio Table Pad
Old Hickory Furniture
Old Hickory Tannery
PAMA
Paul Hansen
Pearson
Pennsylvania Classics
Peters Revington
Pinetique
Plant Plant
Port Royal
Porter
Pouliot Designs
Pulaski
Quoizel
Rembrandt
Remington Lamps
Reprodux
Rex
Richardson Brothers
Ridgeway Clocks
Rosecore
Royal Patina
Sedgefield Leather
Salem Square
Sam Moore
Samsonite
Sarreid
Sealy Mattress
Serta Mattress
Sherrill
Shuford
Sligh
Southampton
Southwood
        Reproductions
Spring Air
Stanford
Stanley
Stanton Cooper
Stark Carpets
Statesville Chair
Statton
Stiffel Lamps
Stone International
St. Timothy
Style Upholstery
Swaim
Thayer Coggin

Theodore Alexander
Thomasville
Tradition House
Tropitone
Trosby
Trouvailles
Universal
Vanguard
Venture By Lane
Virginia House
Virginia Metalcrafters
Waterford
Weiman
Wellington Hall
Wesley Allen
Wesley Hall
Wildwood Lamps
William Alan
Winston
Woodard
Woodmark Originals
Yorkshire House

Pulaski Factory Outlet

1134 East Main St.
Pulaski, VA 24301

Phone:	(540) 980-0436	**Hours:**	**Mon, Tues, Thurs, Fri, & Sat 10:00-6:00. Closed Wed and Sun.**
Toll Free:	None		
Fax:	(540) 980-1572		
		E-mail:	**dlear@pulaskifurniture.com**
		Web site:	**www.pulaskifurniture.com**

This is the only factory outlet for Pulaski Furniture. Their furniture is very good quality, and many of the pieces here are in good condition. The discounts here start at a flat 65% off retail. If a piece doesn't sell within 30 days, it is marked down further periodically until it sells. This outlet certainly offers good value for money.

Please note that this outlet, unlike the vast majority, will not accept out of state checks. They take Virginia checks only. They do accept most credit cards.

Please be aware that this outlet is not as service oriented as the factory outlets in Hickory and High Point. They can only arrange shipment to the East Coast, primarily from New York to Florida. Before visiting this outlet, you may wish to call their delivery service, Hopkins Delivery Service, at (276) 647-5200 to see if they service your area of the country.

If you bring your own truck or trailer, the outlet will wrap your furniture and load it for you. However, as this outlet is also in a mountainous area at the edge of the Smokies, you may not want to drive a rented truck or trailer on these steep, curving roads unless you have prior experience with this type of driving. You should also make sure you have plenty of time to get out of the mountains before it gets dark, as these roads are for the most part unlit.

If you're planning a trip to the Smokies anyway, you may wish to visit this outlet and the outlet for Henredon in Spruce Pine, NC, not far from here. Pulaski, VA is approximately a two hour drive from High Point and Hickory.

Otherwise, you may wish to concentrate your trip instead on the main outlet centers of Hickory and/or High Point, where you'll be better able to make the most of your travel time.

Phone orders accepted:	**No**
Discount:	**65%-70% off mfrs. suggested retail**
Payment methods:	**VISA, MC, AMEX, Discover, Virginia checks.**
In-house financing available:	**No**
Deposits required:	**Not applicable**
Catalog available:	**Yes, at their Web site**
Clearance center:	**Not applicable**
Delivery:	**East Coast only, through Hopkins Delivery Service (276-647-5200)**

Directions: From I-40, take exit 193B (US Hwy. 52) toward Mount Alry. After about 30 miles, take the I-74 west exit toward Wytheville. After about 10 miles, take exit #5 and get on I-77 north. After about 30 miles, take exit #32 and get on I-81 north. After about 15 miles, take exit #94B and get on VA Hwy. 99 north toward Pulaski. After a couple of miles, VA 99 changes name to Main St. You'll see the outlet about two miles after getting on VA 99.

Quality Furniture Market Of Lenoir

2034 Hickory Blvd. SW
Lenoir, NC 28645

Phone:	**(828) 728-2946**	**Hours:**	**M-Sat 8:30-5:00**
Toll Free:	**None**	**E-mail:**	**quotes@qualityfurnituremarket.com**
Fax:	**(828) 726-0226**	**Web site:**	**www.qualityfurnituremarket.com**

Quality Furniture Market Of Lenoir has been in business for nearly half a century in Lenoir, NC. They'll be celebrating their 50th anniversary in the near future. They have a huge store. In fact, it's a lot bigger than it looks from the outside. There is a huge basement gallery that extends under the building and most of the parking lot.

Most of their sales are special order, but they do have some floor samples and discontinued pieces scattered around priced at about 60%-70% off retail, many of which are shown on their Web site!

Quality Furniture Market also has a terrific play area for kids at the front of the store, closely supervised by the office staff at the front. They have a VCR showing cartoons and movies, toys, etc. for all ages. It's a rare benefit in North Carolina for parents trying to shop with their kids in tow.

Their discounts are excellent: 50%-70% off retail. They have had the very best prices I've found on a number of lines. They also have a sterling reputation for service, as the local BBB will tell you as well. I have heard nothing but compliments about this store from readers and friends who have actually purchased here.

In an effort to keep prices low and shipping fast, they do require full payment in advance. This speeds up delivery by leaving out the step of notifying the customer that the order has arrived and waiting a week or two for payment to be sent in. It also helps them keep prices down by eliminating that small percentage of customers who default on the final payment and force the store to sell off their special order furniture (which cannot be returned to the factory) at a cut rate price.

As a general rule, I recommend that consumers not pay in full in advance for any special order product. That is still the best rule to use when dealing with most businesses.

However, as Quality Furniture Market passes the benefits of this policy through to their customers, and they have a sterling reputation in the industry, I have no qualms about recommending to readers that they not allow this policy to prevent them from shopping here. I would personally trust them with a full payment up front if I were placing an order here.

Anyone ordering furniture by phone should definitely compare prices here. Their prices and service are hard to beat.

Phone orders accepted:	**Yes**
Discount:	**50%-70% off mfrs. suggested retail**
Payment methods:	**VISA, MC, Discover, personal checks**
In-house financing available:	**No**
Deposits required:	**Full payment required with order**
Catalog available:	**Yes**
Clearance center:	**No**
Delivery:	**Full service in-home delivery and set-up. Customer pays freight company directly for shipping costs.**

Directions: From I-40, take exit #123 and drive north on Hwy. 321 toward Lenoir, NC. Quality Furniture Market is on the left side of the highway just before you get into Lenoir.

Quality Furniture Market Of Lenoir (cont.)

Quality Furniture Market Of Lenoir

Quality Furniture Market Of Lenoir (cont.)

Lines carried:

Action By Lane	Comfort Designs	James R. Cooper, Ltd.	Reliance Lamps
A La Carte	Conover Chair	Jamestown Manor	Remi
Alexander Julian	Correll	By Statton	Rex
Allusions	Cox	Jasper	Ridgeway Clocks
Ambiance Imports	Craftique	Jeffco	Riverside
American Drew	Crawford Of Jamestown	John Richards Collection	Robert Allen Fabrics
American Of Martinsville	Creative Wood & Metal	Kimball	SEE Imports
Andrew Pearson Designs	Crystal Clear Lamps	Kinder Harris	Sagefield Leather
Ardley Hall	Customcraft	Kingsley-Bates	St. Timothy
Arnold Palmer Collection	D & F Wicker	Koch & Lowy	Sarreid
Artisan House	Dale Tiffany Lamps	La Barge	2nd Ave.
Artistica	Davis & Davis Rugs	Lane	Sedgefield Lamps
Artmark Fabrics	Decorative Arts	Lane/Venture	Serta Bedding
Artmax	Decorative Crafts	Lexington	Sherrill
Aston Garrett	Design Guild	Lloyd/Flanders	Sidney Arthur
Austin Sculptures	Design South	Lyon Shaw	Skillcraft
Baldwin Brass	Dinaire	M & H Seating	Sligh
Barcalounger	Distinctive Designs	MER Rugs	South Sea Rattan
Bassett	Dillon	Mikhail Darafeev	Speer Lamps
Bassett Mirror	Ekornes	Miller Desk	Spinning Wheel Rugs
Bean Station	Elements By Grapevine	Minoff Lamps	Spring Air
Bernhardt	Emerson et Cie	Mirror Fair	Stanley
Best Chair	European Pine	Montaage	Statesville Chair
Blacksmith Shop	Fabrica	Murray Feiss	Stiffel Lamps
Bob Timberlake	Fairfield Chair	NDI	Style Seating
Boling Chair	Fashion Bed Group	Natural Light Lamps	Sustainable Lifestyles
Bradburn Galleries	Fiam	Nautica By Lexington	Tapestries Ltd.
Brett Austin	Ficks Reed	New River Artisans	Thayer Coggin
British Traditions	Fine Art Lamps	Norman Perry	Thief River Linens
Broyhill	Fitz & Floyd China	Oklahoma Imports	Tomlin Lamps
Builtright	Frederick Cooper	Old Hickory Tannery	Trica
Butler Specialty	Fur Designs	Ohio Table Pad Co.	Tropitone
Cambridge Lamps	Gaby's Shoppe	Oriental Lacquer	Universal
Carlton McLendon	Garcia Imports	Osborne & Little	Uttermost
Carolina Mirror	Georgia Art Lighting	Pacific Rim	Uwharrie Chair Co.
Carson's Of High Point	Glass Arts	Palecek	Vanguard
Carver's Guild	Grace	Paper White	Velco
Casa Bique	Great City Traders	Payne	Venture By Lane
Casa Rustica	Guild Master	Pearson	Virginia Metalcrafters
Casual Lamps	Hart Associates	Pennsylvania Classics	Visions
Chapman Lamps	Hammary	Pennsylvania House	Waterford
Charleston Forge	Hekman	Peters Revington	Weiman
Chatham County	Highland House	Phillip Jeffries	Wellington Hall
Chrishawn	Hitchcock Chair	Plant Plant	Wesley Allen Brass Beds
Chromcraft	Homecrest	Pompeii	Wildwood
Clark Casuals	Hooker	Powell	Winners Only
Classic Leather	Howard Miller Clocks	Pulaski	Winston
Clayton Marcus	JSF Industries	Raymond Waites	Woodard
Cochrane	J. Royale	By Lane	Younger

Reflections

Level 3
Hickory Furniture Mart
U. S. Hwy. 70 SE
Hickory, NC 28602

Phone:	**(828) 327-8485**	**Hours:**	**M-Sat 9:00-6:00**
Toll Free:	**None**	**E-mail:**	**hickorysr@abts.net**
Fax:	**(828) 327-8316**	**Web site:**	**www.reflectionsfurniture.com**

Reflections has a great selection of contemporary furniture, which can be in short supply in North Carolina. They have a nice Natuzzi gallery, plus they carry a wide variety of other unique lines, listed below. Prices tend to run 40%-50% off retail. They have a very good reputation for customer service.

September is a great month to shop here. They have a big sale on all leather furniture on Labor Day weekend, and they offer an additional 10% off all special orders throughout the month of September.

If you're looking for unique contemporary furniture, Reflections should be a must visit while you're in Hickory!

Lines carried:

American Leather	Dellarobbia Rugs	Furniture Graphics	Pastel
Andrew Pearson	Dia	Gamma	Rockledge Design
Artisan House	Dinec	Huppe	Studios
Artmax	Ekornes	Johnston Casuals	Shermag
AXI	Elite	Koinor	Silver
BDI	Ello	Lazar Industries	Trica
Calligaris	EXL	Leeazanne	Van Teal
Creative Elegance	Fattori-Star	Natuzzi	Visu
Decorative Arts	Foreign Accents	Nouveau Concepts	

Phone orders accepted:	**Yes**
Discount:	**40%-50% off mfrs. suggested retail**
Payment methods:	**VISA, MC, Discover, and personal checks**
In-house financing available:	**No**
Deposits required:	**50% deposit when order is placed, balance due when furniture is ready to be shipped**
Catalog available:	**No**
Clearance center:	**No**
Delivery:	**Full service in-home delivery and set-up. Customer pays freight company directly for shipping costs.**

Directions: Please see *Hickory Furniture Mart* for complete directions.

Regan's Market Samples Plus

615 Greensboro Rd.
High Point, NC 27260

Phone:	**(336) 882-6631**	**Hours:**	**M-Sat 9:00-6:00**	
Toll Free:	**None**	**E-mail:**	**None**	
Fax:	**(336) 454-1933**	**Web site:**	**www.furniturechoices.com**	

Regan's Market Samples Plus is actually a clearance center for Furniture Choices. They get in a few market samples, but their primary stock comes from Furniture Choices' three North Carolina stores.

Discounts run 50%-70% off retail. They do have some good deals, and Furniture Choices has a good reputation for customer service.

Most of the stock here is medium quality from lines such as Rowe, Bently, Birmingham, and Supple. If you're in the area, you may wish to stop by and see what deals they have in stock.

Phone orders accepted:	**Yes**
Discount:	**50%-70% off mfrs. suggested retail**
Payment methods:	**VISA, MC, Discover, and personal checks**
In-house financing available:	**No**
Deposits required:	**Not applicable**
Catalog available:	**No**
Clearance center:	**Not applicable**
Delivery:	**Full service in-home delivery and set-up. Customer pays freight company directly for shipping costs.**

Directions: From I-85, take exit #111, and head north on Hwy. 311 into High Point Turn right on Greensboro Rd. Boyles is a few miles down on the left.

Robert Bergelin Co.

Level 3
Hickory Furniture Mart
U. S. Hwy. 70 SE
Hickory, NC 28602

Phone:	**(828) 345-1500**	**Hours:**	**M-Sat 9:00-6:00**
Toll Free:	**(800) 345-1599**	**E-mail:**	**hickorysr@abts.net**
Fax:	**(828) 345-0203**	**Web site:**	**www.rbcfurn.com**

The Robert Bergelin Company is a small 4th generation family-owned furniture factory in Morganton, NC, that sells directly to the public through their three showrooms at the Hickory Furniture Mart in Hickory, the Atrium Furniture Mall in High Point, and their newest showroom in Winnetka, IL. They also accept phone orders and ship nationwide.

You can call to request a catalog showing all of their available styles, or you can view a complete catalog with some color photos on their Web site. You can also obtain pricing at their Web site.

Most of their furniture is case goods. Their only upholstered items are a mission-style sofa and chair and two upholstered dining room chair styles. They carry the most popular styles on the market: mission, traditional American, French, etc. They have quite a variety of styles in their dining room sets, in particular. You'll notice pieces in their catalog that are nearly identical to some of the most popular styles from Stickley, Lexington, and Alexander Julian, among others.

The quality of Robert Bergelin furniture is definitely a cut above these lines, however. In past editions of this book, I stated that I believed the quality of Robert Bergelin and Stickley was about equivalent. After a thorough demonstration of the quality points Robert Bergelin Co. uses, I stand corrected. When you visit their showroom, I would suggest that you allow their showroom manager to point out all the little details that set their quality apart from most other companies.

They also offer customization on many items. On dining room tables, you can specify the size, leg style, pedestal style, lazy susan if desired, and number of leaves. They can configure a home office desk and hutch any way you like. You can even choose your hardware and finish for any piece.

Robert Bergelin Co. offers terrific value for money. They offer the kind of heirloom furniture that will still look great when you hand it down to your grandkids.

Phone orders accepted:	**Yes**
Discount:	**Factory direct pricing to the public**
Payment methods:	**VISA, MC, AMEX, and personal checks**
In-house financing available:	**No**
Deposits required:	**50% deposit when order is placed, balance due when furniture is ready to be shipped**
Catalog available:	**Yes**
Clearance center:	**No**
Delivery:	**Full service in-home delivery and set-up. Customer pays freight company directly for shipping costs.**

Directions: Please see *Hickory Furniture Mart* for complete directions.

Robert Bergelin Co.

The Atrium
430 S. Main St.
High Point, NC 27260

Phone:	**(336) 889-2189**	**Hours:**	**M-F 9:00-6:00, Sat 9:00-5:00**
Toll Free:	**(888) 296-7977**	**E-mail:**	**rbchp@mindspring.com**
Fax:	**(336) 889-2190**	**Web site:**	**www.rbcfurn.com**

The Robert Bergelin Company is a small 4th generation family-owned furniture factory in Morganton, NC, that sells directly to the public through their three showrooms at the Hickory Furniture Mart in Hickory, the Atrium Furniture Mall in High Point, and their newest showroom in Winnetka, IL. They also accept phone orders and ship nationwide.

You can call to request a catalog showing all of their available styles, or you can view a complete catalog with some color photos on their Web site. You can also obtain pricing at their Web site.

Most of their furniture is case goods. Their only upholstered items are a mission-style sofa and chair and two upholstered dining room chair styles. They carry the most popular styles on the market: mission, traditional American, French, etc. They have quite a variety of styles in their dining room sets, in particular. You'll notice pieces in their catalog that are nearly identical to some of the most popular styles from Stickley, Lexington, and Alexander Julian, among others.

The quality of Robert Bergelin furniture is definitely a cut above these lines, however. In past editions of this book, I stated that I believed the quality of Robert Bergelin and Stickley was about equivalent. After a thorough demonstration of the quality points Robert Bergelin Co. uses, I stand corrected. When you visit their showroom, I would suggest that you allow their showroom manager to point out all the little details that set their quality apart from most other companies.

They also offer customization on many items. On dining room tables, you can specify the size, leg style, pedestal style, lazy susan if desired, and number of leaves. They can configure a home office desk and hutch any way you like. You can even choose your hardware and finish for any piece.

Robert Bergelin Co. offers terrific value for money. They offer the kind of heirloom furniture that will still look great when you hand it down to your grandkids.

Phone orders accepted:	**Yes**
Discount:	**Factory direct pricing to the public**
Payment methods:	**VISA, MC, AMEX, and personal checks**
In-house financing available:	**No**
Deposits required:	**50% deposit when order is placed, balance due when furniture is ready to be shipped**
Catalog available:	**Yes**
Clearance center:	**No**
Delivery:	**Full service in-home delivery and set-up. Customer pays freight company directly for shipping costs.**

Directions: Please see *The Atrium* for complete directions.

Robert Bergelin Co.

Hubbard Woods
920 Green Bay Rd.
Winnetka, IL 60093

Phone:	**(847) 446-8540**	**Hours:**	**M-Sat 10:00-6:00**
Toll Free:	**None**	**E-mail:**	**rbcwinnetka@rbcfurn.com**
Fax:	**(847) 446-8541**	**Web site:**	**www.rbcfurn.com**

The Robert Bergelin Company is a small 4th generation family-owned furniture factory in Morganton, NC, that sells directly to the public through their three showrooms at the Hickory Furniture Mart in Hickory, the Atrium Furniture Mall in High Point, and their newest showroom in Winnetka, IL. They also accept phone orders and ship nationwide.

You can call to request a catalog showing all of their available styles, or you can view a complete catalog with some color photos on their Web site. You can also obtain pricing at their Web site.

Most of their furniture is case goods. Their only upholstered items are a mission-style sofa and chair and two upholstered dining room chair styles. They carry the most popular styles on the market: mission, traditional American, French, etc. They have quite a variety of styles in their dining room sets, in particular. You'll notice pieces in their catalog that are nearly identical to some of the most popular styles from Stickley, Lexington, and Alexander Julian, among others.

The quality of Robert Bergelin furniture is definitely a cut above these lines, however. In past editions of this book, I stated that I believed the quality of Robert Bergelin and Stickley was about equivalent. After a thorough demonstration of the quality points Robert Bergelin Co. uses, I stand corrected. When you visit their showroom, I would suggest that you allow their showroom manager to point out all the little details that set their quality apart from most other companies.

They also offer customization on many items. On dining room tables, you can specify the size, leg style, pedestal style, lazy susan if desired, and number of leaves. They can configure a home office desk and hutch any way you like. You can even choose your hardware and finish for any piece.

Robert Bergelin Co. offers terrific value for money. They offer the kind of heirloom furniture that will still look great when you hand it down to your grandkids.

Phone orders accepted:	**Yes**
Discount:	**Factory direct pricing to the public**
Payment methods:	**VISA, MC, personal checks**
In-house financing available:	**No**
Deposits required:	**50% deposit when order is placed, balance due when furniture is ready to be shipped**
Catalog available:	**Yes**
Clearance center:	**No**
Delivery:	**Full service in-home delivery and set-up. Customer pays freight company directly for shipping costs.**

Directions: From I-94, take exit #31, and go east on Tower Rd. As you near the lake, turn left on Green Bay Rd. The Robert Bergelin showroom will be less than a mile down on the left.

Room By Room

Atrium Furniture Mall
430 S. Main St.
High Point, NC 27260

Phone:	**(336) 889-0423**	**Hours:**	**M-F 9:00-6:00, Sat 9:00-5:00**
Toll Free:	**None**	**E-mail:**	**roombyroom@northstate.net**
Fax:	**(336) 889-0820**	**Web site:**	**www.atriumfurniture.com**

Room By Room carries a variety of lines for every room in the house. They're fairly new, but I've heard no complaints about them at all. Discounts run 40%-50% off retail. They are special order only.

Lines carried:

Millenium
Ashley
Anthony
Primo

Phone orders accepted:	**Yes**
Discount:	**40%-50% off mfrs. suggested retail**
Payment methods:	**VISA, MC, AMEX, Discover, personal checks**
In-house financing available:	**No**
Deposits required:	**50% deposit when order is placed, balance due when furniture is ready to be shipped**
Catalog available:	**No**
Clearance center:	**No**
Delivery:	**Full service in-home delivery and set-up. Customer pays freight company directly for shipping costs.**

Directions: Please see The Atrium for complete directions.

Rose Furniture

916 Finch Ave.
High Point, NC 27261

Phone:	**(336) 886-6050**	**Hours:**	**M-F 8:30-5:00, Sat 8:30-4:00**
Toll Free:	**None**	**E-mail:**	**See Web site**
Fax:	**(336) 886-5055**	**Web site:**	**www.rosefurniture.com**

   Rose Furniture is one of the oldest and best-established furniture discounters in the High Point area, if not the entire state of North Carolina. Their discounts are quite good, about 30%-50% off retail, depending on the line. They also have periodic sales throughout the year, including their annual winter sale each February when they discount everything an extra 10% off.

   Unfortunately, Rose Furniture has been accumulating complaints at the BBB, including at least one which is unresolved. Until all complaints against this company have been resolved, I must recommend that my readers not shop here.

Phone orders accepted:	**Yes**
Discount:	**30%-50% off mfrs. suggested retail**
Payment methods:	**Personal checks. No credit cards.**
In-house financing available:	**Yes**
Deposits required:	**30% deposit when order is placed, balance due when furniture is ready to be shipped**
Catalog available:	**No**
Clearance center:	**Yes, just across the street**
Delivery:	**Full service in-home delivery and set-up. Customer pays freight company directly for shipping costs.**

Directions: **From Business I-85, take the Surrett Dr. exit in High Point. Go south about 100 yards, and turn right on Finch Ave. Rose Furniture will be immediately on your right.**

Rose On Main

1813 S. Main St.
High Point, NC

Phone:	**(336) 886-8525**	**Hours:**	**M-F 9:00-5:30, Sat 9:00-5:00**
Toll Free:	**None**	**E-mail:**	**None**
Fax:	**None**	**Web site:**	**www.rosefurniture.com**

This used to be Rose Furniture's main clearance center, right on Main St. in downtown High Point. Now, it is an extension of their main store. Rose's main clearance center has moved to a new facility across the street from the original Rose Furniture showroom on Finch Ave.

Unfortunately, Rose Furniture has been accumulating complaints at the BBB, including at least one which is unresolved. Until all complaints against this company have been resolved, I must recommend that my readers not shop here.

Phone orders accepted:	**Yes**
Discount:	**30%-50% off mfrs. suggested retail**
Payment methods:	**Personal checks. No credit cards.**
In-house financing available:	**Yes**
Deposits required:	**30% deposit when order is placed, balance due when furniture is ready to be shipped**
Catalog available:	**No**
Clearance center:	**Yes**
Delivery:	**Full service in-home delivery and set-up. Customer pays freight company directly for shipping costs.**

Directions: From I-85, take exit #111 (Hwy. 311), and head northwest into High Point. After several miles, when you reach downtown High Point, Hwy. 311 will become S. Main St. Rose Furniture Main Clearance Center is on the right side of Main St., across from Kagan's Furniture.

Simex Factory Outlet

Level 4
Hickory Furniture Mart
U. S. Hwy. 70 SE
Hickory, NC 28602

Phone:	(828) 327-0244	**Hours:**	M-Sat 9:00-6:00
Toll Free:	None	**E-mail:**	moutlet@charterinternet.com
Fax:	(828) 327-4544	**Web site:**	www.hickoryfurniture.com

The Simex factory outlet is part of Manufacturer's Outlet, a very reputable company with a long-standing reputation for service. Manufacturer's Outlet also operates the factory outlets for Hickory White and Theodore Alexander at the Hickory Furniture Mart.

The stock is made up of floor samples, discontinued styles, and customer returns. All of the furniture here is upholstery: sofas and occasional chairs. The discounts run from 50%-70% off retail. Virtually all of the furniture here is in new first-quality condition.

This factory outlet also features LeatherTrend, Clayton-Marcus, SofaTrend, and Mirador. In addition to furniture, they also have a line of European oil paintings at good prices and some Asian antique pieces.

They also participate in the regular mall-wide sales run by the Hickory Furniture Mart in February, May, July, and November. Please check out Web site at www.smartdecorating.com for upcoming sale dates.

Phone orders accepted:	No
Discount:	50%-70% off mfrs. suggested retail
Payment methods:	VISA, MC, personal checks
In-house financing available:	Yes
Deposits required:	Not applicable
Catalog available:	Not applicable
Clearance center:	Not applicable
Delivery:	Full service in-home delivery and set-up. Customer pays freight company directly for shipping costs.

Directions: Please see *Hickory Furniture Mart* for complete directions.

Sity Slicker

Level 2
Hickory Furniture Mart
U. S. Hwy. 70 SE
Hickory, NC 28602

Phone:	**(828) 325-0092**	**Hours:**	**M-Sat 9:00-6:00**
Toll Free:	**None**	**E-mail:**	**bsityslicker@aol.com**
Fax:	**(828) 325-0969**	**Web site:**	**www.hickoryfurniture.com**

Sity Slicker's main line is Paul Robert upholstery. They also carry a variety of case goods and accessories, listed below. They've got a nice showroom, and a good catalog on CD. Just call or email the showroom to receive a copy. Discounts here run 25% off retail on Paul Robert upholstery.

Their stock is primarily new. They will sell you any item off the floor if you wish at the same 25% discount offered on special orders of new furniture. They sometimes mark these floor samples down further during the regular mall-wide sales run by the Hickory Furniture Mart in February, May, July, and November. Please check out Web site at www.smartdecorating.com for upcoming sale dates.

Lines carried:

August Jackson	El Paso Import Company	MARA	Stockton Gage
Authentic Models	Fine Art Ltd.	Montaage	Seagull Lighting
Brett Austin Group	Furniture Classics Ltd.	Muti & Co. Ltd.	Shady Lady
CBK, Ltd.	F.O. Merz & Co. Inc.	Ozark Rustic	The Natural Light
Compass Home Furnishings	Gentry's Home and Garden	Ottoman Treasures	Village Court
Country Originals Inc.	Home Decor Plus Inc.	Powell	of Florida
Chicago Textile Company	Indus Design Imports	Paul Robert	VSI
Dragonfly Home	Limited Addition	Picture Source	William Sheppee
Designer Imports	Light Artistry Inc.	Riverwood Inc.	Water Wonders

Phone orders accepted:	**Yes**
Discount:	**25% off mfrs. suggested retail**
Payment methods:	**VISA, MC, Discover, personal checks**
In-house financing available:	**No**
Deposits required:	**50% deposit when order is placed, balance due when furniture is ready to be shipped**
Catalog available:	**Yes, on CD-ROM**
Clearance center:	**No**
Delivery:	**Full service in-home delivery and set-up. Customer pays freight company directly for shipping costs.**

Directions: Please see *Hickory Furniture Mart* for complete directions.

Sklar Peppler Factory Outlet

210 S. Main St.
High Point, NC 27260

Phone:	**(336) 882-7586**	**Hours:**	**M-F 9:00-4:30, Sat 9:00-1:30**
Toll Free:	**None**		**Closed April and October**
Fax:	**336-882-7585**	**E-mail:**	**None**
		Web site:	**www.sklarpeppler.com**

The Sklar Peppler Factory Outlet is located in their main wholesale showroom in downtown High Point. Please note that they are closed to the public during April and October for the International Home Furnishings Market in High Point.

Sklar Peppler does have some high quality upholstery, and this showroom offers some good bargains. Their discounts on new furniture run about 45%-50% off the average retail charged on this line nationwide. Sklar Peppler has no "manufacturers suggested retail". Each retailer nationwide sets the retail price however they wish. Therefore, the retail prices around the country on this line will vary a bit.

Please note that this outlet features new furniture only. They don't have any of the discontinued items, showroom samples, etc. that you normally find at a factory outlet. They will allow you to buy some items off the showroom floor.

Unlike many wholesale showrooms, this one will accept phone orders. They also have a complete catalog available at their Web site above. If you see something you like, just call to place your order here.

If you're in downtown High Point checking out the wholesale showrooms, you should definitely stop in.

Phone orders accepted:	**Yes**
Discount:	**45%-50% off average retail price nationwide**
Payment methods:	**Personal checks. No credit cards.**
In-house financing available:	**No**
Deposits required:	**50% deposit when order is placed, balance due when furniture is ready to be shipped**
Catalog available:	**Full catalog at their Web site above**
Clearance center:	**No**
Delivery:	**Full service in-home delivery and set-up. Customer pays freight company directly for shipping costs.**

Directions:	**The Sklar Peppler Factory Outlet is in downtown High Point, NC. From I-85, take exit #111 (Hwy. 311), and head northwest into High Point. After several miles, when you reach downtown High Point, Hwy. 311 will become Main St. The Sklar Peppler Factory Outlet will be just past the Visitor's Center on the left.**

Smokey Mountain Furniture

3281 Hickory Blvd.
Hudson, NC 28638

Phone:	**(828) 726-1434**	**Hours:**	**M-F 9-5, Sat 9-6**
Toll Free:	**None**	**E-mail:**	**None**
Fax:	**(828) 726-1152**	**Web site:**	**None**

Smokey Mountain Furniture is located just a few miles north of Hickory, NC. They have a limited selection of lines in stock (American Drew, Lexington, Pulaski, etc.), but they can special order many more.

Unfortunately, this store has been accumulating complaints with the BBB, some of which have not been answered. Until Smokey Mountain Furniture again has a clean record with the BBB, I must recommend that my readers not shop here.

Lines carried:

Action By Lane	Broyhill	Jetton	Riverside
American Drew	Chromcraft	Kingsdown	Universal
Athens	England Corsair	Lexington	Vaughan
Benchcraft	Hood	Null Industries	
Bob Timberlake	Howard Miller	Pulaski	

Phone orders accepted:	**Yes**
Discount:	**35%-50% off mfrs. suggested retail**
Payment methods:	**VISA, MC, personal checks**
In-house financing available:	**No**
Deposits required:	**50% deposit when order is placed, balance due when furniture is ready to be shipped**
Catalog available:	**No**
Clearance center:	**No**
Delivery:	**Full service in-home delivery and set-up. Customer pays freight company directly for shipping costs.**

Directions: From I-40, take exit #123 and drive north on Hwy. 321 to Hudson. Smokey Mountain Furniture is on the right side of the road.

Sobol House

Richardson Blvd.
Black Mountain, NC 28711

Phone:	**(828) 669-8031**	**Hours:**	**M-Sat 9:30-5:00**
Toll Free:	**None**	**E-mail:**	**sales@sobolhouse.com**
Fax:	**(828) 669-7969**	**Web site:**	**www.sobolhouse.com**

Sobol House is located in Black Mountain, NC, just east of Asheville. They have a good selection of medium to high-end lines, including Bevan-Funnell, Flexsteel, Barcalounger, and Braxton Culler.

They have floor samples on display at a discount of 55-60% off retail. A few of these in-stock pieces are shown on their Web site. They also have great deals on many lines sold over the phone.

They do accept VISA and MC for in-store purchases and deposits on special orders, but they require a certified check, cashier's check, or money order for the balance due on delivery of any special order furniture. Please be aware that if you choose to pay with VISA or MC, you will be charged an extra 3% "processing fee". This is not a typical fee in this industry. I am unaware of any other furniture discounter which has this policy.

In the 2003 edition of this book, I reported that Sobol House had been accumulating complaints at the BBB regarding delivery delays. The BBB has confirmed that all such complaints have since been resolved.

Phone orders accepted:	**Yes**
Discount:	**40%-60% off mfrs. suggested retail**
Payment methods:	**VISA, MC, personal checks, certified funds**
In-house financing available:	**Yes**
Deposits required:	**50% deposit when order is placed, balance due when furniture is ready to be shipped**
Catalog available:	**Yes, limited information at their Web site**
Clearance center:	**No**
Delivery:	**Full service in-home delivery and set-up. Customer pays freight company directly for shipping costs.**

Directions: **From I-40, take exit #64, and go north on Hwy. 9. Turn left on Sutton Ave. Sobol House is about a mile down on the left.**

Sobol House (cont.)

Lines carried:

American Drew
Athol
A.P. Industries
Arte De Mexico
Barcalounger
Bard Intl.
Bassett
Bassett Mirror
Berkline
Bevan-Funnell
Braxton Culler
Builtright
Cambridge
Capel
Capris Furniture
Carolina Mirror
Century
Cochrane
Colibri Furniture
Colonial
Conover Chair
Cooper Classics
Craftique
Davis Cabinets
Decorative Crafts
Designz Unlimited
Destinations
Eddy West
Environment
Fairfield
Fairmont Designs
Flexsteel
Flat Rock
Generations
Hammary
Hammerton
Hickory Springs
Homecrest
Howard Miller
Johnston Casuals
Karges
Kessler
Key City
King Hickory
Kushwood
Lea Furniture
Legacy Bedding
Lloyd Buxton
Miller

Old Biscayne
Old Hickory Furn.
Ozark Cedar
Passport
Pompeii
Pulaski
Reprocrafters
Riverside
Sarreid
Scheibeco
Serta
Stakmore
Stein World
Superior Furniture
Taylor King
TeenaIron Works
Three Coins
Timmerman
Universal
Vaughan Furniture
Vietri
Waterford
Weiman
Wesley Allen
Wesley Hall
Whitaker
WildWood Lamps
Yorkshire House

SofaTrend Factory Outlet

Level 4
Hickory Furniture Mart
U. S. Hwy. 70 SE
Hickory, NC 28602

Phone:	**(828) 327-0244**	**Hours:**	**M-Sat 9:00-6:00**
Toll Free:	**None**	**E-mail:**	**moutlet@charterinternet.com**
Fax:	**(828) 327-4544**	**Web site:**	**www.hickoryfurniture.com**

The SofaTrend factory outlet is part of Manufacturer's Outlet, a very reputable company with a long-standing reputation for service. Manufacturer's Outlet also operates the factory outlets for Hickory White and Theodore Alexander at the Hickory Furniture Mart.

The stock is made up of floor samples, discontinued styles, and customer returns. All of the furniture here is upholstery: sofas and occasional chairs. The discounts run from 50%-70% off retail. Virtually all of the furniture here is in new first-quality condition.

This factory outlet also features Simex, Clayton-Marcus, LeatherTrend, and Mirador. In addition to furniture, they also have a line of European oil paintings at good prices and some Asian antique pieces.

They also participate in the regular mall-wide sales run by the Hickory Furniture Mart in February, May, July, and November. Please check out Web site at www.smartdecorating.com for upcoming sale dates.

Phone orders accepted:	**No**
Discount:	**50%-70% off mfrs. suggested retail**
Payment methods:	**VISA, MC, personal checks**
In-house financing available:	**Yes**
Deposits required:	**Not applicable**
Catalog available:	**Not applicable**
Clearance center:	**Not applicable**
Delivery:	**Full service in-home delivery and set-up. Customer pays freight company directly for shipping costs.**

Directions: Please see *Hickory Furniture Mart* for complete directions.

Southern Designs

Level 3
Hickory Furniture Mart
U. S. Hwy. 70 SE
Hickory, NC 28602

Phone:	**(828) 328-8855**		**Hours:**	**M-Sat 9:00-6:00**
Toll Free:	**None**		**E-mail:**	**info@hickoryfurniture.com**
Fax:	**(828) 328-1806**		**Web site:**	**www.hickoryfurniture.com**

Southern Designs in the Hickory Furniture Mart has good bargains on a number of high quality lines, such as Hitchcock Chair and Distinction Leather. Their specialty is solid wood casegoods.

They also have a number of high-quality manufacturers which produce knock-offs of better known brands. Richardson Brothers and Chatham County each produce very nice arts & crafts style furniture similar to Stickley. Brown Street produces a line almost identical to the Bob Timberlake signature series from Lexington. The quality is identical in my experience, but the prices on the lesser-known lines are quite a bit cheaper.

If you're shopping for any of the current "in" styles, such as mission or arts & crafts, you should check with this source to see what they may have from a lesser-advertised brand that may be identical to the heavily advertised pieces you originally chose.

Lines carried:

Ashton Pictures	Distinction Leather	Lt. Moses Willard Lamps	Superior
Big Sky Carvers	Eagle Craft Desks	Mobel	Today's Home Upholstery
Brown Street	Heritage Haus	Null Industries	2 Day Designs
Chatham County	Hitchcock Chair	Oriental Accents	Van Patten Curios
Cherry Pond	Huntington House	Richardson Brothers	Virginia House
Conover Chair	Key City	Shady Lady	Wisconsin Furniture
Cooper Classics	Leather Comfort	Skillcraft	
Craft-Tex	By Viewpoint	Southern Craftsmen's Guild	
Crawford of Jamestown	Lighting Enterprises	Stone County Ironworks	

Phone orders accepted:	**Yes**
Discount:	**40%-60% off mfrs. suggested retail**
Payment methods:	**VISA, MC, personal checks**
In-house financing available:	**No**
Deposits required:	**50% deposit when order is placed, balance due when furniture is ready to be shipped**
Catalog available:	**No**
Clearance center:	**No**
Delivery:	**Full service in-home delivery and set-up. Customer pays freight company directly for shipping costs.**

Directions: Please see *Hickory Furniture Mart* for complete directions.

Southern Style

Level 4
Hickory Furniture Mart
U. S. Hwy. 70 SE
Hickory, NC 28602

Phone:	**(828) 322-7000**	**Hours:**	**M-Sat 9:00-6:00**
Toll Free:	**None**	**E-mail:**	**southernstyle@ctc.net**
Fax:	**(828) 322-7220**	**Web site:**	**www.hickoryfurniture.com**

Southern Style specializes in upholstery by Southern of Conover. They've also got a number of high quality wicker and casegoods lines, listed below. Their discounts run 40%-50% off retail.

They will sell most items off the floor. None of these floor samples are marked down, but I've found that you can negotiate a discount on most items if you try.

If you're interested in any of the lines below, this store is well worth checking out. They have a very good reputation for customer service.

Lines carried:

APA
Boca Rattan
Braxton Culler
Magnussen
Southern of Conover
Stein World
Wynwood

Phone orders accepted:	**Yes**
Discount:	**40%-50% off mfrs. suggested retail**
Payment methods:	**VISA, MC, AMEX, Discover, personal checks**
In-house financing available:	**No**
Deposits required:	**50% deposit when order is placed, balance due when furniture is ready to be shipped**
Catalog available:	**No**
Clearance center:	**No**
Delivery:	**Full service in-home delivery and set-up. Customer pays freight company directly for shipping costs.**

Directions: Please see *Hickory Furniture Mart* for complete directions.

Stanley Furniture Factory Outlet

6496 Virginia Avenue
Bassett, VA 24055

Phone:	**(276) 629-9306**	**Hours:**	**M-F 9:00-6:00, Sat 10:00-5:00,**
Toll Free:	**None**		**Sun 1:00-5:00**
Fax:	**(276) 629-9245**	**E-mail:**	**None**
		Web site:	**www.stanleyfurniture.com**

The Stanley Furniture Factory Outlet in Bassett, VA is the only factory outlet for this brand. It's about an hour's drive from the High Point area. As this area of Virginia also has outlets for Hooker, Bassett, and Lane, it's well-worth a side trip from High Point if you have the time.

This outlet has a good variety of undamaged furniture at discounts of 55%-60% off retail. With the exception of dining room chairs, there is no upholstery here, only casegoods. There are some quite good bargains here.

For example, on my last trip here, I found this pretty bedroom set for a little girl (pictured on the following page) . This entire set retails for $3,928.00 including the poster bed, nightstand, dresser, mirror, and chest. This set in undamaged condition at the outlet was only $1,598.00. That's a savings of 60% off retail.

The outlet also has some damaged pieces at discounts of 70%-85% off retail. If you have basic woodworking skills and want to find some terrific deals on pieces that need a little fixing up, this is a terrific source.

Please be aware that this outlet is not as service oriented as the factory outlets in Hickory and High Point. They can only arrange shipment to the East Coast, primarily from New York to Florida. Before visiting this outlet, you may wish to call their delivery service, Hopkins Delivery Service, at (276) 647-5200 to see if they service your area of the country.

Overall, this is a great source. If you're in the High Point area shopping for furniture, you may wish to take a side trip to all the great outlets in southern Virginia.

Phone orders accepted:	**No**
Discount:	**60%-85% off mfrs. suggested retail**
Payment methods:	**VISA, MC, AMEX, Discover, Virginia checks.**
In-house financing available:	**No**
Deposits required:	**Not applicable**
Catalog available:	**Yes, at their Web site**
Clearance center:	**Not applicable**
Delivery:	**East Coast only, through Hopkins Delivery Service (276-647-5200)**

Directions: From I-40 in Greensboro, NC, take the Hwy. 68/Airport exit (#210), and head north on Hwy. 68. After about 30 minutes, turn onto Hwy. 220 toward Martinsville/Roanoke. Stay on 220 all the way through downtown Martinsville. After about 40 miles on 220, you'll see the Stanley Factory Outlet on your right, just north of Martinsville.

Stanley Furniture Factory Outlet (cont.)

Stanley Furniture Factory Outlet

Child's bedroom set from Stanley Furniture

Retail: $3,928.00   Discounted price: $1,598.00
Savings at the Stanley Furniture Factory Outlet: $2,330.00 = 60% off retail

Stevens Furniture

1258 Hickory Blvd. SW
Lenoir, NC 28645

Phone:	**(828) 728-5511**	**Hours:**	**M-Sat 9:00-5:30**
Toll Free:	**None**	**E-mail:**	**sales@stevensfurniture.com**
Fax:	**(828) 728-5518**	**Web site:**	**www.stevensfurniture.com**

Stevens Furniture in Lenoir, NC, has been discounting furniture by phone since 1964. They have a huge store with large galleries for Stanley, Broyhill, Lexington, and Hickory White, among other lines.

Although you can buy furniture off the floor if you wish, the discount you receive in person is no better than the discount you receive over the phone. Their discounts run about 40%-50% off retail.

There is a small "Value Center" in the basement with some discontinued styles and floor samples discounted up to 75% off retail, but there really isn't much selection. Routinely, they might have a few odd dining room tables, a few occasional tables and chairs, and a desk or two.

Stevens Furniture does currently have a satisfactory record with the BBB, and I have heard no complaints about them. However, their "sister store" (as they call it), Parkway Furniture, has a very poor record with the BBB. As of this printing in February 2004, both stores are owned by the same man, Thomas Shores.

I cannot say whether Stevens Furniture will also begin to have similar problems. They've had a good record for customer service for many years, and may continue to have that good record for many years to come. However, in my experience, when multiple stores are owned by the same person and one store has complaints, soon they all have complaints. Before ordering here, please recheck the BBB report or our Web site, www.smartdecorating.com, to ensure that Stevens Furniture is not experiencing problems at that time.

Phone orders accepted:	**Yes**
Discount:	**40%-50% off mfrs. suggested retail**
Payment methods:	**VISA, MC, AMEX, Discover, personal checks**
In-house financing available:	**Yes**
Deposits required:	**1/3 deposit when order is placed, balance due when furniture is ready to be shipped**
Catalog available:	**No**
Clearance center:	**Yes**
Delivery:	**Full service in-home delivery and set-up. Customer pays freight company directly for shipping costs.**

Directions: From I-40, take exit #123 and head north into Hickory, NC, on Hwy. 321. Go about 10 miles north on Hwy. 321 to Lenoir, NC. Stevens is on the left right past Quality Furniture Market of Lenoir.

Stickley Furniture Showroom

225 North Elm St.
High Point, NC 27260

Phone:	**(336) 887-1336**	**Hours:**	**M-Sat 9:00-5:00**
Toll Free:	**None**		**Closed April and October**
Fax:	**None**	**E-mail:**	**None**
		Web site:	**www.stickley.com**

Stickley has recently opened their wholesale showroom in High Point to the public. Please note that this is not a factory outlet. No discontinued items or other outlet merchandise is in stock. Customers may only special order new furniture directly from Stickley. Discounts are up to 42%, depending on when you call. Also, please note that as a wholesale showroom, this store is closed during April and October for the High Point International Home Furnishings Market.

Unfortunately, although this store advertises in High Point that they are open to the public, they will only sell to you if you are a North Carolina resident. They do not permit customers to pick up their furniture at the store. Everything must be shipped. As soon as you give them any address outside of North Carolina, they will tell you that you must contact your local dealer in your area and pay the retail price charged in your town.

Unless you live in North Carolina, this store is a waste of time. Fortunately, Stickley has a wide variety of manufacturing competitors who do not put such ridiculous restrictions on shoppers. Many other companies manufacture similar or identical styles to the same level of quality.

In particular, if you're interested in the traditional "Stickley look", go check out the Robert Bergelin Company. They make a better quality product at a lower price, and they are delighted to sell directly to consumers.

Phone orders accepted:	**No**
Discount:	**Up to 42% off mfrs. suggested retail**
Payment methods:	**VISA, MC, personal checks**
In-house financing available:	**No**
Deposits required:	**50% deposit when order is placed, balance due when furniture is ready to be shipped**
Catalog available:	**Yes, at their Web site above**
Clearance center:	**No**
Delivery:	**Full service in-home delivery and set-up. Customer pays freight company directly for shipping costs.**

Directions:	**The Stickley Furniture Showroom is in downtown High Point, NC. From I-85, take exit #111 (Hwy. 311), and head northwest into High Point. After several miles, when you reach downtown High Point, Hwy. 311 will become Main St. Turn left at English St., then take an immediate right on N. Elm St. You'll see the Stickley Furniture Showroom right in front of you on the left.**

Studio 70

Catawba Furniture Mall
377 Hwy. 70 SW
Hickory, NC 28602

Phone:	**(828) 322-2800**	**Hours:**	**M-Sat 10:00-7:00**
Toll Free:	**None**	**E-mail:**	**Please see Web site**
Fax:	**None**	**Web site:**	**www.studioseventy.com**

Studio 70 has a great selection of contemporary furniture and accessories, one of the best in Hickory. They're very pleasant to deal with, and they have a good reputation for customer service. Their prices run about 30%-60% off retail.

For instance, on a recent visit, I found a great deal on a bedroom set (pictured on the following page). This set retails for $13,059.00 including the bed, two nightstands, dresser, mirror, armoire, and a seven drawer chest (not pictured). The discounted price on the entire set was only $8,499.00, a savings of 35% off retail.

I have found that this source will work for your business. Ask for an extra 10% off. Depending on which brand you're interested in, they may be able to come down a bit more on the price for you.

Please see the listing in this book for the Catawba Furniture Mall if you are planning a visit here. The Mall offers discounts on hotel rooms and coupons toward your furniture purchase during their big sale weekends four times each year.

If you're in the market for contemporary furniture and accessories, this is a great source!

Lines carried:

ADesso	Comfort Designs	Hjellegjerde	Rossetto
Andrew Pearson	Doimo	Kinder Harris	Studio 99
Artmax	Eurostyle	Laurier	Tempur Pedic
Calligaris	Evans Designs	Leatherworks	Swedish Mattress
Carter Contemporary	Hellenic Rugs	Nayer Kazemi	Weiman

Phone orders accepted:	**Yes**
Discount:	**30%-60% off mfrs. suggested retail**
Payment methods:	**VISA, MC, AMEX, Discover, personal checks**
In-house financing available:	**No**
Deposits required:	**50% deposit when order is placed, balance due when furniture is ready to be shipped**
Catalog available:	**Yes, limited catalog at their Web site above**
Clearance center:	**No**
Delivery:	**Full service in-home delivery and set-up. Customer pays freight company directly for shipping costs.**

Directions: **The Catawba Furniture Mall is in Hickory, NC. From I-40, take exit #123-B and turn right. The mall will be about half a mile down on the right.**

Studio 70 at the Catawba Furniture Mall

Bedroom set at Studio 70

Retail: $13,059.00   Discounted price: $8,499.00
Savings at Studio 70: $4,560.00 = 35% off retail

Tarheel Home Furnishings Outlet

241 Timberbrook Lane
Granite Falls, NC 28630

Phone:	(828) 396-8150	**Hours:**	M-Sat 9:00-6:00
Toll Free:	None	**E-mail:**	tarheelhomefurn@yahoo.com
Fax:	(828) 396-8151	**Web site:**	None

Tarheel Home Furnishings Outlet has some good bargains, particularly on Bassett and Lea. They have a large Bassett gallery, and they claim to have the lowest prices anywhere on this brand. If you plan to special order Bassett, invite this source to beat any competitor's price.

Overall, their pricing runs about 40%-60% off retail. Their reputation for customer service is excellent. I particularly like the fact that they follow up with every customer after the furniture is delivered to make sure everything is correct and the customer is pleased with their order. This is unusual. Most furniture discounters don't take the time to do this.

This source is well worth visiting if you're in the Hickory area. If you plan to order any of the lines below by phone, definitely call them and compare pricing.

Lines carried:

American Drew	Joffran	PeopleLoungers	South Seas Rattan
Bassett	Legacy Classic	Peters-Revington	Stein World
Chromcraft	Magnussen Home	Powell	Sunrise
Homelegance	Master Design	Sealy	Supreme Mattress

Phone orders accepted:	Yes
Discount:	40%-50% off mfrs. suggested retail
Payment methods:	VISA, MC, personal checks
In-house financing available:	No
Deposits required:	50% deposit when order is placed, balance due when furniture is ready to be shipped
Catalog available:	No
Clearance center:	No
Delivery:	Full service in-home delivery and set-up. Customer pays freight company directly for shipping costs.

Directions: From I-40, take exit #123 and drive north on Hwy. 321 to Granite Falls. Tarheel Home Furnishings Outlet is on the left side of the road.

The Showroom
115 East Church Street
Martinsville, VA 24112

Phone:	(276) 638-6264	**Hours:**	M-Sat 10:00-6:00
Toll Free:	None	**E-mail:**	showroom@fm-a.com
Fax:	(276) 638-2719	**Web site:**	www.fm-a.com

The Showroom in Martinsville, VA is a reputable deep discounter with access to some very nice lines. They have a great reputation for service, and I find their staff very pleasant and helpful. Their discounts tend to run about 50% off retail.

Their prices are frequently significantly lower than the deep discounters in High Point and Hickory on identical items. Before placing a special order with another discounter on any of the lines they carry, definitely call The Showroom to compare prices. As The Showroom is significantly outside the main furniture discounting areas and not as widely known, they're willing to work a little harder to get your business.

They also have a very nice line of custom occasional and dining room chairs. Customers can choose from one of 195 styles arranged around the upper walls of the showroom and have their chairs stained and upholstered any way they wish. They also have a few styles of occasional tables that can be custom stained as well. If you like, you can even send them a sample of your own furniture (a drawer or leaf) and they will stain your chairs to match.

If you've found a bargain on a lone dining room table at a factory outlet or clearance center, as I recommend, this is a good place to get special order chairs to match.

If you plan to order custom chairs here, you may wish to stop by 1502 Fabrics in High Point first to pick out a fabric. They stock a huge selection of roll ends and discontinued fabrics from many of the local furniture factories. They have terrific bargains. Some fabrics are as low as $1.50 a yard!

If you plan to visit High Point, you may wish to take a day to drive to the Martinsville, VA area, which also has outlets for Hooker, Lane, Stanley, and Bassett plus a clearance center for The Showroom right down the street.

Phone orders accepted:	Yes
Discount:	**Approximately 50% off mfrs. suggested retail**
Payment methods:	**VISA, MC, AMEX, Discover, personal checks**
In-house financing available:	**No**
Deposits required:	**50% deposit due with order. Balance due before shipment.**
Catalog available:	**No**
Clearance center:	**Yes, please see *Martin Plaza***
Delivery:	**Full service in-home delivery and set-up. Customer pays freight company directly for shipping costs.**

Directions: From I-40 in Greensboro, NC, take the Hwy. 68/Airport exit (#210), and head north on Hwy. 68. After about 30 minutes, turn onto Hwy. 220 toward Martinsville/Roanoke. After about another 20 minutes, you'll enter Martinsville. Be sure to stay on Business 220 through town, not on the 220 bypass which goes around Martinsville. About 10 miles after you get on Business 220, you'll come to Broad St. There's a green "John Deere" dealership sign on the corner. Broad St. will dead end into Church St. Turn right. The Showroom is down the street on the right.

The Showroom (cont.)

Lines carried:

American Drew
APA Marketing
Butler Specialty
Century
Fairfield Chair
Hekman
Hooker
Kessler
King Hickory
Lane
Lane Action
Leather Trend
Passport
Sarreid
Stanley
Sumter
Taylor King
Ultimate Accents
Woodmark
Wynwood

Theodore Alexander Factory Outlet

Level 4
Hickory Furniture Mart
U. S. Hwy. 70 SE
Hickory, NC 28602

Phone:	**(828) 327-3766**	**Hours:**	**M-Sat 9:00-6:00**
Toll Free:	**None**	**E-mail:**	**info@hickoryfurniture.com**
Fax:	**None**	**Web site:**	**www.hickoryfurniture.com**

The Theodore Alexander Factory outlet at the Hickory Furniture Mart is fairly new. It has a good assortment of furniture and accessories, particularly occasional tables and vases. This is the only factory outlet for this brand.

Theodore Alexander is owned by Paul Maitland-Smith, who founded the Maitland Smith Furniture Company. After he sold his original company to a conglomerate and retired, he evidently missed the furniture business and decided to start this new company, named after his two grandsons.

The look of Theodore Alexander furniture and accessories is very similar to Maitland Smith, except that Theodore Alexander leans more strongly toward oriental styles. The quality and styling are top notch.

Most of the stock here is in new first-quality condition: floor samples, customer returns, discontinued items, and stock overruns.

Their normal discount runs between 50% to 80%. In January, the outlet runs a month long sale with even bigger discounts. During the sale, all items are 75% to 80% off retail. The outlet also runs shorter sales in May, July, September, and November with the same discounts.

Please also see the listings under Hickory Furniture Mart for more information on travel bargains to the Mart and ways of saving money on shipping.

Phone orders accepted:	**No**
Discount:	**50%-80% off mfrs. suggested retail**
Payment methods:	**VISA, MC, AMEX, personal checks**
In-house financing available:	**No**
Deposits required:	**Not applicable**
Catalog available:	**No**
Clearance center:	**Not applicable**
Delivery:	**Full service in-home delivery and set-up. Customer pays freight company directly for shipping costs.**

Directions: Please see *Hickory Furniture Mart* for complete directions.

Thomas Home Furnishings

4346 Hickory Blvd.
Granite Falls, NC 28630

Phone:	**(828) 396-2147**	**Hours:**	**M-Sat 9:00-5:00**
Toll Free:	**None**	**E-mail:**	**thomashomefurn@charter.net**
Fax:	**(828) 396-6179**	**Web site:**	**www.thomashomefurnishings.com**

Thomas Home Furnishings in Granite Falls just north of Hickory, NC, has a huge store with large galleries for La-Z-Boy and Pennsylvania House, among other lines. They have recently expanded, with a new 12,000 square foot Lexington Gallery--including many groups from their Bob Timberlake collections.

The one thing that gets your attention first when you walk in the door, though, is the sound of phones buzzing off the hook. This source does a booming order-by-phone business. They do have good discounts, about 40%-50% off retail on most brands. In particular, they have the best deals I've found anywhere on La-Z-Boy.

All of the furniture in stock is new first-quality. They have some floor samples available at deeper discounts, so you may certainly wish to stop in if you're also shopping in nearby Hickory or Lenoir.

If you're ordering furniture over the phone, definitely call them to compare prices. They have the lowest prices available on some lines, including La-Z-Boy, and they have very reliable service. If you plan to visit the Hickory, NC area, definitely stop in. They also have some great deals on floor samples.

Phone orders accepted:	**Yes**
Discount:	**40%-50% off mfrs. suggested retail**
Payment methods:	**VISA, MC, personal checks**
In-house financing available:	**No**
Deposits required:	**50% deposit when order is placed, balance due when furniture is ready to be shipped**
Catalog available:	**No**
Clearance center:	**No**
Delivery:	**Full service in-home delivery and set-up. Customer pays freight company directly for shipping costs.**

Directions: From I-40, take exit #123 and drive north on Hwy. 321 to Granite Falls. Thomas Home Furnishings is on the right side of the road.

Thomas Home Furnishings (cont.)

Lines carried:

AICO
American Drew
Arnold Palmer Collection
Artistica
Athol
Austin Sculptures
Bassett
Bernhardt
Bob Timberlake
Bradington Young
Broyhill
Carolina Mirror
Carsons
Charleston Forge
Clayton Marcus
Conover Chair
Craftique
Crawford
Designmaster
Elliott's Designs
Excursions By Lane
Fairfield
Fairmont Designs
Great City Traders
Hammary
Hekman
Henry Link
Highland House
Hooker
Kessler
Kinder Harris
Lane
Lane/Venture
La-Z-Boy
Leathercraft
Lexington
Moosehead
Palmer Home Collection
Pennsylvania House
Pulaski
Royal Craftsmen
Sam Moore
Sedgefield
Serta Mattress
Southampton
Southwood Reproductions
Stanford
Stanley
Stiffel Lamps

Sumter Cabinet
Universal
Venture By Lane
Virginia Metalcrafters
Wellington Hall
Wesley Allen Brass Beds
Wildwood Lamps
Woodmark

Thomasville Factory Outlet

Westover Gallery Mall
1410 Westover Terrace
Greensboro, NC 27408

Phone:	**(336) 273-2713**	**Hours:**	**M-F 9:30-6:00, Sat 9:30-5:00**
Toll Free:	**None**	**E-mail:**	**info@thomasville.com**
Fax:	**None**	**Web site:**	**www.thomasville.com**

This is Thomasville's newest factory outlet. It has a good variety of Thomasville casegoods (armoires, beds, etc.), upholstery, and leather. There is also a small selection of furniture from Highland House and Hickory Chair.

Please note that all three Thomasville Factory Outlets charge 7% sales tax even on orders shipped out of state. As most customers will owe sales tax to their home state anyway, this should not be a problem. Please see the "Frequently Asked Questions" list in the introduction of this book for a more detailed discussion of sales and use taxes on out of state purchases.

If you're in the Greensboro/High Point area, this outlet is definitely worth a visit.

Phone orders accepted:	**No**
Discount:	**65%-75% off mfrs. suggested retail**
Payment methods:	**VISA, MC, AMEX, personal checks**
In-house financing available:	**Yes**
Deposits required:	**Not applicable**
Catalog available:	**Not applicable**
Clearance center:	**Not applicable**
Delivery:	**Full service in-home delivery and set-up. Customer pays freight company directly for shipping costs.**

Directions: **Travel I-40 toward Greensboro and exit on Wendover Avenue. Proceed east on Wendover Avenue. Exit right onto Westover Terrace. At the end of the ramp, turn left and cross the bridge over Wendover Avenue. The outlet is located in the shopping center immediately on your right.**

Thomasville Factory Outlet

Hwy 321 N.
Hudson, NC 28638

Phone:	**(828) 728-4108**	**Hours:**	**M-F 9:00-5:30, Sat 9:00-5:00**
Toll Free:	**None**	**E-mail:**	**info@thomasville.com**
Fax:	**None**	**Web site:**	**www.thomasville.com**

This is one of Thomasville's three factory outlets. The stock here is an even mix of casegoods and upholstery. There is also a small selection of furniture from Highland House and Hickory Chair. The vast majority of the furniture here is undamaged and in first-quality condition.

They also have a wide selection of upholstery from Thomasville's nearby upholstery manufacturing plant. If you're in the market for a sofa or armchair, this is a great place to visit.

They also have some terrific bargains here. On a recent visit, I found a great deal on a dining room set (pictured on the following page). This set retails for $7,680.00 including the table, six chairs, and china cabinet. This showroom sample in undamaged condition was available for only $2,805.00, a savings of 64% off retail. One of my tour members purchased this set.

Please note that all three Thomasville Factory Outlets charge 7% sales tax even on orders shipped out of state. As most customers will owe sales tax to their home state anyway, this should not be a problem. Please see the "Frequently Asked Questions" list in the introduction of this book for a more detailed discussion of sales and use taxes on out of state purchases.

The outlet is huge. If you're looking for good deals on medium to high-end upholstery and case goods, this is definitely an outlet you should visit.

Phone orders accepted:	**No**
Discount:	**65%-75% off mfrs. suggested retail**
Payment methods:	**VISA, MC, AMEX, personal checks**
In-house financing available:	**Yes**
Deposits required:	**Not applicable**
Catalog available:	**Not applicable**
Clearance center:	**Not applicable**
Delivery:	**Full service in-home delivery and set-up. Customer pays freight company directly for shipping costs.**

Directions: From I-40, take exit #123 (Hwy. 321) and head north through Hickory toward Lenoir. Just before you get to Lenoir, you'll see the Thomasville Factory Outlet on your right.

Thomasville Factory Outlet (cont.)

Thomasville Factory Outlet in Hudson, NC

Dining room set from Thomasville

Retail: $7,680.00   Discounted price: $2,805.00
Savings at the Thomasville Factory Outlet: $4,875.00 = 64% off retail

Thomasville Factory Outlet

401 East Main St.
Thomasville, NC 27361

Phone:	**(336) 476-2211**	**Hours:**	**M-F 9:00-5:30, Sat 9:00-4:00**
Toll Free:	**None**	**E-mail:**	**info@thomasville.com**
Fax:	**(336) 476-2359**	**Web site:**	**www.thomasville.com**

This is one of Thomasville's three true factory outlets. Most of the furniture in stock here are case goods from Thomasville's main case goods manufacturing plant, right next door to the outlet.

They do have some upholstery in stock here, but most of Thomasville's sample and discontinued upholstery is liquidated through their other outlet in Lenoir, NC, which is closer to their main upholstery and leather manufacturing plants in Hickory, NC. If you are specifically looking for Thomasville upholstery, you would be better off visiting their Lenoir outlet instead. There is also a new Thomasville outlet in Greensboro which has some upholstery.

The outlet is quite large, and they have some very good bargains here. On a recent visit, I found a great deal on a solid cherry entertainment center (pictured on the following page). The usual retail on this item is $3,045.00, but the outlet had this floor sample marked down to only $1,155.00. It was in new first-quality condition.

Thomasville does a good job of clearly marking which items are first-quality, floor samples, seconds, or irregulars. The majority of the stock here is in new first-quality condition. Even the few seconds I found scattered around the outlet had very small flaws, and these were marked down to about 70% to 80% off retail.

Please note that all three Thomasville Factory Outlets charge 7% sales tax even on orders shipped out of state. As most customers will owe sales tax to their home state anyway, this should not be a problem. Please see the "Frequently Asked Questions" list in the introduction of this book for a more detailed discussion of sales and use taxes on out of state purchases.

This outlet has a very nice variety of beds, armoires, entertainment centers, chests, bedroom sets, dining room sets, office furniture, and other case goods, as well as some upholstery. This outlet is a "must-visit".

Phone orders accepted:	**No**
Discount:	**60%-80% off mfrs. suggested retail**
Payment methods:	**VISA, MC, AMEX, personal checks**
In-house financing available:	**Yes**
Deposits required:	**Not applicable**
Catalog available:	**Not applicable**
Clearance center:	**Not applicable**
Delivery:	**Full service in-home delivery and set-up. Customer pays freight company directly for shipping costs.**

Directions: **From I-85, take exit #103 and go north on Randolph St. into downtown Thomasville. Just before you reach the railroad tracks, turn right onto E. Main St. The Thomasville outlet will be 4 blocks down on your right.**

Thomasville Factory Outlet(cont.)

Thomasville Factory Outlet in Thomasville, NC

Solid cherry entertainment center from Thomasville

Retail: $3,045.00   Discounted price: $1,155.00
Savings at the Thomasville Factory Outlet: $1,890.00 = 62% off retail

Transit Damage Freight

Cannon Village
251 West Ave.
Kannapolis, NC 28081

Phone:	**(704) 938-9010**	**Hours:**	**M-F 9-5, Sat 10-6, Sun 1-6**
Toll Free:	**None**	**E-mail:**	**info@cannonvillage.com**
Fax:	**(704) 938-9016**	**Web site:**	**www.cannonvillage.com**

Transit Damage is much more than just a typical damaged-freight liquidation center. Yes, they do have a small amount of furniture damaged in shipment or separated from it's original paperwork, but most of their stock at this particular location is made up of floor samples, discontinued styles, and seconds. They can also special order some lines.

This source isn't necessarily worth a separate trip, but if you're in the Kannapolis area anyway, you may wish to stop in. The prices are good, but not as good as in a typical factory-owned factory outlet. Most of the furniture here is priced at about 40%-50% off retail. The bargains here vary widely from not-so-great to fantastic.

This is not a place for an amateur furniture shopper to start out. If you have a good eye for furniture and you can easily judge what it ought to be worth, you can get some spectacular deals here. If you don't know what to take and what to leave alone, though, you could end up paying more than you should.

Expert furniture shoppers and those with the woodworking skills to make minor touch-ups and repairs: run, don't walk, to this outlet. Average consumers: stick with the many less confusing factory outlets and deep discounters elsewhere in North Carolina.

Lines carried:	**Varies**
Phone orders accepted:	**Yes**
Discount:	**40%-50% off mfrs. suggested retail**
Payment methods:	**VISA, MC, Discover, personal checks**
In-house financing available:	**No**
Deposits required:	**Not applicable**
Catalog available:	**Not applicable**
Clearance center:	**Not applicable**
Delivery:	**Customers must make own arrangements to take furniture home.**

Directions: From I-85, take exit #63, and follow the signs to Cannon Village.

Transit Damage Freight

1604 S. Main St.
Lexington, NC 27292

Phone:	(336) 248-2646	**Hours:**	M-Th, Sat 9:00-5:30,
Toll Free:	None		Fri 9:00-7:00
Fax:	(336) 243-2168	**E-mail:**	None
		Web site:	None

Transit Damage is much more than just a typical damaged-freight liquidation center. Yes, they do have a small amount of furniture damaged in shipment or separated from it's original paperwork, but most of their stock at this particular location is made up of floor samples, discontinued styles, and seconds.

Lexington (including Henry Link, Bob Timberlake, and Palmer Home Collection), Stanley, and Bassett all have factories nearby, and they use Transit Damage as a quasi-factory outlet. They have pieces from various other brands here, as well.

This source isn't necessarily worth a separate trip, but if you're in the Lexington area anyway, you may wish to stop in. The prices are good, but not as good as in a typical factory-owned factory outlet. Most of the furniture here is priced at about 40%-50% off retail. The bargains here vary widely from not-so-great to fantastic.

This is not a place for an amateur furniture shopper to start out. If you have a good eye for furniture and you can easily judge what it ought to be worth, you can get some spectacular deals here. If you don't know what to take and what to leave alone, though, you could end up paying more than you should.

Expert furniture shoppers and those with the woodworking skills to make minor touch-ups and repairs: run, don't walk, to this outlet. Average consumers: stick with the many less confusing factory outlets and deep discounters elsewhere in North Carolina.

Lines carried:	Varies
Phone orders accepted:	Yes
Discount:	40%-50% off mfrs. suggested retail
Payment methods:	VISA, MC, Discover, personal checks
In-house financing available:	No
Deposits required:	Not applicable
Catalog available:	Not applicable
Clearance center:	Not applicable
Delivery:	Customers must make own arrangements to take furniture home.

Directions: From I-85, take exit #87, and get on Business I-85 north. Take exit #86 off of Business 85, and take a left at the light. Transit Damage Freight is just up the road on the left.

Triad Furniture Outlet

1589-125 Skeet Club Rd.
High Point, NC 27265

Phone:	(336) 812-8736	**Hours:**	M-F 10:00-6:00, Sat 10:00-5:30
Toll Free:	None	**E-mail:**	JNBusey@yahoo.com
Fax:	(336) 812-9823	**Web site:**	None

   Triad Furniture Outlet in High Point is owned by a long time industry insider. Owner Jay Busey worked in furniture manufacturing for many years. As a result, he knows just where to get the best closeout pieces, market samples, showroom samples, etc. His prices are quite good, about 55%-60% off retail. Discounts can run as high as 80% off retail on selected pieces.

   The store has a good assortment of casegoods and upholstery, but obviously their stock will change significantly between each visit. They have a good reputation for customer service. It's convenient as well, as it's only a few minutes from most of the nice hotels near the airport. If you're in High Point, you really should stop by.

Phone orders accepted:	Yes
Discount:	55%-80% off mfrs. suggested retail
Payment methods:	VISA, MC, Discover, personal checks
In-house financing available:	Yes
Deposits required:	Not applicable
Catalog available:	Not applicable
Clearance center:	Not applicable
Delivery:	Full service in-home delivery and set-up. Customer pays freight company directly for shipping costs.

Directions: From I-40, take the Hwy. 68/Greensboro Airport exit and drive south toward High Point. Hwy. 68 will change name to Eastchester. About 5 minutes south of I-40, you'll come to Oak Hollow Square on the right just before the intersection of Eastchester and Wendover Ave. Triad Furniture Outlet is in the corner of the Oak Hollow Square shopping center to the left of Harris Teeter.

Triplett's Furniture Fashions

2084 Hickory Blvd. SW
Lenoir, NC 28645

Phone:	**(828) 728-8211**	**Hours:**	**M-Sat 8:30-5:30**
Toll Free:	**None**	**E-mail:**	**tff@twave.net**
Fax:	**(828) 726-0171**	**Web site:**	**www.triplettsfurniture.com**

Triplett's Furniture Fashions has a very nice store in Lenoir, NC, just north of Hickory. They have a good selection of medium to high-end lines, such as Lexington, Hekman, Hooker, and Universal. They can also special order many lines over the phone. Triplett's has an excellent reputation for customer service.

The discounts on new furniture in first-quality condition, whether purchased in person or over the phone, run from 40%-50% off retail.

They generally don't have any floor samples or discontinued styles on display. Also, the Clayton-Marcus factory outlet which used to be located here has moved to the Hickory Furniture Mart under new ownership.

Anyone planning to buy furniture by phone should make a point of calling here to compare prices. They have great discounts and good service.

Phone orders accepted:	**Yes**
Discount:	**40%-50% off mfrs. suggested retail**
Payment methods:	**VISA, MC, Discover, personal checks**
In-house financing available:	**No**
Deposits required:	**50% deposit when order is placed, balance due when furniture is ready to be shipped**
Catalog available:	**No**
Clearance center:	**No**
Delivery:	**Full service in-home delivery and set-up. Customer pays freight company directly for shipping costs.**

Directions: From I-40, take exit #123 and drive north on Hwy. 321 to Lenoir. Triplett's Furniture Fashions is on the left side of the road.

Triplett's Furniture Fashions (cont.)

Lines carried:

American Drew
Andrea By Sadek
Athol
Austin Sculptures
Bakers Heritage
Bassett Mirror
Barcalounger
Bevan Funnell
Berkline
Boston Rockers
Builtright Chairs
Cape Craftsmen
Carolina Mirror
Charleston Forge
Chromcraft
Clayton Marcus
Cochrane
Colonial Furniture
Cooper Classics
Cox
Crawford of Jamestown
Crystal Clear Lighting
Dalyn Rugs
Denny Lamps
Design Master
D. R. Kincaid
Fairmont Designs
Fashion Bed Group
Fashion House
Frederick Cooper Lamps
Glober
Hammary
Harris Furniture
Heather Brooke
Hekman
Hillsdale Barstools
Hollywoods
Hooker
Jasper
Johnston Casuals
Koch's
Lea
Legacy
Leisters
Light & Sight Lamps
Master Designs
Medlift
Natural Light Designs
Nichols & Stone

Noble
Null Industries
Ohio Table Pad
P & P Chair
Parker Southern
Peters Revington
Powell
Pulaski
Regency House
Ridgeway Clocks
Riverside
Sam Moore
Sarreid
Sedgefield
Serta
Sidney Authur
Stein World
Statesville Chair
Sumter Cabinet
Temple
Toyo
Two Day Designs
Universal
Vineyard
Walker Mirror
Weathercraft
Wesley Allen Brass Beds
Whitaker
Westwood Lamps

Tyson Furniture Company

109 Broadway
Black Mountain, NC 28711

Phone:	**(828) 669-5000**	**Hours:**	**M-Sat 9:00-5:30**
Toll Free:	**None**	**E-mail:**	**tysonfurniture@aol.com**
Fax:	**(828) 669-8292**	**Web site:**	**home.att.net/~h535/Tysons.htm**

Tyson's Furniture Company in Black Mountain, NC, just east of Asheville, is huge. It occupies about a dozen interconnected buildings covering more than a city block in downtown Black Mountain. They have huge galleries for many high-end lines, including Hickory White, Baker, Century, Henredon, and others.

On my most recent visit here, I found a terrific deal on a Hickory White solid cherry highboy (pictured on the following page). It normally retails for $5,264.00, but Tyson's had this one in stock for only $2,099.00. It was brand-new and in perfect condition.

Most of the furniture here is new first-quality, priced at about 40%-50% off retail. All lines can be ordered over the phone at about 5%-10% less than the regular showroom prices, plus phone customers don't have to pay North Carolina sales tax, so there's really no reason to travel here in person. Should you decide to shop here in person for any reason, though, be sure to ask for their extra 10% discount for cash purchases made in-person at the store.

Tyson Furniture has a record of complaints regarding their advertising policies, particularly the discounts they advertise. As always, when comparing prices among sources, be sure to compare actual dollar amounts instead of percentages off retail. They have no complaints that I'm aware of regarding delivery.

Lines carried:

Barcalounger	Hekman	Karastan	Sealy
Bassett	Henkel Harris	Kincaid	Simmons
Bernhardt	Hickory Chair	Lane	Statton
Broyhill	Hickory White	La-Z-Boy	Stiffel
Clayton Marcus	Highland House	Lexington	Wildwood
Crescent	Howard Miller	Pennsylvania House	Woodmark

Phone orders accepted:	**Yes**
Discount:	**40%-60% off mfrs. suggested retail**
Payment methods:	**VISA, MC, Discover, personal checks**
In-house financing available:	**Yes**
Deposits required:	**50% deposit when order is placed, balance due when furniture is ready to be shipped**
Catalog available:	**No**
Clearance center:	**No**
Delivery:	**Full service in-home delivery and set-up. Customer pays freight company directly for shipping costs.**

Directions: From I-40, take exit #64, and go north one mile into Black Mountain, NC. Tyson's Furniture Company is right downtown on Broadway.

Tyson Furniture Company (cont.)

Tyson Furniture Company

Solid cherry highboy from Hickory White

Retail: $5,264.00   Discounted price: $2,099.00
Savings at Tyson Furniture Company: $3,165.00 = 60% off retail

Utility Craft Fine Furniture

2630 Eastchester Dr.
High Point, NC 27265

Phone:	**(336) 454-6153**	**Hours:**	**M-F 9:00-5:30, Sat 9:00-5:00**
Toll Free:	**None**	**E-mail:**	**Available at Web site**
Fax:	**(336) 454-5065**	**Web site:**	**www.utilitycraft.com**

Utility Craft Fine Furniture on the north side of High Point has a very nice store with a good selection of high-end lines: Hickory White, La Barge, Wellington Hall, Lexington, etc.

All of the furniture here is in new first-quality condition. The discounts run from 40%-50% off retail. There are no floor samples or discontinued styles here. These are all sent to their clearance center downtown.

On a recent visit here, I found a great deal on a Hickory White dining room set (pictured on the following page). The hutch, table, and six chairs normally retail as a group for $18,060.00, but Utility Craft's price on the same set was only $7,345.00. The set was brand-new and in first-quality condition.

Since you save just as much over the phone as you do in person, there really isn't much reason to travel here in person to shop. However, if you plan to order furniture by phone, you really should call here to compare prices. Utility Craft has some great deals.

If you do travel directly to High Point to shop, don't miss Utility Craft's clearance center downtown. There's more information about that source under the listing for *Furniture Clearance Center*.

Phone orders accepted:	**Yes**
Discount:	**40%-50% off mfrs. suggested retail**
Payment methods:	**VISA, MC, AMEX, Discover, personal checks**
In-house financing available:	**Yes**
Deposits required:	**1/3 deposit when order is placed, balance due when furniture is ready to be shipped**
Catalog available:	**No**
Clearance center:	**Yes - See *Furniture Clearance Center***
Delivery:	**Full service in-home delivery and set-up. Customer pays freight company directly for shipping costs.**

Directions: From I-85, take exit #111 (Hwy. 311), and head northwest into High Point. After several miles, when you reach downtown High Point, Hwy. 311 will become Main St. Follow Main St. north all the way through High Point. When you come to the intersection of Eastchester, turn right. Go about 10 miles, and turn left on Penny Rd. Utility Craft Furniture is on the corner.

Utility Craft Fine Furniture (cont.)

Utility Craft Fine Furniture

Dining room set from Hickory White

Retail: $18,060.00   Discounted price: $7,345.00
Savings at Utility Craft Fine Furniture: $10,715.00 = 60% off retail

Utility Craft Fine Furniture (cont.)

Lines carried:

Action By Lane
Allusions
Ambiance
American Drew
Andrew Pearson
A.P. Generations
Ardley Hall
Artistica
Arttra
Baldwin Brass
Benecia Brass Beds
Big Fish
Bob Timberlake
Bradington Young
Braxton Culler
Broyhill
Butler
California Kids
California House
Canadel
Cape Craftsman
Capel
Carver's Guild
Casa Bique
C.B.S. Imports
Cebu
Century
Chapman
Charleston Forge
Clark Casual
Classic Leather
Classic Rattan
Clayton Marcus
Cochrane
Colonial Furniture
Cooper Classics
Comfort Designs
Councill
Cox
C. R. Laine
Craftwork
Crawford
Creative Elegance
Crescent
CTH Sherrill
C.W. Choice
Currey & Co.
Custom Craft
Dauphine Mirror

Decorative Crafts
Dinaire
Designmaster
Distinctive Designs
Eastern Accents
Eddy West
Elements by Grapevine
Elliott's
Ello
Evans Designs
Fairfield Chair
Faithwalk Designs
Fashion Bed Group
Fine Art Ltd.
Fine Art Lamps
Flat Rock
Frederick Cooper Lamps
Fremarc
Friedman Brothers
Garcia Imports
Grace
Guildmaster
Habersham Plantation
Hammary
Harden
Hart
Hekman
Henry Link
Hickory Chair
Hickory White
Hitchcock Chair
Hollywoods
Hooker
Howard Miller
Hurtado
Ital Art Design
J. Royale
J.H. Craven
Johnston Casuals
John Richards Collection
Karges
Kentwood
Kimball
Kinder Harris
Koch
La Barge
La-Z-Boy
Lane
Lane/Venture

Lea
Lexington
Lloyd/Flanders
Lyon Shaw
Madison Square
Maitland Smith
McKay Table Pad
Michael Thomas
Mikhail Darafeev
Miles Talbott
Montaage
Moosehead
Motioncraft
Natural Light
Nichols & Stone
Ohio Table Pad
Palacek
Passport
Paul Robinson
Plant Plant
Phoenix Art
Pompeii
Prestige Arts
Quiozel
Riverside
Robin Bruce
Royal Patina
Salem Square
Sam Moore
Sarreid
Schnadig
Sealy Mattress
Sedgefield/Woodcraft
Serta Mattress
Shadow Catchers
Shady Lady Lighting
Sitcom Furniture
Sligh
Soicher Marin
Southampton
Southwood Reproductions
Stanford
Stanley
Statesville Chair
Statton
Stonelee
Superior
Swaim
Telescope

Textillery
Thayer Coggin
The Elegant Earth
Theodore Alexander
Tomlin Designs
Tropitone
Universal
Uttermost
Vanguard
Vaughan
Venture By Lane
Vitale
Waterford Lighting
Wesley Allen
WHOA!
Wildwood
Winston
Woodard
Woodmark
Yorkshire House

Village Furniture House

146 West Ave.
Kannapolis, NC 28081

Phone:	**(704) 938-9171**	**Hours:**	**M-Sun 9:00-6:00**
Toll Free:	**None**	**E-mail:**	**sales@cannonvillage.com**
Fax:	**(704) 932-2503**	**Web site:**	**www.cannonvillage.com/villagefurn.htm**

Village Furniture House in Cannon Village has a very good selection of high-end lines. They have furniture in stock from Lane, Lexington (including Bob Timberlake), Stanley, Flexsteel, Godfrey Thomas, Broyhill, Kincaid, and others. They can special order many other lines.

Most of the furniture in stock is priced at 30%-50% off retail. Usually, the salespeople will tell you as you come in that they are willing to go even lower than the prices marked and that they will beat any competitor's discounts, so take them up on it!

On a recent visit here, I found a great deal on a Bob Timberlake five-piece bedroom set: queen sleigh bed, dresser, mirror, chest, and nightstand (pictured on the following page). This group normally retails for $9,435.00, but Village Furniture House had this set for only $5,249.00, a discount of 45% off retail. The set was brand-new and in first-quality condition.

Village Furniture House has a great reputation for service. If you're interested in any of the brands they carry, definitely call them for a price quote.

Phone orders accepted:	**Yes**
Discount:	**30%-50% off mfrs. suggested retail**
Payment methods:	**Personal checks. No credit cards.**
In-house financing available:	**Yes**
Deposits required:	**1/3 deposit when order is placed, balance due when furniture is ready to be shipped**
Catalog available:	**No**
Clearance center:	**No**
Delivery:	**Full service in-home delivery and set-up. Customer pays freight company directly for shipping costs.**

Directions: From I-85, take exit #63, and follow the signs to Cannon Village. Village Furniture House is on West Ave. inside Cannon Village.

Village Furniture House (cont.)

Village Furniture House

Bob Timberlake bedroom set from Lexington

Retail: $9,435.00   Discounted price: $5,249.00
Savings at Village Furniture House: $4,186.00 = 44% off retail

Village Furniture House (cont.)

Lines carried:

Action By Lane
Alexander Julian
Alexvale
American Drew
American Of Martinsville
Ashley
Athol
Baldwin Brass
Barcalounger
Bassett
Benchcraft
Berkline
Bevan Funnell
Bob Timberlake
Blacksmith Shop
Bradington Young
Brady
Braxton Culler
Broyhill
C. R. Laine
Capitol Leather
Carolina Mirror
Carson's
Casa Bique
Casual Concepts
Chapman Lamps
Charleston Forge
Chromcraft
Clayton Marcus
Colonial Solid Cherry
Councill-Craftsmen
Craftique
Craftwork Guild
Dansen Contemporary
Design Horizons
Design South
Dillon
Dinaire
Distinction Leather
Ducks Unlimited
Ello
Emerson Leather
Fairfield Chair
Fashion Bed Group
Flexsteel
Friedman Brothers Mirrors
Habersham Plantation
Hammary
Hekman

Henry Link
Hickory Fry
Hickory Hill
Hickory White
Highland House
Hitchcock Chair
Hooker
Howard Miller
J. Royale
Jasper
JTB
Keller
Kessler
Key City
Kimball
Kincaid
King Hickory
Kingsdown Bedding
Klaussner
Knob Creek
La Barge
Lane
Lane/Venture
Lea
Lexington
Link Taylor
Lloyd/Flanders
Lyon Shaw
Madison Square
Master Design
Michael Thomas
Millennium
Moosehead
Nathan Hale
National Mt. Airy
Nichols & Stone
Norman Rockwell
Old Hickory Tannery
Pearson
Pennsylvania Classics
Peters Revington
Pulaski
Ridgeway Clocks
Riverside
Rowe
Royal Patina
Salem Square
Saloom
Sam Moore

S. Bent
Schwieger
Shuford
Simply Southern
Singer
Skillcraft
Sligh
S. K. Dinettes
Southern Of Conover
Southwood Reproductions
Stanley
Statesville Chair
Statton
Stiffel Lamps
Swaim
Tradition France
Tradition House
Tropitone
Universal
Vanguard
Vaughan
Vaughan Bassett
Venture By Lane
Virginia House
Waterford Furniture
Weiman
Wellington Hall
Wesley Allen Brass Beds
Wildwood Lamps
Winston
Woodard
Woodmark

Wellington Hall Factory Outlet

Hwy. 70
Lexington, NC 27293

Phone:	**(336) 249-4931**	**Hours:**	**M-Sat 9:00-4:00**
Toll Free:	**None**	**E-mail:**	**info@wellingtonhalldesigns.com**
Fax:	**(336) 249-7798**	**Web site:**	**www.wellingtonhalldesigns.com**

Wellington Hall manufactures absolutely gorgeous high-end traditional furniture. In fact, they even make some styles for Baker and Henredon, two better-known high-quality lines.

The Wellington Hall Factory Outlet is a bit different from the rest, however. It's located in the back of the actual factory, rather than being at a separate location. Many people don't even know that there's an outlet here. You have to go all the way to the back of the factory building (toward the extreme right in the picture on the next page), and ring a bell by a little door. Then, you wait patiently for someone from the front office to walk all the way to the back of the factory to open the little door.

It's well worth the wait, though. The outlet is actually just a back corner of the factory floor itself. It's quite an interesting eyeful to see all of the works in progress further forward in the plant.

As of this printing in February 2004, Wellington Hall has is only actively manufacturing their Wellington Walls wall systems, which can be seen at their Web site. They still do have some stock in their casegoods lines which they are continuing to sell off at this outlet. They may resume manufacturing their dining room sets, bedroom sets, and other casegoods at a later time. It would be a good idea to call and find out what type of stock they currently have before driving out to the outlet.

On a recent visit here, I found a beautiful mahogany table (pictured on the following page) that normally retails for $1,247.00, marked down to $575.00. It was a discontinued style with no damage.

This is a terrific outlet. If you're traveling to the Lexington area, near Hickory, you have to see this place!

Discount:	**60%-75% off mfrs. suggested retail**
Payment methods:	**VISA, MC, Discover, personal checks**
In-house financing available:	**No**
Deposits required:	**Not applicable**
Catalog available:	**Not applicable**
Clearance center:	**Not applicable**
Delivery:	**Customer must make own arrangements to take purchases home**

Directions: The Wellington Hall Factory Outlet is right on Business 85, just north of Lexington, NC.

Wellington Hall Factory Outlet (cont.)

Wellington Hall Factory Outlet

Mahogany table from Wellington Hall

Retail: $1,247.00   Discounted price: $575.00
Savings at the Wellington Hall Factory Outlet: $672.00 = 54% off retail

Wellington's Fine Leather Furniture

7771 Valley Blvd.
Hwy. 321 S.
Blowing Rock, NC 28605

Phone:	**(828) 295-0491**	**Hours:**	**M-F 9:00-6:00, Sat 9:30-5:00**
Toll Free:	**(800) 262-1049**	**E-mail:**	**hampwell@fineleatherfurniture.com**
Fax:	**(828) 295-0495**	**Web site:**	**www.fineleatherfurniture.com**

Wellington's Fine Leather Furniture has a very nice leather showroom in Blowing Rock, NC, about 40 miles north of Hickory. They also sell by phone. They guarantee prices of at least 30%-40% off the manufacturers retail price.

All of the furniture displayed in their showroom is new first-quality. There are no floor samples or discontinued styles available, which means there really isn't any reason to travel here in person. Also, this store is quite far from the main cluster of factory outlets and discounters in Hickory and Lenoir, NC.

You may wish to check out their online leather auctions at www.leatherfurniturebids.com. Leather is so popular that most pieces bid up to market value, but occasionally you can find a real bargain here.

If you're planning to order leather furniture by phone, you may wish to compare prices here. There are many other discounters, primarily in Hickory and High Point, who generally have better bargains on leather upholstery, though.

Lines carried:

Distinction
McKinley
Palliser

Phone orders accepted:	Yes
Discount:	**30%-40% off mfrs. suggested retail**
Payment methods:	**VISA, MC, AMEX, Discover, personal checks**
In-house financing available:	**No**
Deposits required:	**50% deposit when order is placed, balance due when furniture is ready to be shipped**
Catalog available:	Yes
Clearance center:	No
Delivery:	**Full service in-home delivery and set-up. Customer pays freight company directly for shipping costs.**

Directions: From I-40, take exit #123, and drive north on Hwy. 321 about 40 miles to Blowing Rock. The store is on the left side of the highway.

The Wild Pear

Hickory Furniture Mart
2220 Hwy. 70 SE
Level 3
Hickory, NC 28602

Phone:	**(828) 326-9296**	**Hours:**	**M-Sat 9:00-6:00**
Toll Free:	**None**	**E-mail:**	**thewildpear@earthlink.net**
Fax:	**(828) 326-9296**	**Web site:**	**www.hickoryfurniture.com**

The Wild Pear at the Hickory Furniture Mart is a cute little shop with some good deals on linens and a few lines of furniture. They have a good reputation for customer service.

They generally do not sell furniture off the floor, but I've found that if you make an offer on a piece in stock, sometimes they'll take it. Shoot for 20% below the price marked.

If you're interested in any of the lines listed below, you may wish to give them a call.

Lines carried:

Anichini	Fleur de Lis	MU/H	Shabby Chic
Bonjour	KOKO	Paper White	Traditions
Eastern Accents	Mayland Court	Savoy	White Linen

Phone orders accepted:	**Yes**
Discount:	**40%-50% off mfrs. suggested retail**
Payment methods:	**VISA, MC, AMEX, Discover, personal checks**
In-house financing available:	**No**
Deposits required:	**50% deposit when order is placed, balance due when furniture is ready to be shipped**
Catalog available:	**No**
Clearance center:	**No**
Delivery:	**Full service in-home delivery and set-up. Customer pays freight company directly for shipping costs.**

Directions: Please see *Hickory Furniture Mart* for complete directions.

Wood Armfield Furniture Co.

The Atrium
430 S. Main St.
High Point, NC 27260

Phone:	**(336) 889-6522**	**Hours:**	**M-F 9:00-6:00, Sat 9:00-5:00**
Toll Free:	**None**	**E-mail:**	**woodarmfield@atriumfurniture.com**
Fax:	**(336) 889-5381**	**Web site:**	**www.woodarmfield.com**

Wood-Armfield Furniture Co. has a very nice store in the Atrium Furniture Mall in High Point. Their stock is an even mix of traditional and contemporary. All stock is new first-quality.

It would be a good idea to check Wood Armfield's BBB report before ordering. As of this printing in February 2004, they have one unresolved complaint. I would only recommend shopping here when all complaints have been resolved.

Wood Armfield does have great deals on furniture sold over the phone. If you do plan to travel to High Point, NC, to buy furniture, don't miss Wood Armfield's clearance center several blocks away.

Phone orders accepted:	**Yes**
Discount:	**40%-50% off mfrs. suggested retail**
Payment methods:	**VISA, MC, personal checks**
In-house financing available:	**No**
Deposits required:	**50% deposit when order is placed, balance due when furniture is ready to be shipped**
Catalog available:	**No**
Clearance center:	**Yes - See *Furniture Clearance Center***
Delivery:	**Full service in-home delivery and set-up. Customer pays freight company directly for shipping costs.**

Directions: Wood Armfield is located inside the Atrium complex in downtown High Point. Please see *The Atrium* for complete directions.

Wood Armfield (cont.)

Wood Armfield Furniture Co.

Lines carried:

Ambience
Ardley Hall
Arttra
Berkline
Bernhardt
Bob Timberlake
Bradington Young
Broyhill
Cambridge
Canadel
Cape Craftsman
Capel
Carsons
Casa Bique
Casa Stradivari
Century
Chapman
Classic Leather
Councill
Colonial Furniture
Craftwork
Crescent
Designmaster
Florita Nova
Fine Art
Frederick Cooper
Friedman Bros.
Garcia Imports
Great City Traders
Guildmaster

Habersham
Hart
Hekman
Henry Link
Hickory White
Hilda Flack
Hollywoods
Howard Miller
Jasper
John Richards
Kinder Harris
Koch
La Barge
La-Z-Boy
Lexington
Ligna
Maitland Smith
Miles Talbott
Montaage
Nichols & Stone
Nora Fenton
O. L. F.
Palecek
Pennsylvania Classics
Phillips Collection
Phoenix Art
Rex
S. Bent
Sarreid
Sedgefield

Shadow Catchers
Silkwood
Soicher Marin
Southwood
Stanley
Statesville Chair
Statton
Swaim
Tapestries Ltd.
Thomasville
Vanguard
Wesley Hall

Worthington Furniture Gallery

237 Timber Brook Place
Granite Falls, NC 28630

Phone:	**(828) 396-6343**	**Hours:**	**M-Sat 9:00-5:00**
Toll Free:	**None**	**E-mail:**	**None**
Fax:	**(828) 396-6345**	**Web site:**	**None**

Worthington Furniture Gallery is located just a few miles north of Hickory, NC. They have a limited selection of medium to high-end lines, including Hammary, Lexington, and Universal. They have an excellent reputation for customer service.

They have some good deals on the lines they sell by phone. So, if you're planning to order your furniture by phone, give this source a call to compare their prices.

They also have a small clearance center in their basement with some good bargains. If you're in the Hickory area, you may wish to stop in.

Lines carried:

Hammary
Hekman
Leatherworks
Lexington
Sam Moore
Sedona Leather
Universal
Waterford Furniture

Phone orders accepted:	**Yes**
Discount:	**35%-50% off mfrs. suggested retail**
Payment methods:	**VISA, MC, personal checks**
In-house financing available:	**No**
Deposits required:	**50% deposit when order is placed, balance due when furniture is ready to be shipped**
Catalog available:	**No**
Clearance center:	**No**
Delivery:	**Full service in-home delivery and set-up. Customer pays freight company directly for shipping costs.**

Directions: From I-40, take exit #123 and drive north on Hwy. 321 to Granite Falls. Worthington Furniture Gallery is on the left side of the road.

Zagaroli Classics

Level 3
Hickory Furniture Mart
U. S. Hwy. 70 SE
Hickory, NC 28602

Phone:	**(828) 328-3373**	**Hours:**	**M-Sat 9:00-6:00**
Toll Free:	**(800) 887-2424**	**E-mail:**	**customerservice@zagarolileather.com**
Fax:	**(828) 328-5839**	**Web site:www.zagarolileather.com**	

Zagaroli Classics is a family-owned business based in Hickory, NC, that sells high-end custom leather upholstery directly to the public through their showroom in the Hickory Furniture Mart in Hickory. They also sell through their own catalog, and online through their Web site (above). Their prices are typically about half of what a retailer would charge for comparable furniture.

I was very impressed with the service at their showroom. The furniture is very high quality, with solid maple frames and 8-way hand-tied springs. They use only aniline-dyed leather, which is the best quality you can buy.

It isn't necessary to visit their showrooms in order to buy from them. They have a free full-color catalog showing all of the various sofa and chair styles they manufacture. They have a nice selection of contemporary and traditional styles. You can also view their entire catalog online at their Web site, www.zagarolileather.com.

They will send you leather samples in the mail, so you can easily decide in your own home what color and grade of leather you would like. They do require a $10 deposit before sending you a leather sample kit, but this is refunded when you return the leather samples to them.

They have also recently added outlet selections to their Web site. You can see and buy one-of-a-kind samples at their Web site at up to 75% off retail.

I was very impressed with the quality and service at this source. Anyone who is considering purchasing new leather upholstery by phone should definitely request their free catalog and compare their prices. You are unlikely to find better prices on leather upholstery without actually traveling to North Carolina and shopping in person for floor samples and discontinued styles.

Phone orders accepted:	Yes
Discount:	**Up to 60% off mfrs. suggested retail**
Payment methods:	**VISA, MC, personal checks**
In-house financing available:	**No**
Deposits required:	**50% deposit when order is placed, balance due when furniture is ready to be shipped**
Catalog available:	**Yes**
Clearance center:	**No**
Delivery:	**Full service in-home delivery and set-up. Customer pays freight company directly for shipping costs.**

Directions: Please see *Hickory Furniture Mart* for complete directions.

BRAND INDEX

A

C

D

De Nunzio   81
Decorative Arts   226, 227
Decorative Crafts   51, 81, 84, 89, 116,
      128, 133, 163, 205, 210, 226, 240, 270
Deitz and Sons   128
Dellarobbia Rugs   227
Demdaco   133
Denny Lamps   51, 89, 95, 133, 136, 138, 265
Design Guild   128, 226
Design Horizons   273
Design Source, Ltd   128, 133
Design South   128, 210, 226, 273
Design Systems   128
Designer Imports   236
Designer Wicker   27, 109
Designer's Attic   128
Designmaster   27, 61, 63, 68, 81, 84, 163, 255, 265, 270, 279
Designs By Robert Guenther   128
Designs South   222
Designz Unlimited   240
Destinations   240
Deszign, Inc.   128
Dezine   133
DIA Metal Furniture   20, 227
Dietz   128
Dillon   89, 128, 163, 205, 210, 222, 226, 273
Dimplex   51, 128
Dinaire   51, 84, 123, 128, 156, 163, 205, 222, 226, 270, 273
Dinec   101, 103, 222, 227
Dining Ala Carte   95
Directional   20, 128, 222
Distinction Leather   84, 98, 128, 136, 188, 205, 210,
      222, 242, 273
Distinctive Designs   12, 128, 163, 181, 182, 226, 270
Distinctive Imports   27
Distinctive Oils   128
Dixie   77, 187
DMI   49, 128, 141, 174, 195, 205
Doimo   248
Douglas   79, 100
DR Kincaid Chairs   101, 103
Dragonfly Home   236
Dresher   95
Drexel Heritage   57, 59, 67, 69, 104, 105
DSF   210
Ducks Unlimited   136, 169, 199, 273
Dunmore Furniture   128
Dura Hold   128
Duralee   81, 128, 205, 210
Durham   138
Dutailier   128, 156, 163, 210

E

E. J. Victor   81, 107, 108, 138

Eagle Craft Desks   242
Eastern Accents   16, 17, 27, 128, 138, 270, 277
Eastern Shore Trading Co.   81, 133
Eckadams/Vogel Peterson   128
Eddie Bauer   89, 169, 199
Eddy West   89, 240, 270
Edrich Mills Wood Shop   24, 81
Edward Art   89
Ekornes   141, 210, 226, 227
El Paso Import Company   236
El Ran Motion   192
Elan International   205
Eldred Wheeler   81
Elements By Grapevine   20, 68, 128, 205, 210, 226, 270
Elite   20, 128, 138, 192, 227
Elliott's Design   27, 51, 56, 128, 255, 270
Ellis   70, 128
Ello   20, 77, 81, 84, 89, 128, 163, 205, 210, 222, 227,
      270, 273
Elvis Presley Furniture   51
Emerson   169
Emerson et Cie   20, 51, 81, 128, 177, 210, 222, 226
Emerson Leather   205, 273
Emess Design Group   128
England Corsair   49, 79, 174, 195, 238
Englander   100, 128, 205
English   138
Environment   240
Espino   128
European Pine   226
Euroreps   128
Eurostyle   248
Evan Du Four   128
Evans Ceramics   128
Evans Designs   248, 270
Evans Frame Shop   128
Excel. Office-Contract   89
Excelsior   128, 163, 181, 182, 211
Excursions By Lane   255
Executive Imports   133
EXL Designs Upholstery   51, 227
Expressive Designs Rugs   128

F

F.O. Merz & Co. Inc.   236
Fabric To Frame   128
Fabrica   20, 128, 226
Fabricoate   163
Fairfax   12
Fairfield   12, 27, 51, 56, 84, 89, 95, 123, 128, 136, 163,
      177, 187, 199, 205, 222, 226, 240, 273
Fairfield Chair   81, 122, 123, 210, 252, 270
Fairington   77
Fairmont Designs   89, 181, 182, 211, 240, 265

G

H

I

J

K

L

M

N

O

P

Q

R

S

T

U

Y

Z

Order Form

📞 **Telephone orders:**   Call Toll Free: 1 (800) 829-1203
Visa, Mastercard, and Discover cards accepted.

✉ **Mail orders:**   Send to: Home Decor Press
1000 Peachtree Industrial Blvd., Suite 6333
Suwanee, GA 30024

⚡ **Online orders:**   Log on to **www.smartdecorating.com**

***We also have a wide variety of electronic titles (e-books) available for purchase only at www.smartdecorating.com**

Please send the books checked below:

☐ The Furniture Factory Outlet Guide, 3rd Edition $24.95

☐ The Insider's Guide To Buying Home Furnishings $24.95

Subtotal $
Please add $5.00 shipping for each book ordered $
GA residents please add 7% sales tax $

Total amount enclosed $

$ Payment: ☐ Check   ☐ Mastercard   ☐ Visa   ☐ Discover

Card number:_____

Name on card:_____   Expiration date:_____

✉ **Shipping:**   Name_____

Address_____

City_____   State____   Zip_____   Daytime phone_____

Call toll free and order now